NOT
ALL
HEROES

AN UNAPOLOGETIC
MEMOIR OF THE
VIETNAM WAR
1971-1972

The author sitting on the steps to his hooch in Chu Lai, South Vietnam, 1971. The conduct of the four CID agents who lived in the hooch is suggested by the decorative pin-up girls on the door.

NOT ALL HEROES

AN UNAPOLOGETIC
MEMOIR OF THE
VIETNAM WAR
1971-1972

GARY E. SKOGEN
FOREWORD BY
CLAY S. JENKINSON

The Dakota Institute Press
of the Lewis & Clark Fort Mandan Foundation

Library of Congress Control Number 2013945540
ISBN-13 978-0-9834059-6-2 (Hardcover)
ISBN-13 978-0-9834059-7-9 (Paperback)

Distributed by The University of Oklahoma Press

Created, produced and designed in the United States of America
Printed in Canada

Book layout and design by:
Margaret McCullough corvusdesignstudio.com

The paper in this book meets the guidelines for permanence and durability of the Committee of Production Guidelines for Book Longevity of the Council on Library Resources

10 9 8 7 6 5 4 3 2 1

The Dakota Institute Press
of the Lewis & Clark Fort Mandan Foundation
2576 8th Street South West Post Office Box 607
Washburn, North Dakota 58577
www.FortMandan.com
1.877.462.8535

MIX
Paper from
responsible sources
FSC® C016245

Dedicated to those
who died honorably
in service to our country.

TABLE OF CONTENTS

LIST OF ILLUSTRATIONS

MAPS

DOCUMENTS

PHOTOGRAPHS

FOREWORD

BY

CLAY S. JENKINSON

"Those stories [of the men who actually enjoyed the war] have not entered the canon of Vietnam memoirs. The war that we know, the Vietnam myth, is not their war. If it were, the myth would have no moral; if men could fight in that Bad War and come out of it undamaged and nostalgic, what would the war mean? But they are nonetheless as valid, as truth-telling, as valuable, as the worst accounts of slaughtered innocents and damaged lives. The soldier's tale of Vietnam is all of the stories. We must not choose among them."

—Samuel Hynes

The Soldier's Tale:
Bearing Witness to Modern War

You are not going to like the author of this book. Nor does he care. Gary Skogen (1945–) has a fascinating story to tell about his year in Vietnam (February 1971 – January 1972). It was, he says, the best year of his life. He was twenty-six years old. He served almost entirely behind the scenes as a Criminal Investigation Division (CID) officer first at Chu Lai and then, for three months, at Da Nang. He never entered a potentially hostile South Vietnamese village in search of weapons or concealed Viet Cong guerillas. He never slogged through rice paddies on patrol. He never held watch deep in the interior of Vietnam through an endless nerve-wracking night, in which the mere rustle of a rodent in the brush sent waves of terror through American GIs. His only battle experiences were a couple of brief exchanges of fire as the helicopter taking him to a crime site landed. He was, he freely admits, having too much fun to take the war very seriously.

Two years after his return from Vietnam in 1972, Skogen joined the Los Angeles Police Department, where he served as a drug enforcement officer for twenty-seven years. Today he lives with his fourth wife in Littlerock, California, near Palmdale and Edwards Air Force Base.

Skogen grew up on a farm near Hettinger, North Dakota, in one of the least populated regions of one of the least populated states. His dream was to be a cop. The military seemed to be the quicker path to that end, so he joined the Army on January 25, 1965, shortly after he received his draft notice. After basic training at Fort Ord, California, and MP training at Fort Gordon, Georgia, Skogen wound up not where he desperately wanted to be, in Vietnam, where the action was, but in the backwater of Incirlik, Turkey, where he learned how little cooperation could be expected between American military forces and local law enforcement authorities. In the autumn of 1967, in return for the promise of a more serious law enforcement assignment, he reenlisted for six additional years. Between 1967 and 1969, he was stationed at Landstuhl, fifteen kilometers from Miesau, in West Germany. Four times during this period he volunteered to go to Vietnam, and four times his request was declined. In 1969, he was sent home to Fort Gordon for CID training. Finally, his fifth request to be stationed in Vietnam was approved.

Literally thousands of memoirs have been published about the Vietnam War. Some of them are classics of war literature. Skogen's is certainly not the most important, but it may be the most cheerful. Although he saw plenty of mayhem during his time in Vietnam, most of it occurred on the base at Chu Lai, and none of the cases he investigated involved men killed in enemy action. Skogen is quick to point out that he found nothing particularly disturbing in viewing the bodies of soldiers killed in brawls, knife fights, drug overdoses, or suicide, for that matter:

> Early in my career I learned that one must become hardened
> to the sight of death and accept life's most gruesome spec-
> tacles. One must emotionally deny the humanity of a pile
> of blood, bones, and flesh. One must do away with the idea
> that a dead body is that of a once-living, breathing, sensate
> human being. Frankly, a lifeless body becomes just a slab of
> meat. Obviously, such detachment isn't possible if the lifeless

body is one's spouse or child or anyone else to whom one had an emotional tie. But, some stranger? Somebody that you've never seen before in your life? As cold and callous as it sounds, his or her body becomes a slab of meat.

Arguably, this emotional detachment is the most remarkable characteristic of Skogen's memoir, a detachment that equally characterizes his attitude toward death, suicide, fellow soldiers, America's purposes in Vietnam, women (both Anglo and Asian), his officers, authority, Army regulations, and the suffering of the people of Vietnam. Those who thwart his will or fail to live up to the standards he sets for them he calls "dickheads," a term he uses twenty-two times in this memoir and thousands of times in his informal discourse. While Skogen's detachment may seem strange to some and offensive to others, it is the basis of the value of this book. He expresses no particular attitude toward the war, no quarrel with LBJ or Richard Nixon, or with the way the war was prosecuted. Surely he has opinions on these things, but he has not allowed them to color or interfere with his narrative, a straightforward account of his experience in Vietnam, which he found so satisfying that he requested to stay on after his year's deployment was complete. There is great irony here. Most American servicemen in Vietnam kept calendars on which they literally crossed off each day as they fulfilled their obligation to spend one full year in country. They attended to these calendars as assiduously as if they were in prison or even on death row. As Skogen's term in Vietnam moved toward its conclusion, he found himself lamenting that his joyful sojourn, "the best year of my life," must unfortunately come to an end.

Skogen has only two axes to grind here. First, he argues (and to his own satisfaction proves) that not everyone whose name is incised on the Vietnam Veterans Memorial Wall deserves to be commemorated there. Second, like B.G. Burkett (*Stolen Valor: How the Vietnam Generation Was Robbed of its Heroes and its History*), Skogen believes that an inaccurate and irresponsible mythology of Vietnam has emerged in which all or most veterans are regarded as victims of the war, a lost generation of American men who suffer endlessly from a mixture of physical and psychological maladies including Post Traumatic Stress Disorder (PTSD), human wrecks who have never been able to re-enter American life. Toward the end of his memoir, Skogen writes:

It really is time to get past the victim-veteran mentality that has haunted the Vietnam veterans. In telling my story, I have but one purpose: to tell the truth about one soldier's wartime experiences. The myths, and in some cases the lies, told by veterans or wannabe veterans have captured the headlines and attention of the public, and the money for victims' programs. The truth is that for many of us serving in Vietnam, it really was the best of times. Another truth is that not everyone who served there is a hero.

Those who wish to discredit these theses will point out that Skogen, who spent the war behind the scenes, cannot possibly know what thousands of GIs experienced in actual battle against the Viet Cong or North Vietnamese regulars (NVA), that his experience, while it is certainly valid, is not representative or normative, and that he has no right to impugn the lives of soldiers whose grim experiences in Vietnam left them physically and/or mentally impaired. The reader will decide.

Gary Skogen's memoir is not the story of one man's descent into the heart of darkness in the jungles of Vietnam; nor is it the story of loss of innocence as an earnest and patriotic GI from the American heartland discovers that his government regards himself and men like him as expendable in a war that it has already determined it cannot win, while the people we were in Vietnam to protect proved to be corrupt, inept, or secretly hostile to American interests. Gary does not cradle his best friend in his arms as he dies in battle. He does not witness scenes of raw brutality and inhumanity from which he knows he will never fully recover. Gary Skogen's tale is cheerful and opportunistic.

Skogen appears to be as puzzled as his readers by this emotional detachment. "When I first arrived in Vietnam," he writes, "I had a very strong sense that I had arrived in a war zone and that somehow the fighting, dying, and killing would affect me. However, as the days turned into weeks and the weeks translated into months, I grew more and more detached from the war and felt immune from its consequences."

Although it lacks some of the melodramatic qualities of such Vietnam memoirs as John Ketwig's *And a Hard Rain Fell: A GI's True Story of the War in Vietnam*, and Larry Gwin's *Baptism: A Vietnam*

Memoir, Skogen's *Not All Heroes* has several advantages. First, it was written by a man of exceptional intelligence and observational acumen. Second, Skogen's emotional detachment permits him to observe his little corner of Southeast Asia and his little episode in the war in Vietnam with exceptional clarity. His account is untouched by any aura of self-pity, self-importance, or the pose of heroism or nobility. Skogen can fly back to Chu Lai in the back of a helicopter in which he is the only living being surrounded by a number of dead soldiers and feel no need to wring his hands about the horrors or the futility of war.

> [T]he same emotional detachment that served me well when working around the dead victims of violent crimes assisted me in the back of those helicopters, too. I could as easily detach myself from the dead young GIs taking up space with me in a Huey as I could from the suffering of a victim of some terrible crime. As I sat with those dead men, I never once became philosophical about the obvious loss to our country, about the meaninglessness of the war, about the in-humanity we were perpetuating upon these people and them upon us, or about the tears that would be shed back in the States over these lost lives. I figured we, these dead GIs and I, were soldiers, and all of us did the job Uncle Sam paid us to do. On this particular day, the dead GIs' numbers had come up; it was their day to die. My number might come up the next time I jumped off a helicopter in the bush somewhere, or the next time I entered a hooch full of dickheads and one fired a full clip from his M-16 at me, or the next time I drove my jeep up QL1 and hit a land mine buried inches below the surface. But I never dwelt on those possibilities, because if it happened to me, as it had happened to them that day, someone else would be riding in the back of a helicopter with some dead guy dressed in civilian clothes. No, I didn't dwell on it. After all, I was having too much fun.

Too much fun? Some readers will find this callous detachment objectionable, even appalling, and some will doubt that Skogen's apparent dispassion tells the whole truth about his accumulated experience. But it makes for a strangely compelling narrative. The reader will spend as much time puzzling over what sort of man this is as trying to make sense of the last years of the war as seen through one soldier's eyes.

Skogen's experience may be more representative than it at first seems. Between 1954 and 1975, fully 2.8 million Americans served in Vietnam. Approximately 80 percent of these individuals served behind the lines. There, on naval vessels offshore and at Army bases scattered throughout the country, they were comparatively safe, although they were not entirely immune from mortar and sniper attacks, and from sappers (Viet Cong who burrowed their way into bases and encampments to kill American GIs). Their Vietnam experience was fundamentally different from that of the minority of men who engaged the enemy in the countryside. By the time the war was over, 58,212 Americans had been killed, 153,452 wounded, and 1,678 were missing in action. For obvious reasons, the Vietnam experiences of the 80 percent who did not see action have been under-represented in Vietnam memoirs, which are regarded as more compelling in direct proportion to their depiction of the GIs' descent into the nightmare of the killing fields. As Samuel Hynes rightly argues, the narratives of the 80 percent are not only more likely to be representative of "the American's experience in Vietnam," but they are "as valid, as truth-telling, as valuable, as the worst accounts of slaughtered innocents and damaged lives." Skogen's book proves that memoirs without "slaughtered innocents and damaged lives" can be gripping literature, full of drama and insight, and quite entertaining too.

Nor is Skogen's claim that his time in Vietnam was satisfying as strange as it might at first seem. A 1989 Veterans Administration study reported that 71 percent of the Vietnam veterans polled said they were glad they went to Vietnam. A whopping 74 percent claimed to have enjoyed the war.

Although most of the individuals who went to Vietnam spent the war behind the scenes, few can have had as good a war as Gary Skogen. He dressed in casual colonial clothing. He had his own car, an abandoned jeep that had been painted powder blue, with which he came and went more or less as he pleased. If Vietnam represented sexual opportunity for most American GIs, it was sexual paradise for Skogen, who was able to maintain regular work hours with sufficient time off every day to take advantage of a wide variety of sexual possibilities in Vietnam. He lived apart from the rest of the base population in an isolated hooch on a cliff overlooking the South China

Sea. He shared those quarters with three other hand-chosen members of the CID. They even had a system for letting each other know when they wanted privacy at the hooch—for the endless comings and goings of their Vietnamese sexual partners. Was this the Vietnam War or a college frat house? Skogen's book reads more like the Robert Altman's 1970 film *M.A.S.H,* than a serious war memoir.

Skogen was serious about his work in drug enforcement, however, though he knew the relative futility of trying to stem the flow of marijuana, opium, and heroin among America's servicemen. By the time Skogen reached Vietnam in the spring of 1971, in-country morale was at its nadir. Virtually everyone knew that the American phase of the war was winding down, and most Americans, including most GIs, had come to the conclusion that the war was lost. Retired officer Robert Heinl declared, "Our Army that now remains in Vietnam is in a state of approaching collapse, with individual units avoiding or having refused combat, murdering their officers, drug-ridden and dispirited where not near-mutinous." It was, in short, the Vietnam of *Apocalypse Now,* a moral, military, and psychological shambles in which virtually nobody believed there was any goal higher than counting the days, somehow surviving the ordeal, and returning to the United States to pick up the pieces of one's life. Fragging (deliberate attacks on officers by enlisted men) had climbed from a shocking 271 incidents in 1970 to an even more alarming 333 incidents in 1971. By this time, writes historian Stanley Karnow, "Monkey-wrenching [of military equipment] was epidemic." Drug use, by 1971, had also reached epidemic proportions. When the US government began to crack down on marijuana use, soldiers turned to heroin, which was frequently mixed with common cigarettes to camouflage its use. "I can salute an officer with one hand and take a drag of heroin with the other," a soldier matter of factly explained. Arresting soldiers for drug use was, for Skogen, like shooting ducks in a barrel, but he believed strongly that military drug laws should be enforced when so much was at stake. Several incidents that he investigated during his year in Vietnam cost the lives of innocent American soldiers because a fellow soldier was high while on duty. If the truth be told, however, the war had comparatively little to do with Skogen's purposes. Then and thereafter, Gary Skogen just liked to arrest the "dickheads" who use illegal drugs.

After the Tet offensive (January-March 1968), the American establishment determined that the war was lost or at least that it was unwinnable. In February 1968, the *Wall Street Journal* wrote that "the American people should be getting ready to accept, if they haven't already, the prospect that the whole Vietnam effort may be doomed." On February 27, 1968, Walter Cronkite broke with his habit of careful objectivity and optimism to remark, on the CBS Evening News, that it was "more certain than ever that the bloody experience of Vietnam is to end in a stalemate." Cronkite was just back from a fact-finding trip to Vietnam. "It is increasingly clear to this reporter," he intoned, "that the only rational way out will be to negotiate, not as victors, but as honorable people who lived up to their pledge to defend democracy, and did the best they could. This is Walter Cronkite. Good night." President Johnson privately fumed at Cronkite's "pessimism" and "betrayal," but the majority of the American people, who repeatedly voted Cronkite the most respected man in the United States, regarded his abrupt declaration, at the end of his national broadcast, after the shock of the Tet offensive, to be a definitive and reliable assessment of where things stood in Vietnam.

Vietnamization (replacing US troops with South Vietnamese soldiers) had become the policy of the United States early in 1969. President Nixon announced the first troop reductions in the summer and fall of 1969. The deployment of American forces in Vietnam had started with 23,300 troops in 1963. That number rose in stages to 184,000 in 1966 and peaked at 543,400 in April 1969 shortly after Richard Nixon was inaugurated as the thirty-seventh President of the United States. Nixon, who had campaigned on a promise to end the war in Vietnam, instituted the first troop withdrawals on July 8, 1969, (800 troops), September 16, 1969 (35,000 troops), and December 15, 1969 (50,000 troops). Altogether, the de-Americanization of the war occurred in 14 stages between 1969 and 1973. When Skogen arrived in Vietnam in February 1971, there were approximately 250,000 American troops still in country. By the time he left in 1972, there were fewer than 150,000 American troops, and by the end of the year American troop levels had been reduced to fewer than 25,000 individuals. In other words, when Skogen arrived in Vietnam, the United States was emphatically on its way out.

While Skogen served as drug cop and relaxed on the beach, the war had taken a grim turn back in the United States. The sensational

My Lai trial began on November 17, 1970, and ended on March 29, 1971, just weeks into Skogen's Vietnam adventure. The My Lai incident had occurred on March 16, 1968, when United States Army soldiers of "Charlie" Company of 1st Battalion, 20th Infantry Regiment, 11th Brigade of the Americal Division, massacred between 347 and 504 unarmed civilians in a village on the coast of the South China Sea south of Da Nang. Most of the victims were women, children (including babies), and elderly people. The raid was directed by Lt. William Calley, who, as Skogen notes, had been stationed at Chu Lai. The story was broken in the United States by *New York Times* reporter Seymour Hersh on November 12, 1969, two months after Calley was charged with murder by the United States Army. Calley was convicted of murder on March 29, 1971, but two days later President Nixon, over the objection of his aides and Defense Secretary Melvin Laird, ordered Calley released. The My Lai incident—and the sensational trial that followed—staggered American sensibilities and led to a heated national debate about the wisdom of the war and the validity of the kinds of methods that were used to pacify the Vietnam countryside. The conservative *Wall Street Journal* was emphatic: "This is a young man duly convicted of taking unarmed prisoners entirely at his mercy, throwing them in a ditch, and shooting them. Is this nation really to condone such an act, as a strange coalition of super-patriots seems to urge?"

Calley had reported that when he was first called to Washington, DC, in 1969, just as the My Lai incident had begun to rock the US defense establishment, he thought it was to receive a medal of commendation. At the sensational trial, he explained that in Vietnam it was impossible to differentiate between allies and the enemy, that traditional notions of the distinction between combatants and noncombatants were essentially meaningless in the jungles of Southeast Asia. His defense attorney argued, "This boy's a product of a system, a system that dug him up by the roots, took him out of his home community, put him in the Army, taught him to kill, sent him overseas to kill, gave him mechanical weapons to kill, got him over there and ordered him to kill." Calley himself said, "I was ordered to go in there and destroy the enemy. That was my job that day. That was the mission I was given. I did not sit down and think in terms of men, women and children. They were all classified as the same, and that's the classification that we dealt with over there, just as the enemy. I felt then and I still do that I acted as I was directed, and I carried out the order that I was given and I do not feel wrong in doing so." This was not, as historian Samuel Hynes reminds us, "your father's war."

The American people condemned the My Lai Massacre, but they were less sure that Calley was the right individual to hold accountable. Seventy-eight percent of the people polled disagreed with Calley's sentence (life imprisonment and hard labor at Fort Leavenworth); 51 percent wanted him exonerated altogether. Still, after the conviction of Lt. Calley, 58 percent of Americans believed it was "morally wrong" for the United States to be fighting in Vietnam. Fully 60 percent of the American people favored withdrawal of American troops even if it led to the collapse of South Vietnam. America's commitment to winning the war was an ancient memory; "peace with honor" now seemed like a chimera; the overwhelming desire of America was just to get out and come home.

On June 13, 1971, four months into Skogen's tour in Vietnam, the *New York Times* began publishing the Pentagon Papers, the top-secret Defense Department study that revealed, for the first time, the depth of official duplicity and misinformation that led the United States into Vietnam and prevented the American public (and Congress) from having the information it would have needed to make intelligent decisions about the legitimacy and prosecution of the war. The Nixon administration filed suit in the US Supreme Court to block further publication of the Pentagon Papers. In a landmark decision, handed down on June 30, 1971, the Supreme Court affirmed the *Times'* right to publish the government documents, no matter how they had been obtained.

Meanwhile, returning veterans increasingly spoke out against the war. In April 1971, two thousand members of Vietnam Veterans Against the War staged a four-day march on Washington, DC. Soldiers threw their medals onto the steps of the US Capitol. Future Massachusetts Senator John Kerry, a Navy veteran, testifying at a Senate hearing, said, "How do you ask a man to be the last man to die for a mistake?"

Gary Skogen was determined not to be that man.

At the same time, in secret talks in Paris in May 1971, President Nixon's National Security Adviser Henry Kissinger told his North Vietnamese counterpart Le Duc Tho that the United States was now prepared to withdraw its troops entirely from South Vietnam without requiring a simultaneous withdrawal of NVA troops from below the demilitarized zone. By now, although the Nixon administration stated publicly that it believed that South Vietnamese forces were prepared to prevent a communist takeover of their struggling republic, Kissinger had privately determined that the most the US could really hope for was a "decent interval" before North Vietnam won the war, re-unified the country under communist rule, and meted out whatever reprisals it saw fit to the puppets of America's imperialism.

In other words, it could be argued that the essential policy of the Nixon Administration—from January 20, 1969, to March 29, 1973—was to prolong the war merely for the purposes of saving face. Nixon had famously said, as had his predecessor LBJ, that he would not be "the first president of the United States to lose a war." By 1971 his principal objective was to work the inevitable denouement of America's errand in Vietnam so that it could be argued—for those who would be willing to believe it—that it was South Vietnam, not the United States, that lost the war, that we had done what we could for them, and that if they had really wanted to secure their sovereignty, we had handed them a golden opportunity when we departed. Historian Mark Atwood Lawrence writes, "Under this scenario, Washington would settle for a peace deal that assured a sufficient time lag between the removal of U.S. troops and a communist takeover to enable the administration to avoid the appearance of responsibility for South Vietnam's collapse."

The cynicism of this seemed more appalling at the time than it does now. By the second decade of the twenty-first century, in the wake of Vietnam, Watergate, and all the episodes that have followed, the majority of the American people have a healthy disrespect for their government's pronouncements about its geopolitical purposes. Samuel Hynes speaks of a post-Vietnam American hangover that shows no sign of letting up forty years after the war ended, in spite of President George H. W. Bush's euphoric declaration at the end of the first Gulf War, that "By God, we've kicked the Vietnam syndrome once and for all!"

Skogen's narrative is remarkably detached from these domestic agonies, though surely he knew about them. He does not join other memoirists in decrying the domestic protests or claiming that they emboldened North Vietnamese resolve while undermining American troop morale. He does not fault US policy in Southeast Asia (1954-1975), and he decidedly does not argue that the war could have been won if the politicians had gotten out of the way and let the military do their work. He did not feel judged for choosing to serve in Vietnam at a time when hundreds of thousands of people his age and younger had taken to the streets (though not in Hettinger, ND) to protest the war, burn their draft cards, or slip across the border into Canada.

He did his job. He drank his beer. He sought his sexual pleasures. He lived for the present. He studiously avoided any sustained reflection on the legitimacy of the conflict, the strategy and tactics of the war, the impact on America's standing in the world, or the likely effect the war was having on the world to which he would shortly return.

Gary's joyfulness somehow deepens the awfulness of the war. What kind of man has the best year of his life investigating drug crimes, homicides, and suicides among traumatized young men 13,000 miles from home, draftees fighting a war that by now had essentially been given up as lost, and not even the government of the United States any longer talked of victory? Skogen is remarkably unconcerned with the larger implications of the war. The most he will say is, "By 1971 nothing any soldier could do to aid the war effort would affect the outcome. Despite the grandest or most heroic effort, there would be no turning point battle followed by the pageantry of surrender on a battleship in Haiphong Harbor. There existed a consciousness among the 1970s soldiers of the futility of dying in a thoroughly doomed cause." That, and nothing more. And with that brief foray into contextualization and reflection, Skogen turns to his narrative.

Historian Bill Chrystal has said that "every man is the hero of his own story." In other words, everyone shapes the story of his life, no matter how incoherently or ignominiously it actually unfolds, into a tidy narrative in which he is the exemplar of virtue and good sense, and those around him are, as often as not, "dickheads." Most Vietnam War memoirs exhibit this characteristic. One of the principal strengths of Skogen's book—and certainly its main source of credibility—--is that he has not chosen to portray himself as a hero. Just the opposite, in fact. Although it is hard not to suspect that he is piling it on a little for effect, Skogen presents himself as a pure opportunist who broke all the Army rules he found objectionable, while at the same time zealously enforcing the drug laws and regulations. He resists any temptation to invoke the Catch 22 defense that in a mad world with obscene and irrational policies and a pointless war, anything less than mere selfishness was its own form of madness. The sum total of Gary Skogen's "education" in Vietnam was that he discovered that he had a vocation for law enforcement, and in particular drug enforcement. Why a man of a generally anarchic temperament chose to make drug busts his arena of righteousness is not altogether clear from the narrative. Of course, drug abuse in war is especially problematic, but Skogen continued to serve as a drug cop for the rest of his distinguished career.

Skogen's book not only gives us an unvarnished, unapologetic, and unself-serving portrait of one man's tour in Vietnam, but—thanks to his work as a criminal investigator—a portrait of a number of his contemporaries whose lives miscarried in Vietnam, not on the battlefield, but within the confines of the base at Chu Lai. One of the purposes of this book is to raise the question of the legitimacy of some names incised on the Vietnam Veterans Memorial Wall in Washington, DC. Skogen would be the first to admit that his tour in Vietnam, late in the war when American discipline had largely broken down, should not be regarded as representative of the entire war. Chu Lai was just one of many military bases in Vietnam. Skogen saw only what he saw, and he makes no attempt to extrapolate his Vietnam experience. But he also knows that what he experienced at Chu Lai and Da Nang was by no means unique. A large number of US servicemen died in Vietnam in decidedly unheroic ways: of overdoses, in fights over Vietnamese women, in drunken brawls, some of which were racially motivated, in moronic gunplay, often involving intoxicated individuals, in reckless accidental deaths, and in suicide.

The specific claims made in this book are verifiable, as are each of the criminal incidents recorded here. In writing this book, fully forty years after coming home, Gary Skogen has not merely pulled together a series of plausible stories from the haze of his youth, relying solely on the vagaries of memory to tell the story of the cases he handled while in Vietnam. His brother Larry Skogen, a professional historian, impressed by the stories Gary told in the years following his return, but naturally a little skeptical, ventured to the National Archives and Records Administration in Washington, DC, to substantiate (or disprove) his brother's claims. He discovered that Gary's stories were impeccably accurate. In fact, he found incident reports signed in the field by Gary Skogen at Chu Lai, which elaborated (and verified) Gary's oral accounts of those investigations in fascinating detail. In other words, whatever you think of the author's character, values, and attitudes, the stories told in this book are all true. I have seen and inspected the boxes of records that Larry Skogen obtained from the National Archives, including by liberal use of the Freedom of Information Act (FOIA). The names of the individuals involved in the investigations have been changed in this book to avoid giving pain to surviving family members; but in no instance have the details of the crimes and incidents been altered for narrative effect.

———————

This book is sure to have its detractors. Much of that criticism will come from those who cannot understand how Skogen can have regarded his time in Vietnam as an extended beach holiday with benefits while so many of his contemporaries were living through the greatest nightmare of their lives, while at least two nations were being torn apart by the war, and while many of his contemporaries at the front were being killed or wounded precisely at the same time he sought hedonistic pleasures back in camp. Skogen's selfishness and multi-faceted detachment will perplex and offend many. But there are also specific issues in Skogen's book.

Drug enforcement is important, particularly in the military, where so much is at stake, but many readers, particularly those who grew up in the 1960s, have a healthy contempt for NARCs.

Many readers will also find fault with a drug enforcement officer who routinely broke whatever Army rules he disdained, who drank alcohol in excess, and exhibited no respect for military hierarchy and authority. Some readers will find it hard to locate the particular offensiveness of drugs to a man who wallowed in every other excess, including, of course, legal intoxication, and who by his own admission routinely broke Army regulations when it served his passions and interests.

And then there is Skogen's treatment of Vietnamese women. Only a puritan would shudder at the general sexual opportunism of the American GI in a soul-numbing conflict 13,000 miles away at the other end of the planet. In 1971 Skogen was twenty-six years old, highly sexed, and already apparently a veteran of such sexual satisfactions as were available on the plains of North Dakota in the early 1960s. Like most GIs, he took advantage of the ready availability of sex in Vietnam. He was in Vietnam no more than a few days when he received his first blowjob (for 33 cents, in a squalid off-base hooch), and the sense one gets is that he never endured more than a day or two of celibacy in the course of his year in Vietnam. In addition to the hooch girls, the barmaids, the waitresses, the blowjob girls, Skogen had at least two sustained "relationships" in Vietnam with women that have the narrative status of "girlfriends." But he freely tells the reader that he was not monogamous with those special women even for the duration of those relationships. He told one (Phan Thi San) that he reserved the right to take advantage of other sexual prospects when they came along; and the other (a "B-girl" named Lin) actually arranged to send prostitutes to his rental house in Da Nang when she was otherwise occupied for the night.

All this may strike the reader as a bit excessive, but not fundamentally different from the experiences of thousands of other young American men in the war. The 1960s were a time of unprecedented sexual opportunity, and Vietnam was the mother lode. Still, Skogen happily tells us that he made promises to many of these women (to buy them mail-order gifts from Sears Roebuck, for example) with no intention of keeping them. In other words, in a country where one could buy sex for 50 P (piasters) or 33 cents, somehow, in a place where it might have seemed impossible to be a cad, Gary Skogen found a way.

Then there is the issue of whose names belong on the Vietnam Veterans Memorial Wall in Washington, DC. Skogen's particular objection—that not every one of the 58,272 men whose names are incised on the wall is a legitimate hero—makes sense the minute you stop to think about it. He documents a number of cases, from his time at Chu Lai, to prove that those individuals, at least, did not die in ways that can be considered admirable. But whatever status the wall now occupies in American memory and mythology, it was certainly not intended (in 1982) to serve as a hero's list, or to create a hierarchy of death with chivalrous nobility at the top and postmodern squalor at the base. The purpose of the wall was to list those Americans whose lives were terminated in Vietnam. Surely there were protracted debates, when the memorial was designed, about just what sorts of death earned one a place on the wall. In the end anyone who died in the armed services in Vietnam, Laos, Camobodia, and coastal areas between 1956 and the close of the war, according to criteria articulated in a 1965 Presidential Executive Order, was deemed worthy of inclusion. Those missing in action were also included.

In other words, Skogen's objection to the inclusion of those who died from suicide, drug overdoses, and brawling makes sense if you think of the wall as a hero's list, but it is less persuasive if you regard the wall as a purely statistical list of deaths in Vietnam and surrounding countries. Skogen emphatically stands by his assertion that to include a GI who drank himself to death in Saigon alongside someone who died on the front lines is an abomination.

Some historians, psychologists, veterans, and veteran's families will argue that even if one accepts Skogen's general distinction between heroes and non-heroes, it would be unfair to stigmatize those who died from the trauma of Vietnam rather than from an enemy bullet or booby trap as non-heroes. The term "casualties of war," they insist, surely has a wider definition than those killed in action. Those who drank themselves to death and those who took drug overdoses would be regarded by many as legitimate casualties in a war as problematic, traumatic, and divisive as Vietnam, as deserving to be listed proudly among the war dead on the Vietnam Wall as those killed in battle.

This kind of logic Skogen regards as the thinking of dickheads.

———————

When Gary Skogen left Vietnam on January 24, 1972, there were still 140,000 American troops in Vietnam. Each of them has a story to tell as important to a complete understanding of Vietnam as that of Skogen—or anybody else, for that matter. Skogen's memoir must be seen as one relatively minor piece of the larger mosaic of the war. His story is not definitive, but it is important and legitimate, and it is a welcome relief from the dominant heart of darkness theme that characterizes most books in this genre. No single personal account of the war can adequately represent the complex set of events that occurred between 1954 and 1975, tore at the soul of America's sense of itself, terminated two presidencies prematurely, and indelibly marked a whole generation of American men and women. Many Vietnam memoirs are more dramatic than Gary Skogen's, and they may be regarded as more important narratives. But they are not more representative (arguably less), and they provide what can only be regarded as a distorted portrait of the war, certainly a partial one.

We all see through the glass darkly, and—inevitably—in very localized and selfish ways. The 1960s carried American individualism to its logical extreme. Theoretically, there are 2.8 million uniquely legitimate accounts of Vietnam—on the American side alone. Skogen's memoir helps to fill in a relative void in the Vietnam story. It is to be hoped that it will encourage others who lingered on the leeward side of the front lines to write their memoirs, even if they have not previously felt that their stories were dramatic enough or grave enough to deserve preservation. As Samuel Hynes rightly insists, "The soldier's tale of Vietnam is all of the stories. We must not choose among them." The last American servicemen to die in Vietnam were US Marine embassy guards Charles McMahon and Daniel. L. Judge. They were killed in a rocket attack one day before the Fall of Saigon (April 30, 1975). They occupy that unenviable place in the list of US casualties in Vietnam that hundreds of thousands, including Gary Skogen, worked assiduously to avoid.

They did not live to tell their Vietnam stories.

Clay S. Jenkinson
February 4, 2013

PREFACE

Shortly after Desert Storm in 1991, the first President George Bush declared, "The specter of Vietnam has been buried forever in the desert sands of the Arabian Peninsula." On May 1, 2003, the second President George Bush declared, "Major combat operations in Iraq have ended." Both Bushes were wrong. The Vietnam War still gnaws at the soul of America; and, far more American soldiers died in Iraq following the second pronouncement than before it. Moreover, the second President Bush's Iraq War arguably only lengthened the war in Afghanistan, a result of the terror of September 11, 2001. The specter of these prolonged wars should remind Americans of the evils that permeate an army flailing in the morass of a non-winnable war—from political failings or military failings, or both.

And the morass that sucks in an army is as lethal as fighting the war itself. Less than a year into the second Gulf War, reports of suicides among soldiers serving in Iraq shocked the American public. Flying under the radar screen of the news media, but just as importantly, were the airplane loads of "section eight" patients—those who had mentally broken under the pressures of war—winging their way back to the States. Medicated into a manageable impaired consciousness, these soldiers, airmen, sailors, and Marines would be probed, prodded, evaluated, and, discharged, many diagnosed with post-traumatic stress disorder (PTSD)—a "mental illness" directly descended from the "Vietnam Syndrome." Defense lawyers of American veterans of these modern wars are blaming criminal activities on the veterans' PTSD or some other link to the war, anything to deflect personal accountability for their actions just as the Vietnam Syndrome served my generation.

During these modern conflicts, we also witnessed an increase in the number of criminal acts committed by American service men and women in the region encompassing Iraq and Afghanistan. Before the second Iraq War even began in earnest, a soldier threw a grenade into a tent housing officers, reminiscent of the "fraggings" in Vietnam. We also learned about a plethora of sexual assaults against American military women serving in that area perpetrated by their male comrades in arms. The criminal abuse of enemy prisoners is well documented, by the abusers themselves. And, I suspect, all of these crimes were just the activities that the military hadn't been able to cover up. Only because I spent my life before, during, and after the Vietnam War committed almost wholly to fighting crimes connected to illicit drug use and trade, my guess is that historical researchers will also find an extraordinary increase in activities involving illegal drug abuse.

My suspicions are not unfounded. The poppy crop (the source of heroin and opium) in Afghanistan was larger during the war than since before the rise of the Taliban. In 2006 the Associate Press reported the opium harvest in Afghanistan was worth $3.1B. By 2008 the United Nations was reporting that the Taliban was making more money from the opium trade than before the United States forces and their allies toppled it. By 2011 the United Nations reported that the revenue from opium comprised one-tenth of the country's GDP. If there weren't a global market for the product, Afghani farmers wouldn't be so anxious to raise it. And anywhere that there are young men and women, particularly lonely, depressed, or scared, there'll arise a demand for a quick road to euphoria. Heroin and opium offer such a route. I fear, based on nothing more than thirty years of drug enforcement work, that the longer the United States remains in any part of the world "awash" in drugs the more likely it will be that American service members will smuggle, sell, trade, barter, and use illegal drugs. If we are to believe the Russian news agency Pravda, that happened in Afghanistan much sooner than American authorities were ready to admit. As early as December 2003, Pravda.ru reported:

> US Soldiers are developing a drug addiction problem in Afghanistan, said [Russian] Deputy State Drug Controller Alexander Mikhailov. He said that there have already been several occurrences of drug addiction among US soldiers in Afghanistan, but the US leadership is keeping it quiet. "They don't have control of the situation. . . ," said Mikhailov.

In 2012 the Associated Press reported that the "U.S. military struggles to keep an eye on its far-flung troops [in Afghanistan] and monitor for substance abuse." The same report documented drug overdoses and arrests for drug violations in both Afghanistan and in the Army's far-flung bases around the world. For those of us who worked the drug problem in Vietnam, such reports sound eerily familiar.

From February 1971 through January 1972, I served with the United States Army's Criminal Investigation Division (CID) in the Vietnam War. My CID colleagues and I waged a war within the war. Although all major criminal activities fell under our jurisdiction, narcotics offenses and drug-related crimes earned the lion's share of our time. This book is about those criminal activities. Suicides, homicides, personal and property crimes, and drug overdoses barely begin to paint an accurate picture of the Army during its retreat from Vietnam. Within the following pages you'll witness the depravity of the Army during one of the final years of America's then-longest war.

My story is also about the privileged class of soldiers fortunate to be criminal investigators. Although we enforced the law, we often lived outside the pale of Army rules. To protect ourselves, we acquired a stash of unauthorized weapons. To relieve the tension of the war and our jobs, we immersed ourselves into alcohol and sex. To escape the day-to-day Army, we lived and partied quite apart from the rest of the soldiers. Our story is little known to the general public or students of the war.

The criminal and law enforcement activities (drug busts and violence) along with the sex will, I suspect, entertain some of you. But the truths underlying the entertainment (e.g., the sheer number of American soldiers who died from drug overdoses—a cause of death not even recognized in the official casualty figures for the war) will provoke you to question the war's myths. The fact that every one of the names of soldiers who died from drug overdoses while in Vietnam is now chiseled on to "The Wall" for all Americans to honor will, I believe, raise many an eyebrow.

My argument is that service in the Vietnam War wasn't always the noble undertaking of America's youth: Not everyone who served or died in Vietnam is, or should be, a national hero. I also argue against the image of the victim-veteran who so often represents the Vietnam War veterans. The late American writer Art Buchwald once said about World War II that for those veterans who survived the war unscathed it was the best time of their lives. That's the way Vietnam was for many Vietnam War veterans and me. The din from the Veterans Administration's victim-veterans, however, has drowned us out.

My story should serve as a clarion warning to the American people and to their military leaders. In Vietnam the military reacted too late and with too little to the growing flood of crimes and drug abuse that vitiated American forces. It wasn't until 1970 that the

Pentagon took seriously those real threats to the military's capabilities. Prior to then military leaders ignored (because of patriotism or denial or wishful thinking) the signs of the looming disintegration of the military. I fear that today there is a veneer of patriotism covering Americans' view of their soldiers and that they'll not see the realities of the effects of a prolonged war upon warriors. (This patriotism, too, is connected to Bush the First's "specter of Vietnam." A national guilt emanating from the perception that Vietnam veterans were not properly appreciated by their countrymen has led the country into hero-worshipping all those in uniform.) However, despite the hero-worshipping and the veneer, I suspect that we'll find that in our modern wars, as in Vietnam and all other wars, not all warriors are heroes.

My guess is that, after reading my story, you'll not like me much. In fact, many readers will consider some of my actions in the war downright loathsome. That's okay. I didn't go to Vietnam to impress you, and I certainly don't care what you think about my personal conduct. What I do care about, however, is that you glimpse the underbelly of war and realize, as I do, that all the patriotic fanfare that has come to represent our wars and warriors does not change the nature of the undertaking. In war our normally accepted standards of conduct and expectations are suspended. Only the most rigorous imposition of military order has any luck of keeping the warriors' most primordial instincts in check.

There is certainly nothing new about that conclusion. In *Rubicon: The Last Days of the Roman Republic,* Tom Holland writes, "To the Romans, the passions of youth were violent and dangerous, and only discipline could tame them." And so it is that by the time I got to Vietnam in 1971, military discipline was virtually non-existent— at least in all the parts of Vietnam that I experienced. Without that discipline, the passions of our youth, our warriors, "were violent and dangerous." Let's hope that we don't see a recurrence of that scenario in our current or future conflicts.

One final note: the stories you're about to read are all true. They are based on my personal recollections substantiated with archival research, to include CID and Military Police reports, courts-martial records, unit after-action reports, various unit histories, and the National Archives and Records Administration's Combat Area Casualties Current File from the Records of the Office of the Secretary of Defense, Record Group 330. However, to protect the living and the dead, or their families, I have changed the names of subjects, victims, witnesses, and investigators in the criminal cases. Let families think what they want about the service or loss of their sons, brothers, fathers, and grandfathers in the Vietnam War. Let the rest of us know what did and can really happen.

CHAPTER 1   THE WALL

"It is well that war is so terrible.
We should grow too fond of it."

—*Robert E. Lee*

*Commanding General
Confederate Armies*

On the afternoon of January 24, 1972, the "freedom bird" lifted off from Da Nang Airfield heading back to the "World"—the United States. We sat in stony silence as the chartered commercial jetliner accelerated during its take-off roll, but a boisterous roar—punctuated with vulgarities —greeted the lift off. A couple hundred GIs riotously voiced excitement at having survived their year in 'Nam and heralded anticipation of what awaited them back home. That is, things of the real world such as Big Macs, round-eyed women, real houses—not hooches—and Chevrolets and Fords.

Despite the Army's best effort to transplant American culture to Vietnam, the half-finished hooches, Oriental women in ao dais, rice grass conical hats, mopeds, handcarts, pedicabs, rice paddies, and water buffaloes never let the illusion take root. The map might indicate you were taking a trip from one spot on earth called Vietnam to another called the United States, but everyone on the freedom birds knew that the trip was from somewhere grotesque and unearthly back to the World.

Our freedom bird was but one of thousands that transported American service men and women from Vietnam. Altogether, 2.8 million of us circulated through Southeast Asia between the mid-1960s and 1973 when the United States ended its longest and most divisive war. Because the war lasted so long, the wartime experiences of Vietnam veterans differ vastly. Troops arriving in-country early in the war could proudly claim to be the standard-bearers of a powerful nation united behind its soldiers paying the price of liberty for less fortunate people of the world. "We shall pay any price, bear any burden, meet any hardship," President John F. Kennedy had said. By the time I arrived in Vietnam in February 1971, that view of the war had long since evaporated. The 1968 Democratic Convention in Chicago dispelled any illusion of national unity on the war effort. Richard Nixon won the presidential election that year by promising to extricate America from the Vietnamese quagmire. On June 8, 1969, he announced the first withdrawal of United States troops (25,000) from Vietnam. Thereafter, the number of Americans in the war spiraled down sharply. When I arrived there less than two years later, roughly 250,000 troops remained in Vietnam, down from a peak of over 540,000 in 1969. A year later when our freedom bird lifted off from Da Nang, we left behind fewer than 150,000 American troops. Fourteen months later, most of them, too, had departed Vietnam on freedom flights heading home.

Those of us who served in Vietnam from February 1971 to January 1972 held no patriotic illusions about winning the war. We served only as a rear guard protecting a full-scale American retreat that President Nixon dubbed "peace with honor." Our time in the war laid sandwiched between Nixon's visit to China in February 1971 and the North Vietnamese Army's Eastertide Offensive—an all-out attack against South Vietnam—that began in March 1972. These two events foreshadowed the future: normalized US-China relations and an unrelenting North Vietnamese conquest of the South. These events also demonstrated that the United States's priorities as a world power had shifted dramatically from a pugnacious idealism against the communists to a pragmatic accommodation with them.

Despite the political realities differentiating the experiences of earlier war veterans from us later ones, we did share with them the reality that our individual war in Vietnam lasted one year after our arrival in-country. The end of that year was marked by what the military called our "DEROS," Date Eligible for Return from Overseas. All of us counted on returning to the World on our DEROS. Given this realization, soldiers across the full timeline of America's involvement in the war sought only to survive that one year and leave Vietnam with all body parts securely attached.

Beyond this similarity, however, distinctions in the wartime experiences of Vietnam veterans abound, including, for example, the attitude of the soldiers toward the war. During the early escalation of it, many soldiers thought we could win the war. They carried to Vietnam an arrogant optimism bathed with the glow of America's past military successes. No one could withstand American might. By the early seventies, during the ebbing tide of the war, none of us, except perhaps the fieriest and most inveterate patriot, thought we could win in Vietnam. This attitude had a demoralizing effect on America's warriors. No one wants to be the last soldier to die in a country's war. By 1971, nothing any soldier could do to aid the war effort would affect the outcome. Despite the grandest or most heroic effort, there would be no turning-point battle followed by the pageantry of surrender on a battleship in Haiphong Harbor. There existed a consciousness among the 1970s' soldiers of the futility of dying in a thoroughly doomed cause.

This reality cast a pall of cynicism and depression over American forces in Vietnam, with a resulting deterioration of what is called military discipline. Instead of counting on obedience from their enlisted troops, officers often feared them. Soldiers wore love beads while in uniform, smoked marijuana both on and off duty, and frequently fought among themselves, widening destructive racial fissures running through units. It would not be fair, though, to blame such conduct only on the fact that they were fighting in a lost war. Events on the home front also molded the behavior of the individual American soldier. The racial divisiveness of the 1960s, the crash of the counter-culture, the growing cynicism toward authority, and an epidemic of drug abuse—just to name a few—all came to Vietnam in the ruck-sacks of individual soldiers.

By 1971 the war had spun completely out of control. Not only had the United States lost the war, but also the military establishment had lost control of the warriors. No one knew this better than those of us sent to Vietnam as special agents with the US Army's Criminal Investigation Division (CID). We were assigned there as part of the Army's attempt to regain control of the plummeting military establishment. We represented the Army's effort to impose order over chaos.

You might say that the CID waged a war within the war. Although we investigated all major crimes committed by soldiers, we spent most of our time fighting the "drug war," that is investigating narcotics offenses and drug-related crimes. In 1968, the CID estimated that 48 percent of its workload in Vietnam involved drug cases. During 1971, that figure climbed to 71 percent. I never saw the Viet Cong (VC) or North Vietnamese Army (NVA) as my enemies. Except for occasional rocket attacks that were more nuisances than threats and one firefight in the bush, I cared little about them. The war against them was not my war. More often than not, I found my enemies in Army uniforms or among Vietnamese nationals proclaiming friendship to the Americans. Drugs dominated my war. By abusing or trafficking narcotics, these GIs and Vietnamese posed a greater threat to CID agents, not to mention other American soldiers, than did either the VC or the NVA. Drug overdoses or violent crimes related to drug abuse or trafficking claimed the lives of many of the GIs that I knew who died in Vietnam.

My perspective on the war, therefore, is admittedly far different than that of the combat soldiers who fought in the bush or "Indian Country" —the jungle and elephant-grassed areas outside the support bases. My perspective is also different from those of the far greater number of soldiers who served at the large support bases. Contrary to popular myth, often perpetuated by those who served in Vietnam, most soldiers did not fight in the jungles and rice paddies of Vietnam, but spent their time in the relative security of large bases. Not many Vietnam War veterans admit to their drinking buddies (and now to their grandchildren) that they spent the war typing daily reports in air-conditioned offices, not sloshing through rice paddies.

My Vietnam experience as a CID agent also colors how I view national symbols of the war, such as the Vietnam Veterans Memorial in Washington, DC. The Wall, as it's commonly called, contains the names of more than 58,000 Americans who died in Vietnam. Many of them died in combat or other war-related military activities and deserve a memorial in their honor. Many of the names that I recognize on the Wall, however, memorialize men who died of drug overdoses, in drunken brawls, as a result of criminal activity, or by their own hands for a variety of reasons, none noble. Not everyone who served or died in Vietnam is a national hero.

For example, take the case of Private Nat Johnson, an eighteen-year-old African American from Washington, DC. He arrived in Vietnam in March 1971 and was assigned to the 544th Transportation Company at Chu Lai. At about 5:30 p.m. just eight days after arriving in-country, Johnson asked one of his new buddies if he wanted to share some "skag," a vernacular term for heroin. His buddy refused— or so he told me later. Johnson assured him that it was safe, "he had used it for a long time, and he knew how to handle it." Not well enough, as it turned out. Shortly after midnight, a soldier found Johnson on his back in his bunk with foam oozing from his nose and mouth. Another soldier in the barracks tried to revive Johnson. An ambulance took him to the emergency room of the 91st Evacuation Hospital where he was pronounced dead on arrival. An autopsy and toxicology report showed that he'd died of a drug overdose. The death certificate says that Private Johnson died from respiratory and cardiac arrest, "2nd degree to aspiration of vomitus." He drowned in his own puke. Today he's memorialized on the Wall.

Compare Johnson's death to that of Private Robert Wallace. In 1968, Wallace and I served together as Military Police (MPs) at Lundstahl, Germany. He was a lanky, white Southern boy with a deep drawl. He stood 6'1" and barely made MP weight standards. He was a nineteen-year-old on his first assignment after basic training and MP school. One evening after working a dayshift, some of us went drinking at the local gasthaus. We got drunk; stumbling down stupid drunk—a rather normal occurrence for us. When we got back to the barracks, Wallace was so inebriated he couldn't put himself to bed. His buddies just dropped him in his bunk. He went to sleep on his back, vomited, and drowned in his own puke. (Quite frankly, the most vivid thing that I can remember about Wallace is the memorial service. That was the first time I'd ever really heard taps. Of course, I'd heard taps before, but never when it caused a lump in my throat as it did that time.) His death was as tragic and stupid as the death under similar circumstances of any young person anywhere. But because Robert Wallace died in Germany and not Vietnam, there isn't a Wall with his name on it.

Does the geographic location of Johnson's drowning in vomit make him worthier of such recognition than Private Wallace? And Johnson isn't alone. Far too many of the names on the Wall memorialize soldiers who died similar deaths. In 1970, the year before I arrived in Vietnam, the Army officially, but quietly, claimed 103 deaths by drug overdose. In 1971, we far outstripped 1970 figures. One study estimates that, during the later years of the war, drug overdoses accounted for more than two deaths per day. If that's true, and I believe it is, then simple mathematics tells us that at least a few thousand of the names on the Wall are there because soldiers overdosed on drugs—an action neither patriotic nor noble, and certainly not one worth honoring. Yet, the official death tally for the war doesn't even list "Drug Overdose" as a cause of death. In the non-hostile category, it lists 1,207

"Drowned/Suffocated," 273 "Heart Attack," 1,371 "Other Accident," 842 "Accidental Self Destruction," and 258 non-hostile "Other Causes." Drug overdoses were, in fact, counted under all of these categories and many more. But doing so only whitewashes the reality: many Americans died from drug overdoses or drug-related causes in Vietnam. (Private Johnson's cause of death is officially listed as "non-hostile—died of other causes" and "accidental self-destruction.")

In memorializing the names that I recognize on the Wall or those that died under such circumstances, we're detracting from the honor rightfully bestowed on those men and women who died in the service of their country, and not drowning in their own vomit from alcohol binges or drug overdoses. Henry D. Thoreau wrote, "The impure can neither stand nor sit with purity." With our choice of a national symbol to memorialize those who died in the war, we've etched in granite the names of far too many who do not deserve our respect. We've made the decision that the pure and the impure will be honored together. The nation needs to ask itself if those Private Johnsons who drowned in their own puke (or similar ignoble deaths) should be honored in the same fashion as those heroes who died in the Battle of Ia Drang fighting with Lieutenant Colonel Hal Moore—and countless more battles with countless more commanders. Read Hal Moore's and Joseph Galloway's *We Were Soldiers Once... and Young*, then compare the stories of the heroes recounted in that book to the soldiers' stories in this book. Then ask yourself if they should be honored similarly. I don't think they should be and, frankly, I think it's a national disgrace that they are.

I'm also angry about society's tendency to grant without skepticism victim status to those of us who served in Vietnam. Most Vietnam vets returned home, got jobs, went to school, raised families, and paid taxes. We didn't grovel in self-pity about having to serve our country in some hellhole halfway around the world. A small vocal minority of us—or, as is often the case, pretenders to our status—have set the national agenda regarding Vietnam War veterans. With the complicity of the Veterans Administration (VA) and quacks in the field of psychiatry and psychology cheered on by the media and the entertainment industry, this vocal minority has created an image that we are all victims of the terrible experiences we suffered during the war. As the story goes, we victims require continuing care by a nation that hadn't shown us enough compassion or gratitude decades ago. The now-remorseful nation has created a plethora of compensation programs allowing victim-veterans to collect money and participate in a number of federally funded programs.

For an excellent study of this hoax foisted on the American public, read B. G. Burkett's *Stolen Valor: How the Vietnam Generation Was Robbed of its Heroes and its History*. His argument is quite poignant:

> In ten years of research in the National Archives ... I discovered a massive distortion of history, a poisonous myth created by an entertainment industry so enamored of sensationalism that it had no qualms about presenting a false stereotype to generate profits, by a Department of Veterans Affairs as concerned with its own power base as America's war-wounded, by a legal system manipulated by unscrupulous attorneys motivated not by justice but by a need to win at all costs, by social welfare advocates and mental health professionals willing to support a lie to further their own agendas, and by print and television journalists unwilling to examine their own politics and preconceptions.

This hoax has gone so far as to add to this tormented class of veterans those service members who served during the Vietnam War, but never served in Vietnam. Burkett writes, "To be eligible for compensation, the veteran needs only to have one day of service during the Vietnam era and be certified by a VA psychiatrist as traumatized by an event during military service, not necessarily during combat." In other words, stateside service with one traumatic event—say, the fear that one might be sent to Vietnam—is enough to allow a victim-veteran to receive compensation. As the year 2000 approached, the VA ran advertisements to encourage Vietnam-era veterans who had not served in Vietnam to sign up for its programs because January 1, 2000, was the cutoff date for them to register for some VA services. For the VA, more clients means more money. It's a whole new twist to the Vietnam War's notorious body counts.

And what about all those pretend victim-veterans? Once being a Vietnam veteran became the vogue, these pretenders emerged from the carcass of the war to garner undeserved rewards, such as VA benefits and recognition. A Pulitzer-prize winning historian, politicians, educators, actors, baseball managers, the guys next door, and the homeless bums all claim they served during the war and want to be recognized as national heroes. Thankfully, true veterans such as Burkett and retired Navy Captain Larry Bailey are smoking out these fakers and exposing their fraud. Even so, the sheer number of counterfeiters makes the task formidable. One report suggests there are more than 7,000 fake Navy SEALs—special forces—hawking themselves to an unwitting public. *Caveat emptor*—let the buyer beware—is appropriate advice for anyone encountering an alleged Vietnam veteran, especially one who claims to be the "only survivor of a secret mission," or a prisoner of war, or a Medal of Honor winner. Generally speaking, the more heroic the war story, the more likely it is a fraud.

Of course, there are real prisoners of war and Medal of Honor recipients. In *Stolen Valor* Burkett provides appendices with complete lists of veterans holding these distinctions. Before one invites a Vietnam War hero to talk to any group about his war exploits that won him the Medal of Honor or a similar distinction, one ought to check Burkett's lists. (As a result of Burkett's bringing this problem to light, in 2006 Congress overwhelmingly passed the Stolen Valor Act making it a federal crime to make false claims about the military's highest medals. In 2012 the United States Supreme Court overturned the act as unconstitutional.)

As a minor consolation to my generation, I must add that every war has had its fake heroes. From the American Revolution to the Indian wars of the nineteenth century, the Civil War, and the world wars, there have always been men—and sometimes women—making false claims about having fought gallantly against the nation's foes. Their motives have always been the same: financial gain or a yearning to be something they weren't, heroic individuals. Rather than live a life worthy of such recognition, they have always appropriated the true heroism of real soldiers and fighters for their own pathetic lives.

America's Middle Eastern conflicts in this new century will have generated more military fakers. As the *Navy Times* reported in May 2010, "A former sailor charged with killing his wife ... opted for an insanity defense, saying he suffers from post-traumatic stress disorder stemming from nine years as a [Navy] SEAL." The Navy SEALs are the elite, best of the best Special Forces in the Navy. The problem is that this accused killer never was a SEAL, but that didn't stop him from telling relatives and the police that he suffered from his heroic military exploits as a SEAL. In the twenty-seven years that I served as a Los Angeles policeman after my own return from Vietnam, I saw an increasing number of these victim-veterans, fake or real. They refused to take responsibility for their own actions and, instead, blamed the military, government, or society for their shortcomings. Most of them looked or acted like bums and dressed in old uniforms embellished by an array of military patches and medals. As soon as we would start to question them, they would invariably act indignant because they'd been to "Nam" and we should treat them with respect.

"You're fucking with me 'cause I'm a vet," they'd say. "I've been to Nam, man, and you don't know what that was like."

Well, I did know what it was like, and let them know it. Once we got that fact out of the way, we dealt with the business at hand. And years ago, many of my partners were also Vietnam veterans. But by the time I retired from the LAPD, there were very few Vietnam veterans left in the department. But then, too, there were far fewer Vietnam veterans or pretend veterans running afoul of the law.

When I was in Vietnam, however, running afoul of the law was extremely common among America's soldiers. As a result, I found my whole Vietnam experience quite fun. In fact, the greatest of ironies for me is that the Army's loss of control in Vietnam and the subsequent lack of military discipline with its attendant drug abuse, trafficking, and violent crimes is precisely what made serving in the war such a great experience.

When our freedom bird lifted off from Da Nang, I didn't cheer with the rest of the soldiers. I had tried unsuccessfully to extend my tour in Vietnam. I didn't want to go back to the World because I was having too much fun. I hadn't come to the war as a combat soldier, but as a cop. I had been trained to investigate crimes, a job I thoroughly enjoyed. I went to Vietnam, not in olive drab (OD) green fatigues and combat boots, but wearing a sports shirt, trousers, and loafers. I enjoyed practically every day I spent in Vietnam. Fighting criminals and living in an environment where we enforced the law, but didn't always abide by the rules, was an incomparable high. For me, the Vietnam War was truly the best of times.

CHAPTER 2   TROOPSHIP

NORTHWEST

AIRLINES

I stood out. Everyone standing with me on the tarmac at Travis Air Force Base, California, waiting to board the chartered aircraft wore US Army OD green fatigues. I alone wore loafers and sports pants topped with a square-bottomed, short-sleeved, light cotton, white shirt. The only commonality between the rest of them and me that bright February morning in 1971 is that we all had orders to Vietnam.

Most of the faces around me still showed the unmistakable signs of youth. A few old-timers were heading back for another tour in the war, although some of the lifers—those having served in the Army for more than four years—were embarking on their first trip to Vietnam. Statistically, the age of twenty-six with five years in the Army put me in this last group. My clothes, however, set me apart.

In the military, the uniform and its rank insignia define one's status. Because of the uniform, everyone knows one's place in the military hierarchy and, more importantly, knows that place relative to every other soldier. The lower one's rank, as indicated by the insignia, means fewer privileges. A higher rank accords one more privileges and a greater degree of respect. At a glance, soldiers know, relative to all other soldiers, whether they are to give or receive deference. It's all very comfortable.

That's why I stood out. Special agents of the Army's CID wear civilian clothes. The theory behind agents not wearing standard Army uniforms is twofold. First is the belief that there should be no rank distinction in a criminal investigation. The rank of someone they are investigating should not intimidate CID agents, and no one should know the rank of an investigator on a case. Therefore, no one knows where the investigator fits in the Army's pecking order.

Second, civilian clothes segregated CID agents from the rest of the troops to avoid conflicts of interest during investigations. Agents never know whom they'll be investigating. The Army doesn't want agents striking up friendships with soldiers who later become subjects of investigations. So agents wear civilian clothes and live, work, and play in a world separate from the rest of the Army. This rank anonymity and segregation, I admit, makes agents quite cocky, if not downright arrogant.

For me, at least, there existed a third, unintended, and much more important effect of segregating me from the rest of the Army. Because of it, I felt detached, if not insulated, from the war itself. When I first arrived in Vietnam, I had a very strong sense that I had arrived in a war zone and that somehow the fighting, dying, and killing would affect me. However, as the days turned into weeks and the weeks translated into months, I grew more and more detached from the war and felt immune from its consequences. My civilian shirt had become a magic garment protecting me from the bullets and rockets of the Viet Cong (VC) and North Vietnamese Army (NVA). My job as a criminal investigator and my civilian clothing detached me from the realities of the war and, no doubt, colored my perspective of it.

CID agents stationed in the United States or Europe chose business suits or sports coats and ties for their civilian attire. I knew enough about Vietnam to know that a coat and tie would make an intolerable wardrobe in the tropics. From CID agents who had served in the war, I learned that in Vietnam they wore light cotton shirts, sports pants, and loafers. The whole sum of my girding for war involved shopping at a San Francisco men's clothing store to buy casual wear. So on February 23, 1971, looking quite like a colonial administrator, I stood in a long line of uniformed soldiers waiting on a tarmac at Travis Air Force Base—near Oakland, California—to board a chartered flight to Vietnam.

In the short-term, my trip to that tarmac was as distinctive as my clothing. For the vast majority of Vietnam-bound GIs, their journey to Travis began with orders to Oakland Army Base. There they spent three to five days standing in lines, listening to briefings, and filling out paperwork in a pageant the military calls out-processing. They loitered away their evenings in Spartan transition barracks. The Army choreographed all of these activities to its "hurry up and wait" dance: a tedious process of hurrying from one location to another just to spend hours waiting for something to happen, usually listening to another briefing or filling out more forms. When done at that location, soldiers would rush to a different location, there to wait again. Thus, "hurry up and wait." Eventually, the out-processing at Oakland ended with everybody boarding military buses for the trip to Travis.

My experience held few similarities to that of the typical soldier. I received orders to Vietnam while stationed at the Presidio in San Francisco. During my out-processing at Oakland Army Base, I drove back and forth between Oakland and the Presidio and spent every night in my own room on the Presidio. Being in civilian clothes, I came to and left from the out-processing dance whenever I pleased. I signed the right papers and got credit for the required briefings. As much as possible, I controlled the rhythm of my out-processing. My arrival at the tarmac at Travis, however, snatched me back into military reality.

On the morning of February 23, a CID agent drove me from the Presidio to Oakland Army Base where we exchanged farewells. I threw my duffel bag full of civilian clothes (I packed not one article of military clothing) on the back of a waiting deuce-and-a-half truck and boarded the bus to Travis. As we stepped off the bus at the Air Force base, a crusty old Army Noncommissioned Officer (NCO) armed with a bullhorn commanded us to line up by rank: officers, first; warrant officers (WOs), next; NCOs, after that; and then the lower enlisted grades. I didn't particularly cotton to that idea. Since becoming a CID agent in September 1969, only my closest associates knew my rank. Such rank anonymity helped create the CID mystique and, frankly, I liked it. As inconceivable as it sounds, while about to board an airplane to Vietnam my primary concern was that I would now have to reveal my rank to those unknown GIs around me.

As the sea of OD green rushed past me, each little group forming a pool, one of officers, one of NCOs, and so forth, I contemplated my limited options. I could use my CID credentials to convince Sergeant Bullhorn that I should have my own position in the line. As the only one in civilian clothes, it didn't seem to me that it would be much trouble putting me directly behind the officers or, for that matter, letting me board the airplane separately. Sergeant Bullhorn, though, didn't look like the type who tolerated either negotiations about or deviations to his master plan. I quickly dispelled that idea. My only other option: get in line. With a well-concealed reluctance, I walked over to the line and took my place with the other NCOs. This position put me considerably ahead of most of those in line, but also put me behind a small cadre each of officers, WOs, and senior NCOs. Glances of indifference from the troops around me, however, told me that I had been overly sensitive about the rank issue.

Nevertheless, although I didn't know it then, my sudden integration back into the military hierarchy proved to be short-lived.

As Air Force airmen took our duffel bags off the deuce-and-a-half truck and loaded them into the belly of the Northwest Airlines jet, we began filing up the ramp to board the airplane. I thought it odd that I would be going to war in an airplane belonging to the same airline that had at earlier times taken me home. I frequently flew with Northwest because it served Bismarck, North Dakota, the nearest major airport to my North Dakota hometown, Hettinger, a town of little more than 2,000 people in the southwest corner of the state. Northwest Airlines and many of the other major carriers (Continental, United, TWA, for example) had contracted with the federal government to provide jet-age troop transport for the Vietnam War. Very early in the war, naval troopships ferried soldiers across the Pacific Ocean to Southeast Asia, primarily because that's how soldiers had gone to war in the past and the Army isn't one to mess with tradition. It didn't take long, however, for military leaders to realize that weeks of seasickness and boredom could be avoided by contracting with commercial air carriers. Thus, the major airline companies stripped the amenities out of some Boeing 707s and Douglas DC-8s, filled the voids with seats, and contracted to carry up to three hundred soldiers per flight to Vietnam.

Fortunately, the airline companies preserved the stewardesses as one of the amenities not eliminated on troop flights. As each of us reached the top of the ramp and stepped into the airplane, a smiling stewardess welcomed us aboard. At a time when airlines still imposed age and weight restrictions on their attendants, it was obvious to me that the gray-headed woman greeting us had long ago passed those limits. I have always suspected that all of the flight attendants on our airplane had been hired out of retirement by Northwest specifically to work troop flights to Vietnam, probably to lessen the chances of what today we call sexual harassment against much younger and more appealing women.

Seating on the airplane, as our previous lining up on the tarmac, followed a hierarchical arrangement. The officers filled in the first seats, followed by the WOs, and so on. Just as I walked through the door, however, the stewardess greeting us pointed to another attendant standing at the very back of the cabin and said to me, "Go back to where she's standing." I walked past the filled seats, then the empty seats to where the other stewardess stood. She greeted me, opened an accordion door directly behind her, and invited me to take a seat. The open door led to the galley. When the airplane had been stripped of its amenities, including first-class, the galley had been modified by making it larger and adding extra seats. As I soon learned, the stewardesses spent most of the twenty-plus-hour flight to Vietnam sitting in the galley, talking, playing cards, and sleeping. My civilian attire had earned me a seat with them in the galley. I would be their diversion from the same stories they had told each other on previous flights.

As we took off from Travis and began our journey, my traveling companions and I exchanged introductions. They thought that I worked for the State Department or as a civilian contractor for Philco Ford. No, I told them, and identified myself as an Army CID special agent. Before long, the four stewardesses and I fell into a routine of talking, card playing, and sleeping. I earned my keep in the galley by entertaining them with my crime-fighting stories (some of which were actually true).

The stewardesses' stash of alcohol proved to be one of the many perks of sitting in the galley. Not wanting an airplane load of drunks landing in Vietnam, the Army prohibited the serving of alcoholic beverages on troop flights. This policy changed at times during the war, but on my flight, the attendants offered only coffee and soft drinks to the GIs. When offered a soft drink, I made a passing but quite serious comment about needing some bourbon to go along with it. One of the stewardesses obliged me and opened a galley cabinet filled with miniature liquor bottles. For the rest of the trip, the five of us enjoyed mixed drinks.

The wheels of our airplane touched down only once before reaching Vietnam. In Alaska we stopped to refuel. During the refueling, we soldiers departed the airplane to take advantage of a vending machine snack bar. We had left California on a bright, moderately warm February day. We landed in the cold evening darkness of an Alaskan winter. My thin sports shirt offered little protection from Alaska's frigid breath as I walked from the airplane to the terminal—there were no enclosed piers connected to the passenger gates back then; one walked out an airplane, down the ramp, and across the tarmac to get to the terminal. During my brisk walk to the terminal, I quickly gained a fondness for the idea of tropical Vietnam.

The sea of OD green made the vending machines and pay telephones in the terminal all but inaccessible. By now my preferential treatment on the airplane had transformed glances of indifference into glares of animosity from a few GIs. Most of the soldiers, however, cared little about whether this one guy in civilian clothes received better treatment than they. Besides, I had become accustomed to glares of animosity from GIs in my five years in the Army, all of which I spent enforcing military law and investigating crimes committed by troops in OD green fatigues.

Back in 1965 I was twenty years old and in the classic dead-end job going nowhere. Repairing and delivering appliances for a hardware store in Coeur d'Alene, Idaho, left me frustrated. I looked for a way to add excitement to my life. I telephoned the personnel officer for the Spokane (Washington) Police Department and learned that I had to be twenty-one years old before I could apply for a job as a policeman. Police work beckoned me because I thought it would be exciting. In my own mind, I became the central figure in vignettes involving fast cars, gun fights, fist fights, and, of course, pretty women. Being twenty years old, however, left me whiling away my time until my twenty-first birthday in October 1966.

Two events in 1965 changed the course of my life, as well as the lives of 2.8 million young Americans and their families. A year earlier the United States had increased its role in defending South Vietnam to include launching air attacks against the North from airfields in the South. In early 1965 the communists struck back by attacking the US airfield at Pleiku. President Lyndon Johnson reacted to this communist insolence by evacuating American families from South Vietnam and dramatically increasing US ground forces to protect the airfields. (By the end of 1965, more US forces served in South Vietnam than when I left Da Nang six years later.)

On the black-and-white television in the living room of my Coeur d'Alene apartment, I watched both the evacuation of the American families from South Vietnam and the landing of US Marines on the beaches at Da Nang. The images screamed with excitement. Under the watchful eye of US soldiers, American women and children rushed to helicopters and airplanes to be spirited out of the country. Marines, looking lethal and determined, splashed through the surf of the South China Sea and took up positions on Da Nang's sandy beaches (a location later glamorized in a television series called *China Beach*). Nothing crossing the television screen in front of me looked mundane. Everything I saw looked more exciting than delivering appliances.

The television reports from Vietnam began my transformation from civilian to soldier. The politics didn't motivate me. I cared nothing then, as well as today, about the causes of the war or America's purposes in fighting in it. I wasn't attracted to the ideas of containing communism, of the domino theory, or of defending US allies—particularly South Vietnam, a place I knew nothing about before the 1965 television news stories. It was the idea that I could fly in helicopters or land on the beaches of some far off land that excited me.

Just as the images on my television drew me toward the military, a second event in 1965 determined my fate. For those of us coming of age during the 1950s and 1960s, registering for the draft had become an accepted tribal ritual. Although historically the government had used conscription to fill the ranks of the military during wartime, in 1948 the United States adopted a peacetime draft. By the time I turned eighteen years old in 1963, registering for the draft had become an unquestionable duty for young men.

President Johnson used this pool of young American males to escalate the ground war in Vietnam without activating or calling up the reserves or the National Guard (which is why it became such a haven for that era's politically-connected sons). A call-up of the reserves or Guard would have signaled to everyone that President Johnson seriously wanted to fight that war, thus diverting the nation's attention from the Great Society, his more important domestic agenda. Moreover, such a call-up would bring hardship to Main Street America as citizen-soldiers marched off to Southeast Asia. Johnson didn't want to face the political fallout from such a call-up. Instead, to support his buildup of forces in South Vietnam in 1965, he increased draft quotas to the country's nearly 4,100 local draft boards.

Draft boards—eliminated by President Nixon's lottery system in 1970—held meetings in backrooms where they selected the young men, among the 1-A classified registrants, they would offer up on the draft quota altar. I presented an easy choice for the Adams County draft board meeting in the county courthouse at Hettinger. I hadn't been the scholastic type; I hardly made it out of high school in 1963, and everyone sitting on the board knew it—just one of the many disadvantages of living in a town with a population numbering barely 2,000 souls. Furthermore, in the summer of 1964, I had demonstrated my contempt for my parents by eloping with a divorced woman, much older than me, to Idaho where an eighteen-year-old could marry without parental consent. So, by 1965 I worked and lived in faraway Coeur d'Alene, contributing nothing to the social or economic life of Adams County, North Dakota. My selection must have set a record for the least-discussed decision by the Adams County draft board.

The pull I had been feeling toward the Army suddenly became a push when I received my draft notice in the late fall of 1965. Many young men of my generation viewed their draft notices as death sentences or, at best, sentences to hard labor. I found my invitation to the induction center quite liberating. No longer did I have to wait for my twenty-first birthday to make my life exciting. My draft notice heralded the arrival of a whole new life.

My father was less excited about my impending change of life. He contacted the draft board about getting a medical deferment for me. My wife at the time suffered from numerous medical problems. Dad tried to convince the board to defer me because of her medical condition. The board argued that she would receive better and less expensive medical treatment as my dependent in the Army than she was then receiving. The issue died as quickly as Dad had raised it.

With my draft notice in hand, my only concern was to figure out how to make the best of my situation. I knew that if I went through the conscription process, I faced two years in the Army with little control over my life. Suddenly, the images on my television screen and my perceptions of police work converged. The induction notice showed me that the Army possessed more interest in me than the city of Spokane.

I drove to the Army recruiting station in Spokane and told the recruiter that I wanted to be a cop. He told me that the Army never assigned draftees to its Military Police. If I wanted to be an MP, I had to meet height and weight restrictions, pass a number of other qualifying physical and mental examinations, and enlist for three years. The additional year seemed a small price to pay to maintain control of my life. At 5'10" and 145 pounds, I just met the physical qualifications; I passed the other physical and mental tests; I agreed to the terms of enlistment; and, on January 25, 1966, I enlisted for three years.

Eight weeks of basic training at Fort Ord, California, convinced me that I made the right decision. Dragging an M-14 rifle through the mud, under barbed wire, over concertina wire, up one wall, down the next, then running in formation back to the barracks only to get up the next morning to do it all again wasn't my idea of excitement. Officially, basic training instilled military discipline in us, hardened our bodies, and prepared us to fight the nation's wars—or, more specifically, the Vietnam War. That all may have happened to me, but more importantly, it convinced me that I never wanted to be a grunt, an 11-Bravo, an infantryman. Basic training only foreshadowed what awaited the grunts in their advanced infantryman training, and I pitied the poor bastards about to become 11-Bravos.

Army jobs are assigned a Military Occupational Specialty (MOS) code. The MOS for infantryman was 11-B, stated as "11-Bravo." In Vietnam, leaving the security of the large installations meant being in the "bush." Getting an MOS of 11-B almost assured one an assignment to the Vietnamese bush. Because of that, by the late 1960s, "11-Bravo" became "11-Bush."

On the day I enlisted, five other men enlisted with me at the induction center in Spokane. Of us six, two became surveyors, one an engineer, one an administration specialist, one an air defense artilleryman, and one (me) an MP. Not one of us became an infantryman. Virtually from the outset we enlistees were segregated from the draftees. Those uniformed folk processing us into the military moved us enlistees to one side of a large processing room and had all the draftees lined up against the wall at the other side of the room. "Who wants to go into the Navy?" someone asked the draftees. A couple of guys raised their hands and were then segregated into their own small group. The question "Who wants to go into the Marine Corps?" brought no reply. Nobody raised a hand. Then the sergeant in charge told the draftees to count off: one, two, three, one, two, three, and so on until everyone was just a number. Then he said, "All you twos line up with the gunny sergeant." The twos were now Marines. They nearly established a suicide watch for the twos from that point on because not one of them wanted to be a Marine. The ones and threes considered themselves lucky; they ended up in the Army.

So when we six enlistees took the oath of enlistment in the regular Army that day, another sixty or so men who chose not to enlist were drafted into the Navy, Marine Corps, or Army. The vast majority of those going into the Army became 11-Bravos and replacements for combat units in Vietnam. The same fate awaited our hapless Marines.

One recent study found that, in 1965, draftees made up 21 percent of the country's combat forces and 16 percent of the combat deaths. As the war continued, both those figures increased. By 1970, draftees made up as much as 70 percent of some combat units and accounted for 43 percent of the nation's combat deaths. Of course, these statistics meant nothing to the six of us who enlisted together in 1966, but we did benefit from the military's trend to put enlistees in the good jobs and to consign draftees to less-desirable positions, such as infantryman.

This trend became a virtual policy. Writing for *Newsweek* in 1970, Stewart Alsop said, "The Army has adopted a more or less explicit policy of encouraging well-qualified and intelligent young men to 'volunteer' for non-combat supply and administrative jobs, to avoid being drafted into the infantry. ... Hardly anyone volunteers for Eleven Bravo, for that's where people get killed."

I don't know that I was particularly "well-qualified and intelligent," and being an MP was neither a supply nor administrative job, but basic training convinced me that being an MP was a plum job. Basic training also provided the last combat training I ever received, a fact I regretted only once in Vietnam.

After basic training, I attended MP school at Fort Gordon, Georgia. I quickly found myself at home in the Military Police culture. Nothing seemed foreign to me. The language, the attitude, and even the rough-and-tumble of the self-defense classes all fit me so comfortably. My classmates and I enjoyed being told that we made up an elite group, that our physical and mental tests had demonstrated our superior abilities, and that it would be our job to maintain good order and discipline in the US Army. Good guys and bad guys divided the world, we learned, white hats verses black hats. That the Army issued white hats to the MPs was no coincidence. The bad guys we derisively called "dickheads." MP school taught us how to deal with and to defeat the dickheads. Nothing mundane crept into any of the MP training. Not a day went by that I didn't sense it: I stood at the threshold of an exciting world.

Because the Vietnam War had first served to pull, then to push me into the Army, I volunteered to go to Vietnam when I finished MP training. Had the Army sent me then, at the early stages of the war and as a uniformed MP, my perspective of the war would undoubtedly be different than it is today. The Army, however, instead sent me to Turkey.

Near Incirlik, Turkey, I found myself assigned to an ammunition storage facility. For someone wanting to be a cop, Turkey was nothing but a disappointment. My job: prevent pilfering of US property by Turkish nationals. Instead of being a policeman, I became a guard. To make it worse, the Turkish thieves didn't even target the munitions we so faithfully protected. Their tastes proved less sophisticated, but much more practical than that. They wanted the building materials and tools at the site, and even stole the perimeter fence along which we walked our posts.

One night I caught one of these thieves. No one ever expected us to catch one. If they had, they would have issued us handcuffs and two-way radios to summons backup, but they didn't. As I dutifully walked my post in the darkness of a Turkish evening, a man ran in front of me—a man stumbled in front of me, I should say. His load of four empty jerry cans off-balanced him, making him less than fleet of foot in his hasty retreat from our compound. I yelled, "Halt, Military Police!" as I had been trained to do at Fort Gordon. I'm sure he didn't understand me, but my yelling told him he was in trouble. He picked up his pace, all the while holding on to his prized gas cans. I judiciously decided not to shoot him, but reverted to my high school football days and tackled him. We fell together on the desert floor. I jumped up as quickly as I could, drew my issued .45 caliber semiautomatic pistol from its holster, and motioned him to remain prostrate on the ground.

My heart pounding, I now began to ponder my situation. No one ever told us what to do if we actually caught a thief, and without a radio or handcuffs there wasn't much I could do. I had, however, seen my share of cowboy movies. First, I fired two rounds from my pistol into the air. The blasts scared the shit out of the Turk on the ground. Given what little I know about Turkish justice, he can't be faulted for thinking he was my target. After firing the two shots, I confidently thought, "That'll bring somebody."

Too confidently it turned out. After a very long fifteen-minute wait, I still stood there alone guarding my very scared prisoner. I then took off my belt and tied his hands behind his back—cowboys, again. I helped him to his feet, pointed the direction to go, and the two of us, me now burdened with the four jerry cans I held as evidence, headed to a manned guard shack over a mile away.

Any exuberance I felt for having captured a Turkish desperado quickly faded upon arriving at the guard shack. Through a blizzard of profanity, the NCO of the guard informed me that my job was to keep Turks from coming onto our compound, not to catch them on their way out of it. I now realized that part of the master plan included the absence of handcuffs and radios for the guards. No one intended for us to catch anybody.

The NCO turned my prisoner over to a local policeman. My guess is they went to a local café and, over a thick cup of Turkish coffee, my ex-prisoner recounted my John Wayne antics to the uncontrollable laughter of his lifelong neighbors. As I later learned in Vietnam, co-operation between local police and the US military existed often as a facade serving political, not law enforcement ends. Understandably, local policemen had much stronger ties to and affection for local nationals caught in the web of American law enforcement than for the Army's MPs or CID. I didn't know it then, but the consequences of my capture of a Turkish thief began my education for duty in Vietnam.

Fortunately when I arrived at the storage facility near Incirlik, the Army had already begun dismantling it and removing the munitions. After a disappointing three months in Turkey, the place resembled any other uninteresting spot in the Turkish desert, and the Army sent me to France.

At the same time, French President Charles de Gaulle had pulled his country out of the military structure of the North Atlantic Treaty Organization (NATO) and kicked its forces out of France. As a consequence, most tourists see more of France than I did. I remained there just long enough to see the Eiffel Tower, to wonder why it caused so much excitement, and to receive orders to Miesau, West Germany.

To my chagrin, Miesau turned out to be another ammunition storage assignment. The Germans, however, had no interest in the munitions or the perimeter fence we guarded. I grew nostalgic for Turkish thieves. My Army bosses knew I had a burning desire to be a cop, not a guard. In the fall of 1967, only eighteen months into my three-year enlistment, they offered me a quid pro quo: if I agreed to re-enlist for six additional years in the Army, I would receive an assignment to a law enforcement unit at Landstuhl, fifteen kilometers from Miesau. I eagerly accepted the offer and finally became a cop. Ironically, my real police work began just nine days before my twenty-second birthday. By then I could have been a Spokane policeman for almost a year, except, of course, for my draft notice. For the remainder of my time in Germany, I worked as a patrolman, a desk sergeant, and, finally, an MP Investigator (MPI)—a uniformed investigator of military offenses. Busting dickheads exhilarated me. I had found my niche in life.

During the time I spent in Germany, two trends changed the face of the Army. Of these trends, the escalating war in Vietnam ranked first. When I arrived in Europe, few of us had any combat experience, except for a smattering of graybeards from the Korean War. Four times I volunteered to go to Vietnam, and four times the Army turned me down. Other soldiers wanted to go to the war, too. A number of us felt that being in Germany left us out of our generation's war. Our fathers and uncles had licked the Nazis, the Japanese, and then the North Koreans and Chinese. Our turn to lick someone had come around on that great cosmic clock. The Viet Cong and North Vietnamese offered the only game in town. And besides, war is career enhancing, we believed. So we volunteered to go to Vietnam. Some went; some of us didn't. Nevertheless, by 1969 the number of Vietnam War combat veterans in Europe had increased dramatically. The face of the Army took on a war-hardened countenance.

The increase in drug abuse and drug-related crimes in the Army created the second trend. One might argue that this trend was connected to the number of Vietnam War combat veterans in Europe. That conclusion, however, ignores the fact of increasing drug abuse in American society at large. Most of the drug users I saw in Europe had the faces of raw recruits straight from America's streets, not of combat-hardened veterans from Southeast Asia. These drug users, new to the Army and to Europe, would have abused drugs and committed drug-related crimes wherever fortune took them: into the Army, at colleges, or down the street, because that's the way it was in the sixties. Regardless of their stories, they were dickheads as far as I was concerned, and I engaged them in combat.

I found it extremely frustrating as an MPI that whenever I started a good narcotics case against some dickhead, I had to turn it over to a CID agent. As I spent an increasing amount of time bumping up against narcotics offenses, my jurisdiction as an MPI in such cases remained severely limited. I concluded that I needed to become a CID agent to pursue my primary (and, as it turned out, lifelong) interest: narcotics investigations.

In the summer of 1969 the CID accepted me, and I departed Germany to attend school once again at Fort Gordon, Georgia. In September I graduated from school and received orders to the Presidio in San Francisco. Now a full-fledged CID special agent, I knew that the Pacific Ocean separated me from the Army's worst drug problem. Once again, I volunteered to go to Vietnam. Seventeen months later I lined up with three hundred other soldiers on the tarmac at Travis Air Force Base.

After a two-hour refueling layover in Alaska, we began boarding the Northwest airliner for the last leg of our trip to Vietnam. I lingered behind the other soldiers. No special order governed our boarding this time; everyone simply returned to his previous seat. When I entered the airplane, most of the seats were already filled. As I walked back toward the galley, I looked at the soldiers seated on both sides of the aisle. As I did, two thoughts crossed my mind: how many of these poor bastards were 11-Bushes? And how many were dickheads?

CHAPTER 3   FINALLY, THE WAR

I slept for most of the rest of the flight to Vietnam. As we approached the Saigon area, the stewardesses prepared us for landing, actions not much different than if we were landing at a commercial airport in the States. We fastened our seat belts, put our seat backs in the upright position, and stored all our hand-carried items beneath the seats. There, however, the similarities ended as we approached Tan Son Nhut Air Base. One stewardess told me that our landing would be quick and hot. I soon learned that meant we descended not many degrees off vertical, rolled to a stop, and deplaned with the engines still running. As soon as the commercial airplane disgorged its load of GIs and duffel bags, it taxied away and took off. As I left the airplane I thanked the flight attendants for their hospitality. They had made the first leg of my war journey quite pleasant.

A hot, humid stench greeted me as I stepped out of the airplane on to the top landing of the ramp. At first blush, I preferred the heat and humidity of Vietnam to the frigidity of Alaska. I was, after all, dressed for the tropics. As I descended the steps, however, I found myself longing for the fresh air of California or Alaska or North Dakota or anywhere else for that matter. South Vietnam smelled like one large backyard mulch pit, folded into an open sewer and pureed in a smoke-belching blender. The odor of decaying human and animal excrement and vegetables, and the smell of fish, fowl, and exotic cooking condiments blended with diesel and jet fuel fumes, exhausts of every description, burning plastics and rubber, and other aromas of an Americanized, industrialized war to create an indescribable, repugnant stench. My first reaction when deplaning at Tan Son Nhut was to wrinkle up my nose at the smell that greeted me.

The smell of Vietnam was so overpowering that it took me a few minutes to focus my other senses on the new surroundings. Shortly, however, the sights and sounds of a vast war machine punctured their way through the smell. Helicopters whopped-whopped overhead. Jets roared off toward some distant battle. Propeller-driven cargo planes churned the thick Vietnamese air. Armored Personnel Carriers (APCs), jeeps, deuce-and-a-half trucks, forklifts, refueling trucks, and buses traveled to and fro on the aprons in front of hangars and along runways. And stacked in perfectly aligned rows, shipping containers (the war's ever-present CONEXs) brimful of war materiel waited patiently to feed the ravenous war machine. No one shot at me, but I didn't doubt it: finally, I was in the war—my war.

Tan Son Nhut lay in the northwest corner of Saigon. We boarded military buses and took a very short trip to quonset huts serving as open-bay, transient barracks. The buses are memorable because mesh wire covered the windows—for our protection, the driver told us. The barracks are memorable only because I didn't want to be there. In San Francisco, I had been assured that a CID agent would meet me upon my arrival in Saigon, and that he would guide me through the required in-processing (the opposite of out-processing). When I deplaned, I didn't see anyone else in civilian clothes and no one had approached me. Something had gotten screwed up. I had no choice but to get into one of the buses with the rest of the troops and take the short trip to the barracks.

I never liked open-bay barracks. Army-wide, there existed an identical floor plan for them. A single barracks had one room. Down each side of the room sat a row of double bunk beds, usually about twelve to fifteen bunks per side. The beds lay perpendicular to the walls. An aisle ran down the middle of the room between the two rows of beds, and much smaller walking spaces ran between each set of bunks. One end of the room contained a common latrine with showers. Such a floor plan economized space and built camaraderie, or so they said. I didn't like open-bay barracks because they allowed for no privacy. Besides, I never had liked the idea of putting up with the smells and sounds of forty or fifty other guys sleeping in one room.

After unloading from the bus and being reunited with my duffel bag, I walked into the barracks and my temper soared. By marooning me at Tan Son Nhut, my CID colleague had thrust me back into the realities of Army life, realities I never liked. I would be spending the night in a room with forty-seven other GIs. I knew complaining to someone about it wouldn't elicit much sympathy. Open-bay barracks, snoring bunkmates, and so forth were common ingredients of life for most GIs. Why, someone would ask, is this guy in civilian clothes complaining?

Having resigned myself to my fate, I decided to make the best of a bad situation. In my opinion, the best place to sleep in an open-bay barracks is on one of the top bunks. By the time I got into the room, the other GIs had already claimed most of the bunks, both top and bottom. About halfway down the room I saw one unoccupied top bunk. At the same time, the fattest soldier I had ever seen walked from the opposite end of the room toward the same bunk. When our eyes met, I knew I'd be sleeping in a bottom bunk. By then, the only bottom bunk not spoken for lay directly below his bed. I spent a most fitful night. Every movement of the soldier above me generated creaks from the top bunk's steel bedstead, squeaks and cracks from its bedspring, and groans from the bedposts. By daybreak I had grown angrier with the nameless CID agent who marooned me there. I also resolved that before the day was over I would find somewhere else to sleep that evening.

Between in-processing movements, I found a telephone and called the Saigon CID office. My call met with profuse apologies from the agent on the other end of the telephone line and a promise that someone would arrive shortly to rescue me (all CID agents shared an antipathy for Army life and open-bay barracks). The apology disarmed my anger. I felt nothing but relief about an hour later when an agent in a jeep drove up to the line where I stood and, of course, waited. He wore an open collar, short-sleeved, square-bottomed cotton shirt, sports pants, and loafers. I had done my homework well. We exchanged introductions, he apologized again and ushered me to his jeep. We stopped by the barracks, picked up my duffel bag, and headed southeast into the city of Saigon.

In Saigon, the CID had taken over an entire two-story hotel. Architecturally, the hotel radiated French colonial airs. Grand windows, outlined with simple but distinctive embossment, broke up whitewashed outer walls. Inside, the ground floor contained largely an open, high-ceiling lobby ringed by rooms on its outer perimeter. From the center of the lobby extended a magnificent wooden staircase, ten to twelve feet in width (wide enough to march an entire column of soldiers up it, I remember thinking). The staircase reached to the second floor and its roughly thirty rooms.

The rooms of the first floor housed the CID offices. The agent-driver showed me into one of the offices where a Vietnamese woman, a CID secretary, handed me a hotel room key. I would find my room, she told me, at the top of the stairs. Upstairs I located the room, opened the door, and found it modestly, but more than adequately, furnished: a bed, a dresser, and a nightstand. No more open-bay barracks for me. I dropped my duffel bag on the floor, myself on to the bed, and for the first time in over forty-eight hours, I slept soundly.

Now safely ensconced back with the CID, my in-processing mirrored my out-processing at Oakland. For the next five days, a CID agent drove me in a jeep to the in-processing sessions each morning, then picked me up and returned me to the hotel each evening. For the most part, I found little of interest in any of the mandatory briefings: sexual contact with the natives was highly discouraged; venereal diseases, they told us, had reached epidemic proportions. The cancerous black market ate at the fabric of South Vietnam's economic life. Drug abuse had become a major concern and, like good soldiers, we would avoid such conduct. And, as ambassadors of the people of the United States, we should act accordingly. My take on these entreaties was that I had no intention of abstaining from sex (just one day in-country and I found myself sexually attracted to the slight, raven-haired Vietnamese women); I would be the enforcer of black market and drug laws; and, let uniformed GIs be ambassadors; I was a cop.

Only two things of note came out of my in-processing. First, I learned that I would be attached to the 23d MP Company, 23d Infantry Division (Americal), Chu Lai. My original orders said that I would be assigned to the 23d, but until my in-processing at Tan Son Nhut that meant nothing to me. In fact, I knew very little about the 23d or Chu Lai except that when I told my Saigon CID hosts about my assignment, the news evoked much sympathy from them. In turn, they would each close their eyes, shake their heads, and say with a sigh, "That's way up north." I soon learned that Chu Lai, even though a major installation, was, from a CID perspective, in the bush. Saigon CID agents considered themselves big city cops. They believed that being attached to an outpost such as Chu Lai equated to moving to Mayberry and working for Andy Taylor. The crime I witnessed at Chu Lai belied the allusion to Mayberry and, from my perspective, the big city cops in Saigon missed all the fun.

The second thing of note to come out of the in-processing sessions was my getting jungle fatigues. Now that I had arrived in-country, the Army wanted to ensure that I was properly dressed for war. Finding my protests futile, I went to a supply store to pick up two sets of jungle fatigues. I had no idea what I would do with the uniforms, but

I dutifully packed them with the civilian clothes in my duffel bag. (I eventually wore the uniforms for a short period of time while at Chu Lai. Someone had decided that all soldiers should be dressed for war and mandated that CID agents, like everyone else, would wear jungle fatigues. The CID protested the decision and lost. As a concession, however, we didn't wear rank on the uniform. In the rank's place we wore "US" patches on our collars. Unfortunately, the "US" on the collars looked like an officer's rank insignia. This created many military faux pas as enlisted men saluted us and officers didn't know if they or we should salute. After three weeks, the Army cried uncle, and we packed our jungle fatigues away, never to be worn again.)

I spent my evenings in Saigon getting introduced to its nightlife. Three or four of us staying at the CID hotel would find a restaurant or bar and spend a leisurely evening there. Being the newest arrival from the States, I found myself the center of attention as my news-hungry hosts wanted all the latest information from the World. I would fill them in on the latest war protests, which included the planting of bombs at the Provost Marshal's Office—the commander of the Military Police—on the Presidio and one of the barracks at Oakland Army Base. (Army Explosive Ordinance Disposal [EOD] technicians defused both bombs.) In general, they asked questions and I provided answers. I had thought that upon my arriving at the war, someone would give me survival points: don't do this, do that, and so on. Remarkably, during five evenings in Saigon, my first five evenings in the war, rarely did our conversation touch on the war in Vietnam. Almost every conversation I had with the CID agents centered on events back home.

After five torturous days of in-processing and five wonderful evenings filled with drink and exotic foods ("Don't ask what it is" was the most important advice I received in Saigon), I began the second leg of my war journey, the trip to Chu Lai. I returned to Saigon about six times during the next year. Each time I stayed at the same hotel and frequented many of the same restaurants and bars that I did on my first evenings in Vietnam. But it never felt the same. I eventually grew to dislike the haughty attitudes of the Saigon CID agents and never quite found their company as enjoyable as it had been upon my arrival in Vietnam. I would spend a couple of days in Saigon working on the details of a case, then eagerly drive to Tan Son Nhut Air Base to catch a flight back to Chu Lai. That was all ahead of me, though. After my first five days in Saigon, an agent drove me to Tan Son Nhut, I thanked him for his hospitality, grabbed my duffel bag, now loaded with civilian clothes and two sets of Army fatigues, and strode towards the waiting Air Force C-130.

The primary mission of the aircraft was to ferry supplies to Chu Lai; we passengers were merely add-ons. Wooden pallets stacked with supplies dominated the center of the fuselage. Silver-colored metal rollers installed down the center of the airplane's floor made loading the supply-laden pallets easier. An Air Force load master sweated profusely as he oversaw the loading of the pallets and fixed each one securely in place with a combination of straps, clips, and rope attached to tie-down locations embedded in the walls, floor, and ceiling of the aircraft. Not until he secured the last pallet did he allow us to board.

The sweltering heat, a product of a blazing sun and a dripping atmospheric humidity, made standing on the tarmac nearly intolerable. I wondered how the Air Force troops, seemingly oblivious to the heat—except for the load master—could work so diligently at unloading the flatbed truck of its load of pallets that they so carefully slid into the open back door of the airplane. (On a C-130, the door serves double duty as both a door when closed and as a ramp into the back of the aircraft when opened.) After they finished, the loadmaster gave us the signal to walk up the ramp into the airplane. Then we entered the absolutely insufferable environs of the inside of the C-130. The tarmac had been comfortable by comparison.

Every rivet, every bolt and nut, each plate of aluminum, steel, and every other alloy in the aircraft's construction, absorbed and re-radiated all the heat of the blazing sun hitting the airplane in which the crew began to entomb us. "Son-of-a-bitch!" one GI succinctly exclaimed. "Moth-er-fuck!" intoned another, carefully articulating each syllable. In our own ways, we all expressed the same thought: "Let's get this damn airplane off the runway and into the air where, surely, it has to be cooler."

The aircraft crew buttoned up the airplane, started the engines, and prepared the C-130 for take-off. We add-ons took seats that ran the length of the aircraft along each side. Comfort had not been designed into the seats' canvas and aluminum construction. We buckled in while one crew member tried to give us a safety briefing, but the roar of the engines drowned out most of what he said. Eventually, the churning propellers pulled the heavy-laden airplane on to the active runway, and we began our take-off roll.

We ascended from Tan Son Nhut nearly as steeply as we had descended to it in the commercial airplane. I suspected that the pilot flew the C-130 about as steep as he dared. Because small arms fire presented the greatest threat to any aircraft landing or taking off in Vietnam, pilots designed these steep flight paths to get the airplanes out of the range of that threat as quickly as possible. Once airborne, I realized that the steep climbing offered the only defense we had. None of us, except the crew, had any weapons, and the crew only possessed small handguns and maybe one or two rifles.

I had expected that, shortly after my arrival in Vietnam, I would be issued a weapon. I didn't know what I would get, but I was, after all, in a war zone. In the States, I carried a .38 caliber, Colt detective special with a two-inch barrel. One couldn't do much damage with it, but it could be concealed easily and, besides, that's what the Army issued me. Upon arriving in Vietnam, I hoped to get a weapon with more firepower. The MPs carried .45 caliber semiautomatic handguns, the same weapon I had fired into the air when I captured the Turkish thief. Maybe I would get one of them, I thought. Or, I might be issued an M-16 rifle capable of semi or full automatic firing.

When I entered the Army, soldiers still carried the wooden-stocked M-14. During the late sixties, the Army made the transition from the heavy M-14 to the plastic-stocked, much lighter M-16, but I had received no training on the new rifle. Upon arriving in Vietnam, I thought that the Army would issue me an M-16 and teach me how to use it. Nearly a week later, I sat in a troop seat of a C-130, flying over the jungles of Vietnam—jungles concealing our enemy—and I didn't even have a slingshot to protect myself. I thought the uniformed soldiers would be in better shape, but they weren't. They, too, made the trip without any weapons. If that airplane had gone down in the middle of Vietnam, we would have been up that proverbial Shit Creek without paddles.

About thirty of us shared the C-130 heading to Chu Lai. For the duration of the flight, I could see roughly half of the others. Supplies stacked in the middle of the airplane prevented me from seeing the GIs on the other side of the fuselage. The ones I could see were all much younger than me. Despite the sweltering heat that wrung sweat out of our bodies like an old ringer washer, they looked like fresh troops. The fading and frazzling of the uniforms so apparent on the old-timers at Ton Son Nhut hadn't yet marked their uniforms. Their countenances reflected apprehension or, in some cases, fear. In their freshness, they hadn't yet absorbed the cynicism and combat-weariness floating in the Vietnamese air. These "pollens" would eventually transmogrify their faces.

Even their duffel bags exuded newness. My duffel bag proudly carried the wear and tear of an overseas assignment and a couple of moves in the States. My stenciled but fading service number—"RA" followed by a series of eight numbers—and name marked my duffel bag. The RA meant that I had enlisted in the Army; I hadn't been drafted. While the Army replaced the M-14 with the M-16, it also replaced service numbers with social security numbers. The new duffel bags all carried social security numbers and names, neither of which looked faded. My duffel bag looked conspicuously as if it belonged to a lifer.

The recruits with me were replacements for units at Chu Lai. In many ways, they represented what some critics say went wrong with the Vietnam War. Except for the troops arriving early in the war, few soldiers arrived in-country as members of units. They came as individuals. The units they trained with in the States simply sent their graduates to the four corners of the globe to cover the Army's worldwide commitments. Soldiers arrived as individuals in Germany or Italy or California or Vietnam. There they got assigned to units according to their MOSs. Their only commonality with their new comrades might be that they had attended the same military training schools, albeit at different times. Such war management, critics claim, contributed to the demise of cohesion in military units in Vietnam.

The replacements carried on little conversation among themselves, and I didn't talk with anybody. The truth is I never spoke a word during the entire flight. The roar of the engines would have prevented most attempts at conversation anyway. Nevertheless, I felt very uncomfortable. Here I was flying north with a bunch of grunts (11-Bushes, I'm sure) heading to Chu Lai to kill for God and country—if somebody would just give them a weapon. I don't know how many actually felt that way, but that's how I perceived them. And I knew I was going to Chu Lai to be a cop. I began to see then that the concerns of those young men on the flight with me were not my concerns. I had already begun my self-inoculation against the effects of the war. (Had our transport airplane gone down in the jungle, my attitude would have been decidedly different.)

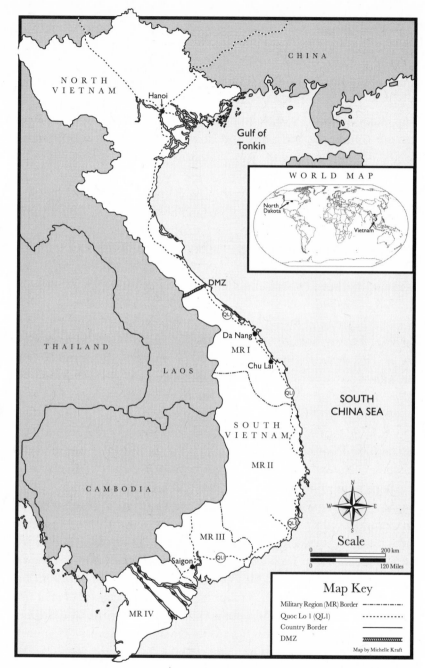

Vietnam was a world away from North Dakota, geographically and culturally. The author was stationed at both Chu Lai and Da Nang, which were in Military Region 1, the very northern sector of South Vietnam. Over half of all American combat deaths suffered between 1967 and 1972 occurred in MR1.

South Vietnam resembled a backward, yawning letter C with its mouth about to close over Laos and Cambodia to the west and its back to the South China Sea in the east. (See Map 1 on page 35.) Saigon (now called Ho Chi Minh City) lay at the bottom of the backward C, right at a point inland from where the bottom lip turned slightly to the southwest. A 425-mile line drawn straight north of Saigon crossed Cambodia and Laos and nearly bisected the Demilitarized Zone (DMZ) separating the two Vietnams, before it terminated in the Gulf of Tonkin of the South China Sea. As a crow flies, Chu Lai lay roughly 150 miles southeast of the DMZ and 350 miles northeast of Saigon, on the outside or coastal side of the backward C. The droning C-130 made the distance seem much farther.

As the flight sauntered north, we became lost in our own thoughts and then drifted in and out of sleep; a GI can sleep anywhere. Contemplation and slumber ended abruptly as we began our descent to Chi Lai airfield.

The US military divided South Vietnam into four military zones. Early in the war, the zones carried the tactical corps-level names of I Corps, II Corps, III Corps, and IV Corps. In 1970, the corps designations gave way to a military region (MR) scheme: I Corps became MR I, II Corps became MR II, and so forth, although the use of I Corps (and the rest) continued throughout the war.

MR IV identified the most southerly and westerly reaches of South Vietnam (the bottom lip of the backward C) including much of the Mekong Delta and all of the Ca Mau Peninsula, South Vietnam's most southern point. Northeast of that was MR III with its headquarters in Saigon. Then came MR II comprising most of central South Vietnam, including Pleiku where the VC attacks in 1965 against the US airfield there prodded President Johnson into escalating the war. Finally, MR I, with headquarters at Da Nang, held the most northerly position and the DMZ. Over half of all American combat deaths suffered between 1967 and 1972 occurred in MR I. Troops assigned to the coastal post of Chu Lai operated predominantly in the southern half of this military region.

Unlike Da Nang, Saigon, and other major Vietnamese communities identified with US installations, the Americans founded Chu Lai. In the spring of 1965, in support of the escalation of US forces in the war, the Marines splashed ashore and built a tent city, complete with a runway, on the South China Sea coast of Quang Tin Province, south of the Bay of An Hoa and the mouth of the Truong River. The name

Chu Lai didn't identify anything Vietnamese in the area. Legend has it that "Chu Lai" is the Chinese Mandarin pronunciation of the initials of Marine General Victor Krulak, Commanding General, Fleet Marine Force, Pacific, at the time the Marines established the base. If a Vietnamese village existed at the site, American construction obliterated it and erased its name from the map. However, many small villages and hamlets with exotic sounding names such as An Hai, Xuan Trung, Khuong Quang, and An Tay remained outside the perimeter of Chu Lai.

From Chu Lai, in August 1965, the Marines launched America's first-ever, full-scale ground offensive against the VC. Most of the fighting of the offensive, dubbed Operation Starlite, occurred nine miles south of Chu Lai. The Marines carried the day, sealing Chu Lai's fate. Quickly buildings replaced tents.

The Navy surveyed the area and selected a spot to build a naval facility about three and one-half miles north of the airfield, on the west side of a small peninsula. (See Map 2 on page 38.) To the east of the peninsula lay the Bay of An Hoa and the open sea. That location left ships susceptible to rough seas, especially during the monsoon season, and would require the construction of extensive breakwater. Coral also dominated the east side of the peninsula. Farther south along the coast, east of the Marines' airfield, sand beaches invited the Navy, but here, too, rough seas could batter ships.

However, to the west of the peninsula, accessible through the mouth of the Truong River, lay a naturally sheltered area. With a little dredging, this area offered protection for the Navy's Landing Ship Tanks (LSTs) and other roll-on/roll-off classes of ships, and provided enough room for a turning basin allowing those ships to sail back out through the mouth of the river and into the open sea. The Navy completed dredging in 1966 and built five sand ramps making sealift operations possible for the nearly 30,000 troops supported by Chu Lai.

The addition of a naval port three and one-half miles north of the airfield meant the extension of Chu Lai's perimeter to encompass both areas and accounted for Chu Lai's peculiar shape. The bulk of the post resembled a rectangle running southeast to northwest about four and one-half miles along the coast and extending a little less than two miles inland. The South China Sea provided the northeast border (one long side of the rectangle); QL1 (for Quoc [nation] and Lo [road]) —South Vietnam's only major north-south highway— marked

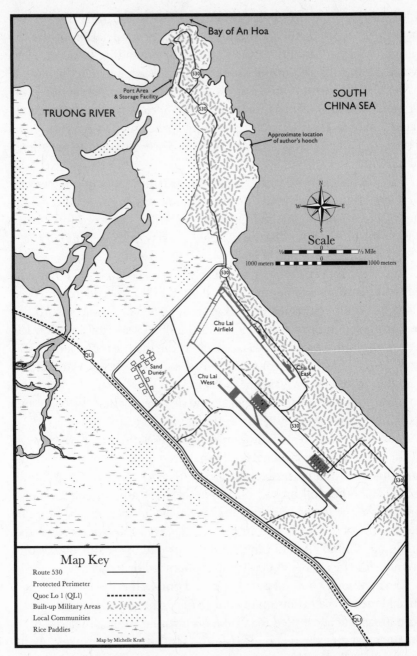

Because of the addition of a naval station at the mouth of the Truong River, Chu Lai had an oddly shaped appendage to the northeast off the otherwise rectangular base. It was along that appendage, that the author spent most of his time in the war living in a hooch overlooking the South China Sea.

the southwest perimeter (the other long side). No such distinguishing natural features demarcated the northwest and southeast boundaries (the short sides) that simply followed two parallel lines, four and one-half miles apart, connecting QL1 to the coast.

At the northern corner of the rectangle, a narrow neck extended north, opening up to about three-quarters of a mile at its widest point. This area encompassed the naval base at the northwest corner of the peninsula. From the northern tip of the peninsula to the southeast perimeter, the base stretched over seven miles.

The Army arrived at Chu Lai on April 20, 1967, when troops of the 196th Light Infantry Brigade (LIB), designated Task Force Oregon, landed at the airstrip and began operations around the Marine base. Shortly, the Army took over the base and extended operations to include all of the provinces of Quang Tin and Quang Ngai (directly south of Quang Tin Province and the most southerly province in I Corps's area of responsibility) and the southerly portion of Quang Nam Province (north of Chu Lai and included Da Nang). On September 25, 1967, Task Force Oregon became the Americal Division, composed of the 196th, 198th, and the 11th LIBs, and the seventh Army division fighting in Vietnam. At first only the 196th resided in Vietnam, but by Christmas, the 198th and 11th had arrived, and the Americal Division became the largest Army division in Vietnam. Chu Lai became the hub of Americal activities.

The Chu Lai our C-130 descended toward had matured into a major installation. Thirty-three miles of lighted perimeter outlined the post, and troops stood guard at 160 perimeter bunkers and twenty-one observation towers. A ten thousand-foot, southeast by northwest concrete runway dominated the very center of the rectangular bulk of the post. Named Chu Lai West, it lay roughly a mile from the coastline. To its east and just a little over one-half a mile inland, another much smaller runway (about 3,500 feet), appropriately called Chu Lai East, served Americal's large helicopter fleet. One main road, #530, snaked its way from the main gate at QL1 in the southwestern corner of the post, ran up the coast east of the runways, and terminated at a gate near the naval facility in the north, in a journey that covered over ten miles.

Off this main artery, veins of roads tied together nearly 4,100 buildings, most of which were east of Road 530 and a few hundred yards from the South China Sea. Among these buildings, GIs found the amenities of home including a Foremost Dairy milk plant, an

American Express Bank, a hospital, a Korean contract laundry, numerous post exchanges (the GI's shopping mall), libraries, clubs, theaters, chapels, and, of course, living quarters. Even an ice plant provided the GIs with the necessary product for an ice chest and cold beer. When I arrived at the installation, fourteen thousand troops lived and worked in the confines of Chu Lai, and every day a Vietnamese civilian work force of 5,057 passed through the gates to work alongside of them. The American taxpayers had invested $50 million to create Chu Lai literally out of nothing.

By the time our lumbering C-130's wheels touched down on Chu Lai West, future luminaries had already served in the ranks of the Americal Division. General Colin Powell, a future chairman of the Joint Chiefs of Staff and Secretary of State, served as an executive officer with the 11th LIB, and later, as a staff director with Americal headquarters during one of his Vietnam tours (1968–69). General H. Norman Schwarzkopf, later the hero of the Persian Gulf War (1991), spent part of one of his Vietnam tours (1969–1970) as a commander with the 198th LIB. Moreover, the division's units' official histories enjoyed touting historic ties to heroism from the days of the Civil War and the Battle of the Little Big Horn, through two world wars and the Korean War. But what most people will remember about Americal derives from its most infamous member, Lt. William Calley.

In March 1968, Lt. Calley and the men of Charlie Company, 11th Brigade, Americal Division, vented their fears and frustrations on unarmed Vietnamese at a small village called My Lai. Estimates vary, as they always do in these cases, but somewhere between one hundred and four hundred Vietnamese died in an orgy of terror orchestrated by Lt. Calley. Not until after I had been at Chu Lai for some time did I make the connection between Calley, Americal, and my previous assignment in San Francisco.

The news about My Lai broke in late 1969 a couple of months after I arrived at the Presidio. The photographs of dead Vietnamese and the stories of wanton carnage sucked the wind out of the sails of America's moral crusade. The My Lai story also created a deluge of allegations of atrocities connected to the war. It's as if the news about My Lai had a cathartic effect on the consciences of war veterans and their families, who now told stories of My Lai-esque massacres and other atrocities that had occurred in the war. Some of these stories involved Americans killing innocent Vietnamese; others involved Americans killing other Americans. A game of one-upmanship increased the ferocity of these atrocities. Oftentimes, these confessions rang with allegations of units going into villages where they murdered babies, pregnant women, and children, all non-combatants.

I'm sure that many of these stories sprouted from a kernel of truth. That is, women and children were probably killed. But were they non-combatants? I know that during my time in Vietnam, it was not uncommon to see a pregnant woman armed with the weapons of war. Also, young children oftentimes became belligerents in the war. I frequently saw twelve-year-old adolescents who were seasoned combat veterans. I'll never forget an incident near Chu Lai when a five- or six-year-old child dropped a miniature fragmentation hand grenade into the gas tank of a jeep and blew it up. The American public had, I believe, a view that war involved professional soldiers against professional soldiers, such as the commonly held view of the fighting in World War II. Americans found it difficult to understand that pregnant women and school-age children could die in war, not as innocents, but as combatants. So when reports of such deaths bubbled to the surface after the My Lai story broke, Americans assumed many more My Lai-type of atrocities had occurred. Not far removed from these stories were tales about Americans murdering Americans. Veterans and their families provided plenty of grist for this mill grinding at America's conscience. As these reports hit congressmen and the Army, the CID ended up with the job of investigating them.

In support of these investigations, I interviewed many veterans and their families in the San Francisco area. Seldom did these interviews result in any valuable information. In fact, I never heard of any of these reports being substantiated. I do, however, remember one case during which a family learned more than they wanted to know about their son's death.

The parents of a young soldier who died in Vietnam wrote to their congressman claiming that they possessed evidence that an American soldier had murdered their son. The congressman sent the charge to the Army, and the case file landed on my desk at the Presidio. The file contained very few details, but what did exist seemed pretty straightforward: the Army notified the parents that their son died in hostile action. I had a copy of the notification letter with the case file. The Army shipped the body home for burial. They should be happy that enough of his body remained to be buried, I callously and cynically thought. And now, the parents claimed he had been murdered.

They lived in Oakland. I drove to their house in a nice middle-class neighborhood overlooking the San Francisco Bay. I introduced myself and they cordially invited me into their home. They impressed me as very nice people who had, unfortunately, lost a son in the war. They believed, however, that someone had lied to them about the circumstances surrounding their son's death. They didn't raise the topic, but the ghosts of My Lai sat with us in that living room.

When I asked them to show me the evidence they had to support their allegation, the mother produced a box of neatly wrapped letters. She held the precious package for some time, explaining that in them her son repeatedly said that he feared for his life. After some persuasion from me, she finally handed me the letters. For the most part his letters contained complaints about the heat, the rain, and the mosquitoes, with homesick notes about missing his mom's cooking and the girl next door. I saw nothing, however, that indicated that he feared for his life and told that to the parents.

"Don't you see it?" the mother asked incredulously.

She then showed me statements in his letters where her son had written about the crazy—not funny, but psychotic—guys he worked with. In one, for example, he wrote, "The sergeant that I work for, he's crazy. Everywhere he goes he carries a gun." Considering that their son was in a war and nearly everyone carried a weapon of some kind, it's hard to image that such a statement flagged any sort of feelings from him. Nevertheless, half dozen similar statements convinced his parents, after his death, that he feared for his life.

Moreover, with equal certainty they believed that the body shipped home to them was not their son's. When the Army's Mortuary Affairs shipped his remains home, it had recommended that his casket not be opened, a standard procedure when a body had been grossly disfigured or when there remained nothing but body pieces zipped up in a bag. The father, however, insisted that the local undertaker open the casket. Too little of the head remained to identify the face, but when the father looked at the arms, he found them nearly hairless. He and his wife knew that their son had very hairy arms. The hairless arms on the body in the casket before them helped raise doubts as to their son's death, or at least the official version of it.

They proceeded with the funeral plans not completely convinced that they were burying their son. They then reread their son's letters and developed their theory that he had been murdered and the Army was covering up that crime, to include substituting someone else's body in his place. I believe the atrocities at My Lai generated their conspiracy theory. These middle-aged parents, products of World War II and previously possessed of an unshakable faith in their government, had been transformed by the news about My Lai. A government whose soldiers could kill innocent women and children at My Lai, then try to cover up the massacre, could lie to them about the death of their son.

I returned to the Presidio, filed my initial report, and sent a message through channels asking for more information on the son's death. What I learned would not console his parents. The Army, through the young soldier's commander, had in fact been lying to the parents. The young man had committed suicide by using an M-16 to blow away most of his head. Not wanting to compound the grief of the parents, the commander decided to report that their son had died in hostile action.

Not surprisingly, my second visit with the parents quickly lost any cordiality. When I told them about their son's suicide, understandably they didn't believe me. I wouldn't have believed me either under the circumstances. Given the evidence, however, I informed them that I would close the case. Today I'm convinced that their son committed suicide; I suspect they're just as convinced that he did not, and that it wasn't their beloved son that they buried. Today, I'm not sure what the truth is, but I do know that in Vietnam I saw enough deception and simple fuck-ups to believe anything could happen.

As our C-130 taxied to a stop near the hangars along Chu Lai West, the temperature in the airplane once again soared, even though, contrary to our expectations at Tan Son Nhut, it never had gotten comfortable in the aircraft. Our first flight in Vietnam taught us that being airborne in Vietnam offered little protection from the country's unrelenting heat and humidity. We impatiently waited for the loadmaster to lower the back door so we could deplane. Fortunately, we had to get off the airplane before he could unload his supplies. At ground level, the buildings, pallets, and machines of war at Chu Lai didn't look appreciably different from what I saw at Tan Son Nhut. But the air had a different smell. Through the mixture of the aromas of modern warfare and Vietnamese culture wafted the faint scent of the ocean. As a North Dakotan, I hadn't grown up around oceans, but in the years since leaving that state I had developed an affinity for the sea. I'm going to find a place to live with a great ocean view, I thought. After all, Chu Lai would be my home for the next year, so why not enjoy it?

DEPARTMENT OF THE ARMY
Company D, 1st Battalion (Mechanized), 61st Infantry
APO San Francisco 96477

Mrs.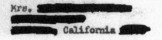
California

Dear Mrs.

I want to extend to you my deepest sympathy concerning the loss of your husband, Private First Class ████████████████, on Sunday morning ████ ██, 1971 at Quang Tri Combat Base, Republic of Vietnam. ███ was pulling the early morning shift of guard duty when his weapon accidentally fired fatally wounding him.

Words never offer consolation after a tragedy, but the people who knew and worked with ███ viewed him with their highest esteem and respect. His initiative and devotion to duty proved, on many occasions, to be an inspiration to every one of his associates. Every man in this unit is deeply grieved by his untimely death.

Last rites and a memorial service were conducted for ███ by our Battalion Cahplain, Major ████████████████, for the men of this company. I extend our sincere regrets for the loss of your husband, and our highly admired comrade-in-arms. If I can be of any additional assistance to you, do not hesitate to contact me.

Sincerely yours,

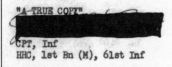
CPT, INF
Commanding

"A TRUE COPY"

CPT, Inf
HHC, 1st Bn (M), 61st Inf

Documents housed with the National Archives and Records Administration demonstrate that Army officials lied to families about the circumstances of their loved ones' deaths. The letter reproduced here with careful redactions claims that an accidental discharge of a weapon caused the soldier's death. The witness statement from the investigator (on the right) shows that he had committed suicide. The question is whether officials lied to protect families or the Army.

WITNESS STATEMENT

For use of this form, see AR 195-10 - TB PMG 3; the proponent agency is Office of the Provost Marshal General.

CE	DATE	TIME	FILE NUMBER
▮▮▮ Tri Combat Base, ▮▮	▮▮ 71	1300 hrs	
NAME, FIRST NAME, MIDDLE NAME	**SOCIAL SECURITY ACCOUNT NO.**		**GRADE** Criminal
	▮▮▮▮▮		Investigator

ANIZATION OR ADDRESS

▮, 1st Inf Bde, 5th Inf Div (M), APO SF 96477

SWORN STATEMENT

I, _____, WANT TO MAKE THE FOLLOWING STATEMENT UNDER

After advising Mr. ▮▮▮ of his rights under Article 31, UCMJ, I then asked him
he following questions:)

▮▮▮▮▮▮

CPT, Inf
Investigating Officer

You were one of the investigators assigned to the ▮▮▮ case, is that correc?
Yes, that's correct.
What additional information can you give me other than that contained in the
CI 1st progress report?
An autopsy report was made by MAJ ▮▮▮▮▮▮▮, MC at DaNang Mortuary,
but the official finding was that ▮▮▮ died from a "gunshot wound to the head
which merely substantiated our own findings. No chemical analysis was taken ▮
his blood so we have no substantial evidence on the possibility of drug abuse.
Did the position of ▮▮▮ body allow the possibility of suicide?
Yes, ▮▮▮ was lying on top of the bunker, face down, head toward the left fr▮
▮▮▮ of the bunker. The weapon he had drawn for guard was to the right of his
body, the same way as the apparent entrance wound, with the muzzle of the
weapon pointed toward his head. There was a pool of blood under ▮▮▮ head
but the muzzle of the weapon, which appeared to have blood on it, was not in
the pool of blood when the body was found. The weapon was lying on its right
side, ejection port down, and there was an expended round under the weapon,
lying between two sandbags. This would tend to indicate that the weapon was
fired from ▮▮▮ right side, and that as he fell, the weapon fell to that
side with the weapon ejecting the expended shell casing straight downward then
falling on top of the casing. The weapon had no shell in the chamber or magazine in the magazine well. The only magazines found were three inside the
bunker.
Were any drugs found at the scene?
Yes, there were several marijuana cigarette butts, 2 empty heroin vials, and
one empty dexedrine vial, all these appeared to be somewhat old. There was
also a plastic bag containing a vegetable material believed to be marijuana
found near the RPG screen in front of the bunker. The bag had apparent bloodstains and there were apparent bloodstains on the RPG screen where the bag hit
it. CPT ▮▮▮ stated that he found the bag lying on top of the bunker and
threw it off, thinking to spare ▮▮▮ family any further grief by connection
▮▮▮ death with drug abuse. He said he gave the bag a back hand flip and th▮
it hit the top of the bunker before it fell to the ground. This could explain
the apparent bloodstains as it may have hit the pool of blood before going off
the bunker.

▮	**INITIALS OF PERSON MAKING STATEMENT**		
	LLF	PAGE 1 OF 2	PAGES

▮TIONAL PAGES MUST CONTAIN THE HEADING "STATEMENT OF___TAKEN AT___DATED___CONTINUED."
▮TTOM OF EACH ADDITIONAL PAGE MUST BEAR THE INITIALS OF THE PERSON MAKING THE STATEMENT AN▮
▮LED AS "PAGE___OF___PAGES." WHEN ADDITIONAL PAGES ARE UTILIZED, THE BACK OF PAGE 1 WILL
▮D OUT, AND THE STATEMENT WILL BE CONCLUDED ON THE REVERSE SIDE OF ANOTHER COPY OF THIS FO▮

CHAPTER 4   SETTLING IN –

A .38, A BLOWJOB,

A HOOCH, AND A JEEP

A quick bus ride brought us to a large hangar serving as an in-processing center. On the way I noticed that there were many more helicopters on Chu Lai than what I'd seen at Tan Son Nhut. UH-1s (Hueys), CH-47s (Chinooks), and Loach helicopters (LOH—light observation helicopter) flew overhead or were parked under the protection of large open-ended hangars. I would come to learn that every day, from sunup to sundown, hundreds of helicopter sorties departed from and returned to Chu Lai East supporting American operations in MR I. From Chu Lai West, C-130 and C-123 transports ferried in tons of war matériel and "cherries," replacements like us. The gray-colored 0-2 FACs (forward air controller aircraft) with their distinctive front and rear propellers and a handful of piper cubs round out the aircraft that are most memorable to me at Chu Lai.

Despite all the flying activity going on, there was a surreal quietude about Chu Lai. I struggled to rectify my perception of coming to a war and now being in the very heart of one. Growing up on a diet of Audie Murphy's "To Hell and Back" and similar WWII movies had prepared me to come into a hostile environment where some faceless, nameless enemy would try to kill me. However, except for aircraft taking off and landing and a lot of front-end loaders, trucks, and jeeps going to and fro along the airstrip, there was nothing going on—nothing, that is, that I expected in a war. I knew I was close to North Vietnam and the infamous DMZ. In the world of Audie Murphy, that meant that I was closer to the front line, and therefore, closer to the action. (In my attempt to understand the surrealism of the moment, I had deluded myself into believe that there was a front line in this war.) I heard no gunfire, no rockets or grenades exploding. Nothing. Nothing sounded like war, but everything around me, the aircraft, the uniforms, and the weapons, reminded me that I was in a war. But no one tried to kill me. Except for the visual landscape, I could have been anywhere in the world.

Once inside the hangar, we were directed through a maze of tables where we turned in our 201 (personnel) files, pay records, and so on. Everyone that came on the C-130 with me was initially assigned to the Division Combat Center where all cherries received newcomer training. I expected to receive some such training as well, but when I told them I was with the CID, I was referred to an MP standing by a jeep parked on the apron in front of the hangar.

I picked up my "lifer's" duffel bag from a pile of bags near the open hangar door and walked over to the MP. I showed him my credentials and we climbed into his jeep. In silence we drove east away from Chu Lai West and on to Road 530, the post's main artery and only paved road, heading toward the ocean. Then the road made a sharp turn north. To our left was Chu Lai East; to our right, an assortment of barracks, hooches, clubs, office buildings, a chapel or two, fuel tanks, and guard towers, and beyond them, about a quarter of a mile from the road, the South China Sea. Between Road 530 and the ocean, earth-moving equipment had decapitated some of the undulating white sand dunes revealing a reddish soil. Reddish veins of unpaved roads intersected Road 530 and snaked through the sand dunes to the buildings. The manmade structures, white sand dunes, and red soil mixed with green scrubs and trees to complete the landscape. In a couple of minutes, the MP stopped in front of one of the buildings, said, "Welcome to the war. Here's your office." I unloaded my bag and he drove away.

The CID building was typical of nearly all the buildings on Chu Lai: plywood sides and metal corrugated peaked roof, and set on eighteen- to twenty-four inch high stilts. Because of the stilts, two or three steps led from ground level into the building. Some of the buildings had sandbags piled around their bases, up about four feet. The CID building did not. For some odd, inexplicable reason, unlike most of the buildings on Chu Lai, the CID building didn't sit square—parallel or perpendicular—to the road. It sat at a forty-five degree angle. It looked like a construction mistake to me. Directly across the street was the Provost Marshal's building housing the MP Law Enforcement Desk and the 23d Military Police Company's administrative offices.

With my duffel bag in tow, I walked up the steps into the building. The first room was a waiting area with a three-foot high railing that divided the open area in half. A small swinging gate at one end of the railing allowed access to the area behind the railing and to a hallway going toward the back two-thirds of the building. The waiting area was spartan, to say the least, furnished only with a bench and a few old metal chairs. Sitting at a desk directly behind the railing was an ARVN (Army of the Republic of Vietnam) NCO. Behind him two Vietnamese women sat at desks, painfully hunt-and-peck typing. (They were our secretaries. Both spoke very little English, but they could read our writing and translate that to the correct keys on a typewriter. I'm sure they never had a clue what they were typing.)

I didn't see any Americans in the waiting area or behind the counter. I stood there looking at the ARVN as he looked at me. This was the first time since coming into Vietnam I wasn't interacting with another American. The silence grew uncomfortably long. Obviously, the ARVN was going to let me make the first move. Finally I said, "I'm Gary Skogen. I just arrived and I was told I was supposed to report in here." Fortunately for me, the ARVN was an interpreter. (I don't know how long he'd been an interpreter before my arrival, but when I left Chu Lai, he was still there.)

The ARVN's countenance changed. He flashed a warm smile, came from behind the railing to where I stood, shook my hand, and welcomed me to Chu Lai. Taking my duffel bag, he grabbed my arm and led me through the swinging gate. He set my bag down by his desk and continued to guide me past the secretaries to the hallway running down the center of the building. Branching off from the hallway were ten or twelve offices.

The first two offices belonged to Second Lieutenant Benjamin Hargrove and Chief Warrant Officer (CW4) James Strawberry, the field office investigator-in-charge. Hargrove was technically the commander, but he wasn't an agent and didn't investigate crimes. He was our chief administrator and that was about it. Strawberry, on the other hand, ran everything. He deferred to the lieutenant on administrative issues, because that's what warrant officers do. But no one in the office every doubted that Strawberry was in charge.

The ARVN interpreter didn't even bother to introduce me to Lt. Hargrove, but directed me into Strawberrry's office and quickly returned to his own desk. Strawberry briefly glanced up from a report on his desk and said, "Have a seat. I'll be right with you." I sat on the gray metal folding chair and studied the ten-foot square room.

Naked two-by-four studs provided the framework for the plywood walls that I saw on the outside of the building and in the hallway. Above me equally naked roof rafters, joists, and a ridgepole framed the roof of corrugated metal. The internal walls stopped just short of the roof framing. One could toss a ball over the wall into the next office or out into the hallway. A small, rectangular four-pane glass window gave one a view of the outside, if he was tall enough. A short guy would have to climb on a chair to see out of it. Plywood floors rounded out the decor.

Not a sheet of plasterboard, a length of floor covering, or a drop of paint covered any of the naked wood. In keeping with this decor, Strawberry hadn't tacked anything, not even a calendar, to any of the walls or studs. He sat at a wooden desk equipped with an in-box, an out-box, and a telephone. A black steel box sat behind him in the corner. It was about eighteen inches wide, two feet high, and three feet long. The lid had a hasp and a large brass padlock stamped "US."

Strawberry jotted something on the report he was reading, threw it into his out-box, stood up and offered me his hand. I stood up and we shook hands. He was both a little shorter and a little heavier than me (5'10", 160 lbs), and black. Not a drop of Caucasian blood coursed through his veins. He was much older than the rest of us and probably had twenty or twenty-five years in the Army—a real lifer. He smiled briefly and got down to business. He assigned all the investigations and approved all the reports, he informed me. "Any questions?" he asked with a tone that said that I should have no questions.

Then he guided me out of his office and down the hall to the other rooms. We stopped in each office for a quick introduction. Uniformed MPIs were doubled up in a couple of the offices. Each CID agent had his own office. My tour ended at the only room with no one in it. It was mine, Strawberry informed me. Like all the other offices, it had naked two-by-fours, roof framing, and a window. Its furnishings included a desk with a chair, an old gray Smith-Corona typewriter, and a couple of extra chairs. Strawberry then told one of the MPIs to get me settled into the barracks and told me to report to work at 7:00 the next morning.

The CID agents shared billets with the MP Company. The 23d Military Police had an authorized strength of just a little over one hundred eighty personnel. The barracks they lived in were typical open-bays with bunk beds. The charge of quarters showed me my bunk and the MP supply sergeant issued linen to me. I spent the rest of the day unpacking my duffel bag and getting everything put away in the wooden footlocker at the end of the bed. Although we CID agents were grouped together in the barracks, it was still an open-bay barracks. I knew as I unpacked my stuff that I wouldn't be staying in this building for long. I made up my mind to size up the other agents and see if I could generate some interest in a CID hooch somewhere on post.

Next morning I went directly to Strawberry's office. He was more talkative than he had been the day before. He formally welcomed me to the unit; he said we had a heavy caseload and "You're expected to carry your own weight"; and, he told me that the MPIs who supported us handled the misdemeanor cases and we handled the felony investigations. In the middle of this orientation, almost absentmindedly, he said, "Oh yes, I guess I better give you a firearm." He got up from his desk and stepped back to the black metal box sitting in the corner of his office. He pulled a key out of his pocket and unlocked the big brass padlock. Inside of the box was a row of little brass hooks. On about half the hooks hung .38 caliber, 2-inch Colt detective specials. He gave me one of the handguns and twelve bullets. I wasn't surprised at getting the .38—it was standard CID issue; the same type of weapon I'd carried at the Presidio. I then expected him to say something like, "This is part of your equipment. Go to the MP armorer to get your helmet, flak vest, and M-16." But he didn't.

It didn't take me long to realize Strawberry had given me the only firearm the Army thought I needed in Vietnam. I saw that none of the other agents had anything but the .38s that we wore in small holsters on our belts, concealed by our square-bottom shirts. The decision to arm CID agents only with .38s left us in the unenviable position of being the good guys outgunned by the bad guys. When that happens, usually a good guy ends up dead. For example, just before I arrived in Vietnam, a CID agent had tried to arrest a man who was sitting at the gun turret with an M-60 machine gun on a V-100 (an armored personnel carrier with oversized rubber tires). The agent tried to outdraw the dickhead and got killed. In typical Army fashion, shortly after his death, 8th MP Group (CI) sent out a directive telling CID agents not to go up against M-60 machine guns.

Simply being outgunned wasn't always to blame for agents getting killed. Also before I got to Vietnam, two agents had gone to a hooch to make an arrest. The bad guy got the drop on them with an M-16 and told the agents to throw down their .38s. The first lesson of survival one learns as a cop is to never, ever give up your weapon. If you have a gun and the dickhead has a gun, there's absolutely no advantage gained by giving up your weapon. Your best option is to shoot it out with him. At least then, you've a chance of survival. Forgetting this lesson, one of the agents dropped his weapon and the other one didn't. The one who kept his pistol opened fire. When he did, his partner went after his .38 on the ground. When he bent down to pick it up, he put his head in front of the weapon his partner was firing, got shot, and died. An inquiry exonerated the surviving partner who had, after all, remembered his survival lesson.

During my first week at Chu Lai, I began wondering why none of the other agents had thought about how outgunned we were or, more importantly, why none of them had done anything about it. My questions on the topic met with everything from disinterest to evasiveness. I realized that as the FNG (fucking new guy) it would take me a while to gain the confidence of the other agents. Not until then would I get honest, straightforward answers from them. There existed a degree of paranoia among agents. Although we enforced the law, we didn't always abide by Army rules. An outsider, therefore, presented a threat—the threat that we'd be held to account for violating the rules. So, the FNG wasn't to be trusted until trust was gained. For the moment, then, I represented the threat to the other agents.

By the end of my first week at Chu Lai, I'd passed the trust test. A little at a time, the other agents offered me glimpses, not intentionally but more carelessly than they had been before, of the unauthorized weapons many had surreptitiously acquired. I saw grenades in a footlocker, a .45 semiautomatic pistol lying on a bed, a sawed-off shotgun in the back of a jeep. Other than the issued .38 we all carried, none of these weapons was authorized. But the Army's decision to give us nothing more than .38s drove us to acquire an unauthorized stash of weapons.

In short order I realized that I needed something besides my .38, too. I started asking some of the other agents and MPIs where I could get another gun. In the process, I did find out that the MP armorer would, on occasion, let an agent unofficially borrow an M-16 when he was going off base. It wouldn't be an authorized weapon issue, but it was better than going off post armed only with a 2-inch detective special. But I didn't think that getting an M-16, which I didn't know how to use anyway, from the armorer would be near as sexy as acquiring my own weapon.

I became friends with an MPI by the name of Ted Keater. A jovial, blond-headed, young mid-westerner, he was a short-timer due to rotate back to the States shortly after I got there. I learned that he had a .45 caliber "grease gun" machine gun. (The MPIs were authorized to carry .45 caliber pistols like all the MPs were. But in a culture where CID agents procured exotic and illicit weapons, the MPIs were caught up in the excitement of obtaining unauthorized weapons, too.) The grease gun got its nickname because it looked like a mechanic's grease gun. Although the Army didn't issue it, the Navy did. Until the summer of 1970, the Navy ran the five sand ramps and sealift activities at the north end of Chu Lai. Then the Army took over most of the Navy area and the Vietnamese Navy assumed the sealift activities. Somehow, during the exodus of the Navy from Chu Lai, Keater acquired a grease gun. One day I asked him, "What are you going to do with your grease gun when you leave?"

"I don't know," he said.

"I'd like to have it."

"OK."

That was it. The deal was sealed. A day or so later we drove to a remote area of the base near sand dunes at the west perimeter. I had never fired a grease gun so Keater went through the process of showing me how to load, shoot, and clear (that's unload) it. I shot a few rounds both on automatic and semi-automatic. What Keater didn't show me was that if you had a magazine in the weapon and the bolt was to the rear, when you pulled the trigger the first time, the bolt went forward, chambered a round, and shot it.

As we were driving away from the sand dunes, I thought I was being safe with the gun: the bolt was to the rear and there wasn't a round in the chamber. I held the gun with the muzzle pointed upward and my finger resting on the trigger. Then he hit a bump. I squeezed the trigger, the bolt went forwarded, chambered a round, and I shot a hole through the jeep's canvas top directly above my head. It surprised the hell out of me and, to say the least, momentarily strained our friendship. The incident embarrassed me as much as it scared both of us. I could have been pointing the gun at Keater just as easily as toward the canvas top. I grew up around guns, and I knew better than to hold a gun with my finger on the trigger. Fortunately for me, Keater was the forgiving type. After his initial anger, he let the incident pass, and I inherited his grease gun anyway. The weapon came with four magazines (taped together in pairs to make them reversible for speedy reloading), a full box of ammunition, and an OD canvas sling. I would only fire the weapon one more time, so I never got close to using all the ammunition he gave me. When I left Vietnam, I passed gun and ammo to another CID agent.

Besides the grease gun, I also scrounged six mini-frag grenades. A mini-frag is a small, round hand grenade about the size of a golf ball. It has a spoon and a ring similar to a normal hand grenade and works basically the same way. To use it one holds on to the spoon and grenade, pulls the ring, and throws the grenade. The spoon flies off and the grenade explodes. To this day, I have no idea why I had them. I had only thrown one hand grenade in my life and that was at basic training. I had never thrown a mini-frag and had no idea if any of the mechanics of throwing one differed from a regular hand grenade. Given my misfortune with the grease gun the first day I used it, I'm undoubtedly lucky I never went to the sand dunes to try one of my grenades.

Nevertheless, now that I possessed a personal arsenal, I felt confident that I wasn't going to be outgunned by the bad guys. I always carried my .38. At times, on base I'd carry the grease gun, but I always left it lying between the two front seats of the jeep. But whenever I left the base, I took the grease gun and the mini-frags with me. I carried the gun and four of the mini-frags in my briefcase along with various forms and drug testing kits that made up the standard CID field kit. For reasons that escape me today, whenever I left the base I put two mini-frags in my pants' front pockets.

Besides being issued my .38 on my second day at Chu Lai, I also received a drive-around orientation from one of the CID agents. Darrell Ross was about my height, a little heavier, and he had wavy, light brown hair. He was probably twenty-three or twenty-four years old and a sexual compulsive if there ever was one. He got the job of showing the FNG around the base.

He showed me the main PX and the bank and pointed out the various stand-down areas. (Troops were rotated from the field to support bases, such as Chu Lai, on a regular basis. While in the support base, they lived in stand-down areas where, theoretically, they were unarmed and could shower and mentally decompress from their field duties before going back out into the bush.) We also drove past the hospital and stopped by the helicopter area at Chu Lai East. He told me that we could catch rides into the bush or to other bases with one of the UH-1 Hueys that seemed to be constantly coming or going. He explained that we'd normally ride on the "slicks"—Hueys stripped of all armament except for two M-60s, one suspended out each door. He also showed me where some of the EM (enlisted men's) clubs were located and offered editorial comments on each: "This club belongs to the engineers; it's an OK club." "This one belongs to the Rangers; it gets kinda rough in there." "There's a lot of problems in this club; it'd be a good idea to stay out of it." And so on.

After we had driven around Chu Lai for a couple of hours, Ross headed for the main gate. Just before we exited the gate, Ross asked, "You had any slant eye yet?"

"No," I replied glancing around nervously as Ross turned north on to QL1. Despite my physical attraction to Vietnamese women, I wasn't yet comfortable enough to think that driving off base was particularly wise. I'd heard all the horror stories about booby traps and bombs and snipers and all sorts of things that could kill me. Now here are two guys going outside the base and, to my knowledge, we've got only two Colt detective specials between the two of us. I knew I only had twelve rounds of ammunition, and I assumed that he had the same. But as unnerved as I felt at the time, I wasn't about to let Ross know it. Any sign of fear on my part would spread like wildfire through the CID and MPI offices. Ross might be taking me to my death, I thought, but I'll be one cool and calm looking corpse. And so he drove on.

As we continued north, Ross explained the monetary system of Vietnam. (That might seem like a strange conversation under the circumstances, but it was shortly to become relevant.) American money was contraband. For currency, GIs used MPC (military payment certificates) or piasters. MPC was exchanged at a rate of one-to-one. One hundred dollars MPC was worth one hundred dollars US. The color of MPC changed frequently in an attempt to prevent the Vietnamese from using it as a black-market currency. If they traded in MPC, whatever amount they had on-hand would become worthless as soon as the color changed. Furthermore, it was illegal for Vietnamese to possess either MPC or US dollars. On the other hand, a piaster was the basic monetary unit of South Vietnam. One hundred and fifty piasters, or 150 P, amounted to $1.00 US. Thanks to Ross, I now knew the basics of the monetary system.

(In reality, there were two basic problems with Ross's economics class. First, the currency of South Vietnam was the dong. Piaster was a holdover term from colonial days. But for the year I was in Vietnam, I never once heard the term "dong" applied to the South Vietnamese currency. Ross's second problem was in his exchange rate. A piaster [dong] was worth much less than 150 to $1.00 US. In Saigon at this time, the rate was around 450 per $1.00. But fluctuating international monetary rates made little impact on the hinterlands. To my recollection, the whole time I was at Chu Lai, $1.00 US bought 150 P.)

In an effort to thwart the black market, service members were paid in Military Payment Certificates (MPC). MPC held the same value as US currency, i.e., $1 MPC = $1 US. American officials often changed the color of MPC currency, which made preceding colors of MPC worthless. The dong was the South Vietnamese currency, although GIs usually called it "piaster"—a holdover from French colonial days. During the author's time in Chu Lai and Da Nang, a 50P note equaled 33 cents US.

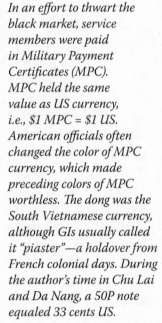

A few miles north of the main gate, we turned off the pavement of QL 1 on to a narrow dirt road. We weaved our way through a little hamlet. Ross stopped on the side of the road and told me, "Wait here." He got out of the jeep and walked on a dirt path through some trees and heavy vegetation to a thatched-roof, stucco-looking hooch about twenty-five yards away. The hooch was small, probably twelve feet square. He walked around the side of the hooch and out of my view. In a couple of minutes, Ross reappeared from around the corner of the hooch walking with a young, pretty Vietnamese girl. She wore a bright, green two-piece, what we would call a pair of pajamas. It wasn't the ao dai I had seen many women wearing in Saigon; it had a much shorter top. She also wasn't wearing one of the conical hats that I'd seen nearly all the other women wearing. I had no idea about her age. She could have been fourteen for all I knew. Or, she could have been twenty-four. My view of Vietnamese women was that they had only three ages: child, beautiful woman, and old lady. I didn't know at what age they made the transition from one to the other, but it was distinctive. The woman walking with Ross toward the jeep was clearly at the beautiful woman age.

As Ross approached the jeep, he walked over to the driver's side and sat down. The woman walked straight to my side of the jeep, took me by the hand, and tugged. I got out of the jeep and walked hand-in-hand with her to the hooch. She led me around the corner of the hooch to the side not visible from the jeep. There a thatched-roof lean-to about six feet high sloped out from the hooch. Under the space covered by the lean-to sat a small, round table three or four feet in diameter. Three or four little three-legged stools completed the table set. We walked past the table and into the open door of the hooch. In the middle of the first room of the hooch, an old woman sat on the dirt floor weaving a bamboo basket. In chronological years, she might not have been that old, but she certainly looked weathered. She paid no attention to us. She continued her weaving as the young woman guided me toward a curtained door (really nothing more than an old rag hanging in front of the door) toward the back of the hooch. She pulled back the curtain and led me into a small room. She still hadn't let go of my hand. As we entered the room, she dropped the curtain, and it fell into place filling in the doorway.

The room was sparsely furnished. A small, homemade table sat next to a short, single bed. A few nondescript items lay in disarray on the table. The bed couldn't have been over five feet long. It had a wood frame and a three-inch thick, homemade mattress, stuffed with whatever the Vietnamese stuffed in their mattresses. A crumpled up blanket lay on the bed. We stopped at the foot of the bed and the young woman turned me around and pushed me backwards on to the bed. At first I just sat down, but she pushed me again until I lay on the bed with my legs and feet hanging over the edge. She then unzipped my pants, dropped down on her knees between my legs, and gave me the best blowjob I had ever experienced. After we finished, she picked up a rag that was lying on the bed, wiped me off, and zipped up my pants. She stood up, took me by the hand and pulled me into a sitting up position. Then she tugged and I stood up. We left the hooch the same way we came in, past the old woman who again ignored us and continued her weaving. The young woman walked me out to the lean-to and let go of my hand. She stood under the lean-to as I disappeared around the corner of the hooch and headed back toward the jeep.

As I walked along the path, I realized that during the whole time we had not spoken one word to each other and, more importantly, I didn't pay her. I got back into the jeep and we drove away. For some time, neither Ross nor I said anything. After a couple of minutes, Ross chuckled and said, "Well, how was it?"

"Fantastic! But she didn't charge me anything."

"It was only 50 P and I already took care of it. Consider it my Welcome Wagon gift to you," he said laughing.

50 P. Well, it didn't take a mathematician to figure out that, at 150 P per dollar, that great blowjob cost thirty-three cents. Better yet, someone else had paid for it. I had a shit-eating grin on my face as I sat there contemplating my new environment. I knew I was going to like this tour. My war was going to be great.

There ended my war orientation course. Unlike the other GIs coming to Chu Lai, I didn't go to the Division Combat Center to learn about defending myself from the enemy's lethal weapons. My war orientation had nothing to do with the war itself. In retrospect, I believe that, like me, the other CID agents had insulated themselves from the war. Our war, the argument seemed to go, didn't involve booby traps or mortar or sapper attacks. If anyone thought about those things, as I did on my first excursion off Chu Lai, he didn't share such thoughts with anyone else. We weren't fatalistic about it either. I never had or encountered an attitude of fatalistically accepting the results of war if it came our way. We were more in denial: the effects of the war weren't coming our way. Or, maybe we were rationalizing through the calculated risks we knew we would take. But positively, we believed we wouldn't have to contend with the real war going on around us; we only had to deal with "our war" involving dickheads, drugs, and 50P whores—not necessarily in that order. We were having a great time in a world where we were a class apart, and a privileged class at that, from the other soldiers. (Despite our arrogance and disdain toward the war around us, when rockets or mortars fell into Chu Lai, as they did often in the evening, we ran to the bunkers at the same speed as the rest of Chu Lai's frightened soldiers. British physicist Stephen Hawking famously said, "I have noticed even people who claim everything is predestined, and that we can do nothing to change it, look before they cross the road." In spite of our overweening confidence, we did look both ways when crossing the road.)

I had decided after our visit to the 50P whore's house that Ross was the kind of guy with whom I wanted to share a hooch. Within a couple of weeks of arriving at Chu Lai, I approached him with my plan. He declared it a great idea and suggested two other agents to join us: Tom McSwain, another "cherry," and Ken Thompson. They were both just as depraved as Ross and I, Ross thought, and they'd jump at the chance to live elsewhere. We asked them and, as always, Ross was right. For the next week or so, we directed our energies to finding a hooch and scrounging everything we needed to make it our home. We were successful beyond our greatest expectations.

Americans imported the word "hooch," also spelled "hootch," to Vietnam. GIs used the term in Korea where it had been imported from Japan. In Japanese uchi means house. Ask a mid-westerner to say it and the "i" is dropped, an "h" is added, and we have hooch. Practically every structure in rural Vietnam (except large edifices, which were few and far between), temporary or permanent, Vietnamese or American, became a hooch. Whatever its origin, "hooch" served the GI well in Vietnam, and we four CID agents set out to get one. (The words "mama-san" [for a GI, any older Vietnamese woman] and "papa-san" [any older Vietnamese man], the first "Vietnamese" words a GI learned, made the same journey from Japan through Korea to Vietnam.)

We found our hooch on the north neck of Chu Lai halfway between the airfields in the south and the sand ramps at the far north end. The vacant hooch sat on the ocean-side edge of a promontory elevated about ten meters above sea level and a couple of meters above nearby buildings. While standing in front of our hooch surveying the surrounding area, the roofs of nearby buildings were at eye level. The top of the once heavily vegetated promontory had been bladed flat and scarred deeper by a road connecting two dozen buildings. All the other buildings were clustered in two spots, but our hooch sat by itself balanced at the lip of a thirty-foot, vegetated cliff that terminated at an outcropping of black coral. The coral meandered a couple of yards before descending into the sea. There was a sand beach about a football field's length to the northeast.

The hooch, probably abandoned eight months earlier when the US Navy left, was in excellent condition and already had electricity. Structurally, it mirrored nearly all the other buildings on post: plywood sides, corrugated metal peaked-roof, and set on twenty-four-inch stilts. An interior wall divided the twenty feet by forty feet structure exactly in half. Three steps led into the front room that we turned into a living room of sorts complete with four small, personal refrigerators for Budweiser beer, a sofa against the wall, a few chairs, and a television to watch AFVN (Armed Forces Vietnam Network). We also had a table and a propane camp stove. We didn't do much cooking there; we normally ate in the mess hall. But, in the evening the stove was good for heating up some beans if one of us got hungry. We decorated the walls and inside of the door with pin-ups from *Playboy* and *Penthouse*.

For the back room we scrounged air force bunk beds, the Cadillac of military bunk beds—unlike Army cots, they had real mattresses. We put one in each corner. For storage we moved in our wooden footlockers from the MP barracks and jury-rigged four wooden bars on the wall for each of us to hang clothes. Next to our beds, we had small tables for nightstands and our personal stereo equipment. We had a fifth small table for our telephone. We'd convinced a troop in the Signal Corps to run a telephone line to our hooch. That detail was the linchpin to our getting permission to move out of the MP barracks. We made up nearly 50 percent of the CID agents on post. One agent or MPI had to be on-call twenty-four hours a day to respond to calls from the MP Desk Sergeant. The guy on-call would sleep on a cot in the CID office. When an MPI was on-call, he'd handle his own investigations excluding the major crimes such as rape, homicide, suicide, and so forth. So on a night when an MPI took his turn on-call, he had to be able to contact one of the CID agents. The on-call roster always listed one of us as the MPI's on-call backup.

That's why we needed a telephone in our hooch. When we decided to move from the MP compound, we had to guarantee to Strawberry that the on-call MPI could contact us. A telephone from the Signal Corps cinched our receiving his permission to move to the hooch. The telephone had an extra-long cord on it, so we could move it around the room to place it next to the bed of whoever was on-call that night.

I connected a mosquito-net frame over my bed. When I slept, I dropped the netting around me. Mosquitoes weren't the problem, though; geckos were. I hated those little fucking lizards crawling all over me at night. The net kept them off. Directly above my bed, stapled to the roof joists, I had a South Vietnamese, yellow and red garrison flag. I stapled it on all four corners, so it ran parallel to my bed directly below it. I don't remember where I procured it. I got it because it personalized my space in the hooch.

We had a shower off our living room. It measured four feet by four feet, had a slatted floor, a showerhead with spigot, and a faucet about knee high. We didn't have a sink, so we used the faucet for such things as washing hands, shaving, washing dishes, and so on. You could look straight through the slats of the shower floor to the ground below. Our water came from a tank on stilts located on a small raise behind the hooch. We made arrangements to have water delivered once a week. We didn't have a water heater, so the water temperature for our shower was whatever the temperature was in our holding tank.

To make our hooch livable, we scrounged two window air conditioners from Philco Ford, the large civilian contract company on Chu Lai. The units were old and beat up, but serviceable. We installed one in each room.

We had an outhouse ten yards out the front door. Unlike a typical outhouse built over a hole in the ground, our outhouse—as the rest on Chu Lai—sat elevated above the ground with a half of a fifty-five gallon drum under it. Every week, like clockwork, a couple poor sons-of-bitches would show up in a truck with a diesel fuel tank in back. They'd pull that drum out from under the outhouse, fill it with diesel, and light it. Then they stirred the shit to make sure it burned. When they were done with our drum, they'd put it back under the outhouse and move on to someone else's. Theirs had to be the most disgusting and thankless job on Chu Lai.

Finally, not far from our hooch we had a "bunker," a culvert about five feet in diameter. Railroad ties had been stacked over the culvert, and dirt was thrown over the ties. Lastly, piles of sandbags protected its entrance. Whenever we heard the thud-thud of mortars or rockets hitting the airfields (the usual targets), we ran into the bunker.

Now that we had a hooch, we needed a hooch maid. Officially, the job of a hooch maid was defined: "The duties performed by Domestic hires [hooch maids] would include the cleaning of quarters, making beds, cleaning rooms, shining shoes and brass, mopping and sweeping floors, performing laundry duties, and pressing clothes." When you hired a hooch maid, you signed an official form acknowledging that you understood that it was Army policy not to pay a hooch maid more than, I believe it was, five dollars a month. That amount, of course, had to be paid in piasters. This policy was a feeble attempt to harness the economic inflation that accompanied doing business with a post of fourteen thousand GIs. Needless-to-say, inflation ravished the rural area around Chu Lai.

Hooch maids generally made more than allowed by official policy. In some cases, GIs paid more simply because loyalty has a price, and a loyal maid was worth much more than the standard fare. On the other hand, some GIs paid considerably more because they were getting more. In many cases, hooch maid was just a euphemism for 50P whore. These prostitutes got legitimate jobs on post simply to gain access to thousands of horny GIs. They performed normal hooch maid chores and offered their bodies to their employers. In exchange, they received more than five dollars a month. Then, when not servicing their official "employers," they made 50 piaster each time they had sex with GIs in stand-down areas. They made far more than five dollars a month and contributed mightily to the inflation destroying their own communities.

As the mastermind of the hooch idea, my hooch mates selected me to find a maid. I liked the idea of getting an attractive Vietnamese woman to tend to our needs. Through some mutual acquaintances, I found the perfect woman (young, attractive, English-speaking, agreeable) and hired her. She robbed us blind. Everything from cigarettes to food to underwear disappeared. I fired her and changed my tactic. I decided to find the ugliest hooch maid on Chu Lai.

Buom Thi Tran was an incredibly unattractive seventeen- or eighteen-year-old woman. The bottom of her feet looked like elephant footpads. They were as wide as they were long. She had about an inch gap between each toe. She had gold, bucked teeth and heavy acne scars. We certainly didn't have to worry about her spending time consorting with us or any other GIs. But most importantly, Tran never stole any-thing from us. She was grateful to have a job and paid us back with tremendous loyalty. In return, we paid her four times the official rate. Until the day I left Chu Lai, she remained our hooch maid.

Typically, hooch maids started coming to work at between 6:00 and 7:00 each weekday morning. All the Vietnamese civilian employ-ees checked-in through the civilian gate. The MPs would check their identification cards before letting them on base. Once on base, the civilians, called "daily hires," would climb into the back of deuce-and-a-half trucks. When the back of a truck was full, the GI driver would transport his load of daily hires around the base, dropping them off at their work places. In the evening, the process would be reversed as the trucks made the rounds to pick up daily hires to ferry back to the civilian gate. As they departed the base, employees were some-times searched for contraband. Female matrons strip-searched female daily hires, finding everything from contraband currency to blocks of cheese hidden in brassieres and elsewhere. By nightfall, only bar maids, interpreters, and a few other select civilians remained on base. The rest of the five thousand-strong civilian work force would be gone, to return the next morning to start the process over again. (A daily hire remaining on base after hours was declared a security violation. Typically, such violations occurred when a GI hid a female while the charge of quarters or MPs made sweeps of the area looking for secu-rity violations. She would then spend the night with him.)

We saved Tran the trouble of riding the trucks by taking turns meeting her at the civilian gate. We'd bring her back to the hooch where she'd stay all day (Monday through Friday) working for us. Then every evening one of us would give her a ride back to the gate. We never had to worry about her having contraband, and we never ques-tioned her loyalty to us.

One day I was in my office when the telephone rang. The voice on the other end was Tran's, and she was screaming, "Logan! Logan! Logan!" Tran, who spoke very little English, couldn't say Skogen; it always came out Logan. I hung up the telephone, ran out to my jeep, and drove to the hooch. When I got there, I saw Tran lying on the ground outside of the hooch hanging on to a case of beer with her arms and legs completely wrapped around it. A Vietnamese man was dragging her and the beer toward a truck. He was one of the base's garbage men. We had a fifty-five gallon barrel beside the hooch that we used for a trashcan. Once a week a couple of male daily hires would drive around in a truck and empty all the barrels. On this day, the guy went into our hooch to steal some beer. Tran tried to stop him and then called me. When all else failed, she latched on to the case of beer and wouldn't let go. As soon as I got there, the man stopped dragging her, jumped in his truck, and drove off. Tran had saved the day by saving our beer. She was certainly an exceptional hooch maid. We paid her well and treated her right. In turn, she gave us her unquestioning loyalty.

When it was my turn to pick up or drop off Tran at the gate, I drove my powder blue jeep. I'd inherited it from Ted Keater along with the grease gun. He figured I possessed some sort of claim to it because, with the grease gun, I had blown a hole in the black canvas top. The two belonged together. The 4-wheel drive jeep wasn't standard Army issue anymore, if it ever had been. It looked as if it came from an earlier era with its rounded hood. I'm not sure how it ended up in Chu Lai. It undoubtedly had been there a long time. Bailing wire and duct tape held together far too much of it. The doors had long since disappeared. Someone re-upholstered the bucket seats in front and the backbench seat in black vinyl. He'd also spray-painted the interior panel dark blue and the hood, sides, and fenders powder blue. There was no mistaking it; the jeep wasn't checked out of the motor pool. We did have a couple of better MP jeeps assigned to our office, but I was partial to my jeep. The only time I rode in another jeep was when someone else drove. Otherwise my powder blue jeep provided my primary ground transportation while I was at Chu Lai.

Within a month of getting to Chu Lai, I'd received a .38, supplemented it with a grease gun and mini-frags, been introduced to a 50 P whore, found a hooch with a great ocean view, and acquired a personal jeep. In the mornings, I stood outside my hooch and watched the bright sunrays dancing off the waves of the incredibly blue water of the South China Sea. In the clear water, I could see stingrays and jellyfish gliding or floating just under the surface. In the evenings, stars burst out of the coal black sky. The Southern Cross, the symbol on the 23d American's shoulder patch, was visible in the southern sky. Moonbeams bounced off the waves on their way to the shore below me. Vietnam is a beautiful country. I'd often think that someday, when this is all over, somebody's going to build a resort right here and make a fortune. In the meantime, though, I was there to be a cop—a narcotics cop, no less—in an environment teeming with dickheads. My wartime experience was shaping up to be an extraordinarily attractive and gratifying chapter of my life.

CHAPTER 5   VIALS, VIALS

EVERYWHERE

I would not be disappointed in my desire to be a drug cop. Vietnam was awash with drugs, and most of them found their way onto the American military bases. Chu Lai was no exception. The drug problem was so enormous that our efforts to stem the tide had little, if any, effect on the situation. In 1970, over eleven thousand GIs were apprehended for illegal possession of drugs in Vietnam, and 1971 was a far worse year. And, that's just the ones who got caught. Far more GIs were using heroin than we ever apprehended.

So whether it was basic law enforcement efforts to curtail drug possession and use or programs intended to rehabilitate users or the American government's attempts to move the corrupt and ineffective government of South Vietnam to take action against drug trafficking, the programs failed. In what surely must be the quintessential understatement of all times, one Army officer assessed the drug rehabilitation program as ineffective because "Vietnam has some negative aspects concerning a good rehabilitation environment." He could have said the same thing about any of the counter-drug programs. "Negative aspects" of Vietnam prevented any efforts from stemming the typhoon-size tide of drug abuse by US soldiers.

One shouldn't assume, however, that the drug problem of Vietnam began there. Rather, it began on the streets, school yards, and college campuses back in the States. One study of heroin users in Vietnam found that three-quarters had used at least one illicit drug before they joined the Army. Twenty percent of them had tried heroin before coming to the war. In another study of 555 soldiers known to use illegal drugs in Vietnam, 76 percent said they used marijuana, 36 percent admitted using amphetamines, and 41 percent acknowledged taking barbiturates, all before they arrived in-country. Admittedly, the easy availability and cheap cost of drugs in Vietnam provided a ready supply for the soldiers, but American culture of the 1960s and 1970s provided the demand.

Although nearly every drug imaginable found its way to the war, the two drugs most demanded by the GIs (not counting alcohol—which was legal) were marijuana and heroin*. Marijuana was so common that one expected to smell it while walking through the company areas. Unless we in the CID thought we could bust a trafficking operation, we seldom bothered ourselves with marijuana-related cases and turned such investigations over to the MPI. Official statistics show that marijuana use was the major drug problem in Vietnam up to 1970 when heroin use began to exceed it. By February 1971, according to an official report, heroin abuse "actually surpassed marihuana [sic] abuse." The reality is that marijuana use continued unabated, but because heroin had become so prevalent, the enforcement of laws against marijuana simply ran out of steam. Why spend valuable investigative time chasing after some soldier toking a marijuana cigarette when there were so many GIs using heroin, a far more dangerous illicit drug?

The statistics on CID investigations in Vietnam demonstrate the phenomenal growth in heroin cases and the corresponding decline in marijuana investigations. In 1970, the CID handled 3,687 marijuana cases and 534 heroin cases. The next year, by August, the CID had investigated 1,113 marijuana cases and 3,054 heroin cases. Marijuana use hadn't dropped by 70 percent in one year, but Army commanders' interest, along with the CID's, had undergone a precipitous decline. On the other hand, a nearly 700 percent increase in heroin cases doesn't mean that abuse of heroin suddenly increased by that percentage. Rather, there was clearly a shift in commanders' and CID's interest from marijuana use to heroin abuse. Moreover, commanders had gotten smarter about how to identify heroin use in a unit, and the CID had gotten smarter about investigating such use. After all, my only

---

* *Much less frequently, but also present, was opium. Heroin actually begins as opium that comes from opium poppies. In places such as Thailand and Laos (and now Afghanistan), poppy farmers score a bulb at the base of the poppy flower. A sap-like substance, usually dark brown, oozes out of the bulb as syrup from a tree. The farmers collect it by scraping it off the bulb. The ooze is pure, unrefined opium. It is shaped into small round buttons about a one-half inch in diameter and one-eighth inch thick. These buttons were sold to GIs who smoked the opium in a variety of pipes. Although I didn't see a lot of opium, it was certainly present anywhere we found the more popular heroin and marijuana. I remember one GI getting busted at the gate by the MPs. He was carrying a hunk of opium the size of a softball that he'd wrapped in a newspaper.*

special training before going to Vietnam was a one-week drug investigation course at Fort Gordon, Georgia. I was in class number five of that course. Only four other groups of CID agents had attended in the weeks before me. So by early 1971, the CID was just getting its first specially trained agents into Vietnam to fight the growing heroin problem.

That problem was most evident in the thousands of vials scattered around Chu Lai. GIs purchased 94 percent to 98 percent pure heroin (the China white variety) packaged in a .25 gram plastic vial for which they paid $2 to $3.50–$10 was the top price in Vietnam, but it was virtually unheard of in the hinterlands around Chu Lai. (By comparison, in the States a user purchased the same quantity of 4 percent to 12 percent pure heroin for around $20.) The clear, hard plastic vials were about one-inch long and half-an-inch in diameter. At the open end, they had recessed necks and snap-on plastic caps.

One saw these vials everywhere on post. During a walk through a company area, one would see heroin vials lying on the gravel, among the vegetation, and on the barracks' floors. They laid discarded in trash cans and under the stilted buildings. I once went to a captain's office and saw his "collection" of vials. He had literally thousands of them on display. He had them lined up on every flat surface in his office. Across the entire length of the top of the door jam, he'd set vials side by side. Across the top of the windowsills, he did the same. On his bookshelves, he arranged them in patterns snaking in and out among his books and manuals. These were just the vials he had collected in his company's area. He told me that one day he decided to channel his frustration into a hobby. "There's nothing I can do about these vials I find," he said, "because I have no idea who threw them away." Because he couldn't legally connect the discarded vials to any of his soldiers, he got frustrated and decided to collect them. With resignation, he said he planned to see how many vials he could collect before he left Vietnam.

The captain wasn't the only one interested in the vials. The Army wanted to know where the vials originated. After all, the use of heroin was shaping up to be a (if not *the*) most effective "weapon" against the Army's efficiency in the war. So the Army Land Warfare Laboratory contracted with a civilian research laboratory to determine the origin of the plastic vials. The contractor determined that the vials were "being fabricated from a low cost, unmodified grade of polystyrene. Method of fabrication was by an injection molding machine probably of a piston type instead of a screw type. Multi-cavity molds were used. The crudeness of the vials strongly suggests that the vials were probably injection molded in Southeast Asia and not imported from a more industrialized country." In other words, they weren't coming from the Soviet Union, one of its satellite nations, or China. The report concluded, "Although the area of fabrication cannot be positively determined, it should be noted that each mold cavity leaves a distinctive characteristic—much like a fingerprint—on each vial formed in that mold. If on investigating injection molding facilities any molds are found which look like they were used to make heroin vials they could be readily checked for definitive correlation with the cataloged vials." To my knowledge, no one ever identified the origin of these vials.

Besides the thousands of empty and discarded vials, in February and March 1971, the CID, MPs, and other police agencies in MR I confiscated nearly three thousand vials still containing heroin. And for every vial we confiscated, dozens more were emptied by users and discarded. The sheer numbers of confiscated and discarded vials pointed to the obvious: thousands of GIs at Chu Lai used heroin. Some Army studies conclude that there were units in which as many as 50 percent of assigned personnel used heroin. Other studies put the figure at between 30 percent to 35percent. The most conservative studies use a 10 percent to 15 percent estimate. In February 1971, Chu Lai had a GI population of 14,000. Even the most conservative figures would put the number of Chu Lai GIs using heroin at between 1,400 and 2,100. On the high end, the figure would be 7,000. The most commonly accepted figures in the middle would indicate that between 4,200 and 4,900 GIs at Chu Lai used heroin at least once. I have no scientific data to counter or to substantiate any of these figures. But given the sheer number of discarded vials I saw and the number of drug cases we worked (nearly three-quarters of our workload), the middle-range studies couldn't be that far off the mark. And that figure doesn't even count the number of GIs who smoked marijuana.

I can't use the phrase "everybody smoked marijuana," because obviously everybody didn't. But a great percentage of the GIs smoked marijuana. One study reported the survey results of about 1,200 departing GIs. Fifty percent of them admitted trying marijuana at least once. Nearly 30 percent of that group of marijuana smokers used the drug at least two hundred times during their year in the war. The survey doesn't reveal how many of the drug users smoked it more than once, but less than two hundred times. The statistics also don't reveal whether they smoked marijuana once a day, twice a day, or more. Nevertheless, that's a lot of marijuana smoked for a group of soldiers fighting a war.

These GIs used marijuana in a variety of ways. They smoked it in water pipes, they smoked it in little hash pipes, or they rolled their own marijuana cigarettes in Zig-Zags (cigarette papers). However, by far, the most popular way of smoking marijuana was to buy commercially rolled cigarettes the Vietnamese nationals sold. The marijuana cigarettes looked like regular, unfiltered tobacco cigarettes, such as Lucky Strikes or Camels. They came ten to a pack (a little clear, plastic sealed bag) that sold for $2. If you saw a GI smoking one, the only way you knew it was a marijuana cigarette was to smell it—there was no hiding the distinctive aroma of marijuana. But if you weren't in a position to smell it, you'd never know he was smoking a commercially rolled marijuana cigarette—unlike the roll-your-own variety that was clearly recognizable. Nevertheless, by 1971 we in the CID weren't that interested in marijuana use. By then our attention focused on the heroin users.

The vast majority of the heroin users in Vietnam smoked it or snorted it. In rare cases, we found troops who injected it. To smoke heroin, a GI would pull most of the tobacco out of a regular cigarette—usually a Kool cigarette. (I don't know why users preferred Kool cigarettes. It may be that the heroin had a bitter taste, and the menthol in a Kool took away the bitterness.) After removing the tobacco from the cigarette, he poured a little bit of heroin into the cigarette tube, tamped in a little tobacco, poured in a little more heroin, tamped in some more tobacco, and so on until he had a heroin-laced cigarette. Then he smoked it. He could be standing in a compound surrounded by other troops, and nobody would notice anything unusual. Smoke from heroin-laced cigarettes, unlike the marijuana cigarettes, had no distinctive smell.

When an abuser snorted heroin, he sprinkled it on the back of his hand, into the palm of his hand, or on a finger and snorted it into his nostril. Sometimes you'd find a guy that poured his heroin into the plastic cap of the vial and snorted it out of the cap.

How often an individual used heroin in a day depended on how much tolerance his system had built up to the drug. When using heroin, as with many drugs, a user develops a tolerance to its effects. So the longer one uses it, the more one needs of it to get high. The best high for a heroin abuser is what is called the "good sick." That occurs when a user has ingested heroin to the point of a borderline overdose, and he becomes physically ill because of this euphoric rush. If a user passes that point, he'll overdose, which may result in his death. The amount of heroin required to achieve a "good sick" or to overdose depended entirely on the individual. I apprehended GIs in Vietnam that said they used eight, ten, or even twelve vials of heroin a day. That is one hell of a lot of heroin going into one's body. That much heroin should have killed them. Then and now, I find it difficult to believe they were using that many vials in a day, but that's what they said.

That GIs were overdosing from heroin use is undeniable. The Army reported 103 deaths in Vietnam from drug abuse in 1970. In the first three months of 1971, it had already reported 35 such deaths. A medical review of over one thousand autopsies conducted in-country between January 1970 and early 1972 determined that drugs, including alcohol, were factors in the deaths of approximately 300 of the GIs, nearly 30 percent—and that's only the in-country autopsies. As well, in 1970, 1,237 soldiers were hospitalized for complications from drug abuse. In the first three months of 1971, half that number had already been hospitalized. Before that year was over, four times as many GIs spent time in the hospital for drug abuse than for combat-related injuries.

I believe that the true number of deaths from these overdoses is higher than that reflected in any official report. Determining that number is, however, impossible because drug-related deaths are not acknowledged in the official casualty figures. The truth is, drug overdoses and heroin-induced deaths were common events. The death of Private Tyron Washington, for example, was typical enough not to surprise us.

Private Washington, an African-American and Bronx, New York native, joined the Army in March 1966. At 6'2" and 207 pounds, he would have been a welcomed addition to any infantry unit, but the Army made him a clerk, and later a driver. He spent his first two years stationed on the east coast. In early 1968, he went to Vietnam. Toward the end of his year, he was wounded and awarded a Purple Heart. He recovered at Fort Dix, New Jersey. In May 1969, he returned to duty, once again on the East Coast. Within a year he received orders to Europe. Private Washington spent one year in Europe before the Army sent him back to Vietnam. He arrived in-country in February 1971. Three days later another soldier found him lying unconscious on a bunk. First a medic, then a doctor tried to revive him. That afternoon, one week before his twenty-third birthday, the doctor pronounced him dead. Investigators found a "small plastic vial containing a white powder substance" in his fatigue shirt pocket.

The autopsy report listed "Probable Heroin Overdose" as the direct cause of death and asphyxiation of gastric contents and pulmonary edema as major findings. In other words, an overdose of heroin had caused a buildup of fluid in his lungs, and he threw up while lying on his back. He had, in effect, drowned. A subsequent line of duty investigation determined that on the day that he died, he had without authority "absent himself from his place of duty…and expired from an overdose of heroin." With that finding, it's doubtful that his wife and son waiting for him back in the Bronx received any of his life insurance money. Today, on the official tally of Vietnam War casualties, the cause of his death is given as "non-hostile—accidental self destruction," and he is memorialized on the Wall.

Although not an everyday occurrence, such deaths at Chu Lai, Da Nang and elsewhere around MR I did not surprise us. We investigated similar deaths a couple of times a week. That's why I think the Army's admission that thirty-five drug-related deaths occurred in all of Vietnam the first three months of 1971 is an undercount. In MR I alone, I'd put that number at twenty to thirty for that time period. Surely, the other military regions were experiencing the same level of heroin abuse as we were. One study estimates that drug overdoses killed more than two soldiers per day during the waning years of the war. I have no evidence to support that claim, but I do know that such deaths were commonplace.

Private Washington's death wasn't surprising and neither was the fact that he overdosed just three days after arriving in-country. The prevalence of heroin meant that cherries were often exposed to it almost immediately upon entering the country. (Technically, Washington wasn't a cherry; he was on his second tour in-country. It's possible that he'd used heroin during his first tour, but I'll give him the benefit of the doubt.) A congressman who visited Vietnam reported back to his shocked colleagues that he spoke to "literally hundreds of privates and corporals, who assured us they were not in Vietnam 15 days when they were contacted by a fellow American or some member of the South Vietnamese population as to the availability of heroin and where they could obtain their source of heroin." Couple the availability of the drug with the increased risk of its use by novice abusers and one has a scenario for a death such as Private Washington's. He was a new troop who easily purchased a couple of vials of heroin. He went to a barracks room to be by himself, listen to some music, and snort the drug. Hours later he was dead. Deaths such as his deprived many American families of their husbands, sons, and fathers, and the Army of its soldiers.

If heroin wasn't the immediate cause of death by overdose, it also caused death by its psychological effects on a user. Such was the case of Private First Class (PFC) Richard Hall.

In October 1969, nineteen-year-old Richard Hall, a white Californian, enlisted for a three-year hitch in the Army. After basic and supply clerk training, he headed to Germany. In less than a year, the Army sent him to Vietnam, where he arrived in January 1971. His immersion into the drug culture was quick and deep. One day in April, he talked to his NCO about his drug problem. After Hall's death the NCO testified that Hall "told me he was using heroin and wanted to get off, but needed some help. At this time he gave me a vial partly filled with a substance which looked like heroin. He stated that because of drugs he couldn't get along with the people in [his] shop where he worked nor with the people he had to deal with in other maintenance units. He said he couldn't stand using it any longer; he knew he couldn't afford it in the United States and was afraid of an overdose."

Sometime during the early morning hours just two days later, while standing guard duty, PFC Hall placed the muzzle of his M-16 on the right side of his head, just above his ear, and pulled the trigger. At about 5:00 in the morning, another soldier saw him lying on top of a bunker and assumed he was sleeping. A little over an hour later, the command post notified all the bunker guards to end their nightly guard duty. The soldier went on top of the bunker to wake Hall. He later testified, "I saw the blood. I rolled him over and saw the large wound, noticing his body was somewhat stiff." The soldier called for help from another GI and then ran to get a medic. The second GI found a bag of marijuana near the body. "I didn't want to make it any worse on his family by having it look like he got high and killed himself," he testified, "so I flipped it off the bunker." A CID investigator later found that bag of marijuana.

PFC Hall's hooch mates testified that he had vast mood swings. "When he was using skag," one stated, "it was as if he didn't have a care in the world. He was much more depressed when he wasn't using it." He received mail from his young wife who was expecting their first child. When in his good moods, he talked about her. During his darker moments, he talked about suicides in his family, including the recent suicide of a cousin. His friends knew that he regularly used heroin and marijuana. One testified that he took drugs to the bunker when he pulled guard duty. Those closest to him believed that he had a sincere desire to quit drugs. When asked if Hall's suicide surprise him, one of the hooch mates responded, "No, when I heard about it, the first thing I asked was if he was high."

Although no chemical analysis of his blood was done, it certainly appeared that PFC Hall had gotten high and killed himself. His concerns about not being able to afford his habit in the States and about a possible overdose were legitimate. If he had a two or three vial-a-day habit, in Vietnam it was costing him $4 to $6. In the States it would cost him $40 to $60 or more every day for 4 percent to 12 percent pure heroin. If he wanted to purchase 94 percent to 98 percent pure heroin in the States, as he was accustomed to doing in Vietnam, his habit could cost $300 to $500 per day!

Also, his tendency to mix heroin and marijuana and use the drugs when alone, for example on bunker guard duty, increased his risk of an overdose. Abusers seldom overdosed when with someone else. A buddy could keep an abuser awake, walk him around, or get him help. Overdosing on heroin was usually a very lonely death. Rather than face the expense of heroin addiction in the States or live with the fear of overdosing or of withdrawal, twenty-one-year-old PFC Hall got high one last time and died a lonely, but quick death on a dark bunker.

His buddy's desire to save Hall's family from further anguish (when he tossed the marijuana bag off the bunker) may have been shared by Hall's commander. In letters to Hall's wife and parents, the captain wrote, "[Richard] was pulling the early morning shift of guard duty when his weapon accidentally fired fatally wounding him." And, "[h]is devotion to duty and strong sincere moral convictions made him an ideal man to work with." These were the official words of condolence offered to a grieving family whose husband and son was a known drug addict who chose to kill himself rather than deal with his addiction. Is this an acceptable perversion of the truth by an Army official wanting to spare a family more grief, or is it an example of an official lying to avoid embarrassing questions and to cover up the realities of a decaying Army? Regardless, the deceit did not carry over to the official tally of Vietnam War casualties. It lists the cause of his death as "non-hostile—suicide." (Four decades hasn't done much to change a culture of misrepresenting facts to a family about the cause of death of a soldier, especially if it's embarrassing to the Army. The tragic death of Army Corporal Pat Tillman, the former NFL player who died from fratricide, proved to be just one example of many cases wherein the Army had to retract its original notice to families. As these misrepresentations of the cause of death were brought to light, the *Christian Science Monitor* reported, "[T]he US military faces a credibility gap.")

Needless-to-say, not every GI who used heroin died of an overdose or by blowing his brains out. But the act of becoming intoxicated by heroin could have dreadful consequences, oftentimes to innocent bystanders. Such was the case with Specialist Four (SP4) Donald N. Hernandez.

On June 23, 1971, at approximately 4:30 p.m., the guard at Tower #62, located along Chu Lai's perimeter running parallel to QL1, observed SP4 Hernandez crawling through the fence heading off post. Hernandez had armed himself with an M-79 grenade launcher and a vest full of M-79 HE (high explosive) ammunition. As he ran across QL1, he began firing rounds at a group of water buffaloes (called "cows" in the first official report) standing off the side of the road. A number of MP units, including two V-100s, responded to the tower guard's call for help. Hernandez evaded the MPs by hiding in the thick vegetation and among rocks southwest of QL1. To intimidate Hernandez into surrendering, the officer in charge ordered the MPs to fire M-60s over the fugitive's head.

Eventually, Hernandez surrendered to the MPs who found him intoxicated and believed him under the influence of heroin. Two MPs handcuffed him and took him to the 91st Medivac Hospital for blood and urine testing. By the time he surrendered, he'd fired five to seven rounds of HE ammo at the water buffaloes. As a testament to his lack of marksmanship, none of the animals was hurt. Before surrendering, he discarded the weapon and vest. The MPs search the area and found the M-79 and vest with five remaining rounds of HE ammo.

While the MPs searched for the weapon, two Vietnamese males carrying a young boy on a stretcher approached them for help. Fourteen-year-old Nguyen Van Lop had been hit in the left hip by one of the M-60 rounds that was fired over Hernandez's head. The MPs transported Lop to Chu Lai's hospital where he was treated. Luckily, the wayward round hadn't injured the young man more seriously, and he recovered from his wound. Unluckily, when Hernandez arrived at the hospital, a "misunderstanding arose when the [medical troops] failed to take" blood and urine samples. With no more evidence than testimony from the MPs that they believed Hernandez was under the influence of heroin, Hernandez's commander could only charge him with illegal discharge of a weapon. Hernandez was busted to private and fined $75 for two months. In August 1971, the Abilene, Texas native returned to the United States after twenty months of wartime service.

How much Hernandez's (alleged) heroin-induced antics played in the death of ten-year-old Ho Thi Lieu is impossible to tell. Lieu lived in Xuan Trung, a small village located just outside the north civilian-processing gate. About thirty minutes after Hernandez began his bizarre rampage, two captains were heading toward the fence line near Bunker #207, positioned considerably north of Tower #62. There's no way of knowing if Hernandez's behavior steeled their determination to do their part in the war on drugs at Chu Lai. Earlier that day they had discussed the problem of Vietnamese nationals selling drugs through the perimeter fence to GIs. On this night they decided to go to the fence line to check out the problem for themselves.

Twenty-eight-year-old Captain Roger Runge from Little Rock, Arkansas, drove the jeep as his partner Captain Paul Manchester from Dedham, Massachusetts, scanned the fence line. Near Bunker #207, Manchester spotted three or four Vietnamese male children standing near the fence. When the children saw Runge and Manchester, they ran away from the fence into nearby trees. For good measure, Manchester fired five rounds of tear gas from his M-79. The rounds landed between the trees and fence. The captains continued on to Bunker #208. There they hid their jeep among trees and entered the bunker where they could remain undetected while observing the fence line.

About an hour later, the captains saw SP4 John Francis jogging on the perimeter road. Francis, a twenty-one-year-old Independence, Kansas native, was on his seventeenth consecutive month in Vietnam. He worked in a radio research company and seldom left Chu Lai. He later claimed he jogged the perimeter road for exercise—never mind that the area was off-limits to him. Just as he passed Bunker #207, the Vietnamese children yelled at him to get his attention. At first he waved at them and continued on. "One of the Vietnamese yelled again," he later testified, "and at this time I saw a girl in the group, and I went over toward the fence. They asked me what I wanted to buy. I told them 'I don't want no Pot, and I don't want no smack [heroin].'

They asked me again, 'What do you want to buy?' After they asked me the second time, I asked if they had a girl. They said 'No.' They acted like they weren't interested [presumably, in selling the sexual favors of the young girl with them], and started angling off." Francis then returned to the road.

The two captains watched Francis talking to the Vietnamese children and believed that he'd see them in their hiding place in the bunker. They feared that he'd warn other troops in the area that they were watching the fence line. To protect their cover, Runge jumped in his jeep to pick up Francis and turn him over to his first sergeant for being in an off-limits area. Manchester lobbed five more tear gas rounds from his M-79 in the general direction of the children.

Thirty minutes later, a Vietnamese man flagged down an MP jeep and told the MPs that someone firing from the base had killed a little girl. Investigation revealed that one of Manchester's tear gas rounds hit Ho Thi Lieu on the right side of the head, killing her instantly. She was not with the children at the fence line, but was standing with another group of children nearly one hundred meters beyond the fence. In his excitement to fire tear gas at the suspected drug dealers at the fence, Captain Manchester had landed at least one of the rounds more than a football field length off target. Young Lieu became an innocent victim of an ill-fated attempt by a couple of overzealous officers to deal with Chu Lai's insurmountable drug problem. (Captain Manchester remained in Vietnam until September 1971. For his service in the war, he received a Bronze Star. He spent the next four years in Germany. Then the Army sent him to a Midwestern university where he earned a Masters of Art degree. In 1978, after completing ten years in the Army, he was discharged from the service.)

Of course, most heroin cases didn't involve death or mayhem. Most of our cases involved simply apprehending GIs, a lot of them, for being under the influence of heroin. We apprehended anyone when he demonstrated the objective symptoms of heroin use, symptoms that not even the most hardened user could hide—and that are still used as evidence of heroin use. For example, a user's pupils will constrict to a pinpoint, and there isn't a thing in the world a user can do to make them dilate. His movements and speech become slow and deliberate. His voice sounds very raspy. So when we saw or someone reported a GI exhibiting these symptoms, we apprehended him and took him to our office.

Once at our office, we had two tests to give him. First, we put him in a dark room. A normal person's pupil will dilate in a dark room to about 6.0 millimeters. When you shine a flashlight in his eye, the pupil will constrict to about 3.0 millimeters. For a person under the influence of heroin, however, you can leave him in the dark and his pupils will not get above 3.0 or 2.5 millimeters. When you shine the light directly in his eyes, his pupils will constrict to 2.0 or 1.5 millimeters. I've seen pupils go down to 1.0 millimeter. It's like looking at a black dot. If a GI failed this eye test, we'd get a urine sample from him and send it to the CID laboratory in Long Binh.

The urine sample was required to substantiate medically and legally that he was under the influence of heroin. This process was not as simple as it might seem. To collect the samples, the Army purchased cases of clear glass bottles shaped like cough syrup bottles. Including the nearly pencil thin neck, they were about six inches high and held six to eight ounces of liquid. When you handed a soldier the bottle and ordered him, "Pee in the bottle," his first reaction was, "You're shitting me!" If he didn't have exceptionally good aim, he peed all over his hand. If he provided you the specimen, you were done with your tests: you'd checked his eyes and you had his urine sample. However, frequently, detainees would respond to the pee-in-the-bottle order with, "Fuck you! I'm not going to do it." If he said that, we put him in a holding tank that didn't have a toilet, set the bottle on the floor, and said, "You're going to stay in here until you pee in the bottle. If you think you're going to get out of this by pissing on the floor, I'm going to take off your pants and mop up your piss with them. Then I'm going to package up the pants and ship them down to the lab. It's your choice." That usually worked.

Once in a while we got a user who said, "I can't go." Sometimes that would be true. One of the objective symptoms of being under the influence of heroin is that bodily functions slow down. One of those functions could be the ability to urinate. In these situations, we put him in a holding cell with the bottle and waited patiently. Eventually we got our sample.

At times we caught the dickheads before they used their heroin. Then we charged them with possession of the narcotic. Examples abound, but the case of PFCs Timothy Jones and Lawrence Sharpe is representative. At 2:45 on an afternoon in March 1971, MPs on town patrol in Quang Ngai City, south of Chu Lai, watched Privates Jones and Sharpe leaving a house of prostitution located on Phan Boi Chau Street. The bordello was notorious for its connection to the area's criminal elements and as a source of heroin. The local commander had placed the establishment off-limits to all US personnel. Jones and Sharpe weren't particularly bright soldiers or they wouldn't have walked out of an off-limits bordello at mid-afternoon. As soon as the MPs saw them, there existed probable cause to apprehend them for violating a written regulation, the off-limits order. The MPs conducted a search of the two soldiers. In the right upper fatigue shirt pocket of Sharpe, a twenty-year-old from Arkansas, the MPs found six vials of heroin. Twenty-three-year-old Jones, a native Texan, proved to be smarter than his younger partner because the MPs found nothing on him.

The soldiers were returned to Chu Lai and released to their unit. The heroin was turned over to us. We confirmed Sharpe's vials contained heroin. He was tried by a court-martial for possession of heroin and violating a written order. He served ninety days in confinement back in the States. His conviction had gotten him out of Vietnam four months early. From his commander, Jones received a ninety-day suspended reduction in grade (meaning he didn't lose his rank, but his commander could reduce his grade anytime during the ninety-day period) and was fined $34 for violating a written order. He served his entire year in Vietnam, returning to the World in November 1971.

Although we arrested many GIs for being under the influence of heroin or in possession of it, our real interest wasn't catching users. We wanted the source, the pusher, to stop the flow of heroin on to the post (a pipe dream, at best). Oftentimes we convinced a user to become an informant for us. We'd make a deal with him that kept him from any punishment for being under the influence or in possession of heroin as long as he cooperated in a bust of his dealer. With our money (called buy-money), the user set up a meeting with his pusher, made a buy, and we nabbed the dealer.

Our most successful informant was a private by the name of Ken Burney, a driver in an engineering battalion. Burney was unlike most of his fellow users because he injected heroin. In his earlier days he may have been of medium build, but when I knew him his emaciated body showed the effects of his heroin use. Probably only in his early twenties, he looked forty. His graying brown hair capped a gaunt face that sought only one thing in life: another heroin fix. Heroin had become his mainstay. He didn't care if he ate; he didn't care if he slept. He constantly craved heroin, and Vietnam provided him a cheap, ready source. I don't remember ever seeing him when he wasn't strung out on it.

His addiction became our boon. Dealers never suspected him of being an informant because they knew how much he depended on their product. However, he knew, as we did, that the apprehension of one pusher, or two, or a dozen, had no effect on the flood of heroin inundating Chu Lai and the surrounding hamlets. So when we agreed to protect him by not charging him for his heroin use, he agreed to cooperate with us. With his cooperation, we made dozens of busts on dealers and we confiscated over a hundred pounds of heroin. As a result, our statistics looked good (how much heroin we confiscated was our version of a body count) and he wasn't denied what he needed most: more heroin. It was, to say the least, a Faustian, symbiotic relationship.

I used him on one of my most memorable cases. I had apprehended him for being under the influence of heroin—again. I asked him if he knew how I could make a big bust. He told me that he knew a Vietnamese woman who was selling heroin, a lot of heroin, to GIs. Although dealers could be male or female, most pushers were Vietnamese women; many of them were prostitutes. For obvious reasons, they possessed an access to the GIs far superior to that of Vietnamese males. When a dealer was male, he was usually pre-teen. I told Burney to negotiate a deal, a large deal, with her. He could have bought us two vials any day of the week, but I wanted quantity. I told him he had $270 MPC to work with. He contacted her and agreed to buy 135 vials, which would take care of all $270 MPC. Normally we used buy-money to make such a purchase. But our buy-money came from Long Binh, and we had to request it in triplicate on such-and-such form and wait several days for the whole bureaucratic process to chug along. On this case, we didn't have the time to fart around with the bureaucrats. Burney had agreed to a meeting with the seller the next day. I didn't want to lose the opportunity to make a big bust, so I used my own money.

Burney agreed to meet the woman in a rock quarry located just off post near Gate #2, the post's southern gate. Our plan was simple: we'd follow him to the quarry, he'd make the buy, and we'd swoop in for the bust. But a convoy of OD green trucks heading to the quarry would undoubtedly scare off the dealer. After much discussion, we decided that Burney would drive a three-quarter ton truck to the quarry, and in a helicopter, we'd follow him at a few thousand feet overhead. A tail vehicle with two CID agents would follow at a safe distance. The tail vehicle would provide transportation back to Chu Lai for the dealer once we apprehended her. So we wouldn't lose sight of Burney (and my $270 MPC), I painted a huge white peace symbol on the canvas canopy covering the box of the truck. The plan called for him to make the buy at the quarry and signal the completion of the deal by raising the hood on the truck. The pilot would auto-rotate (in its simplest form, an emergency landing) the helicopter to the ground, and we'd apprehend the dealer.

Excitement was high as another CID agent, a couple of MPIs, the ARVN interpreter, and I boarded a Huey and departed from Chu Lai East. Burney, with my $270, headed out the gate and turned on to QL1. As planned, we easily spotted the peace symbol. In a few minutes, the peace symbol turned off QL1 and headed toward an obvious scar on the landscape, the rock quarry. We circled impatiently waiting for the signal.

Shortly, we saw three Vietnamese, distinctive in their bright clothing and rice grass conical hats, walk out of the surrounding tree line to the truck. Burney got out of the truck to meet them. After no more than a minute, the Vietnamese walked away and Burney got back into the truck. For a moment I thought the buy hadn't happened. Then Burney got back out of the truck and opened the hood. I yelled into the microphone on my headset, "Go!" The pilot began a quick descent and began to auto-rotate directly to the rock quarry. Adrenaline pumped. "We aren't descending fast enough," I thought. "Come on, Come on, they're getting away!"

Just then, what none of us had expected happened: wind from the blades of the helicopter began swirling the powder-like dust blanketing the quarry. By now I had suspended myself out the door of the Huey, standing on the skid with both feet and hanging on to the doorframe with one hand. What I saw below me looked like a *Grapes of Wrath* Oklahoma dust storm. The ground disappeared, Burney and his truck disappeared, and the Vietnamese disappeared. Everything below me disappeared into a cloud of dirt.

As I stood there, my adrenaline pumping, I thought I saw the ground. Calculating our rate of descent as the pilot began to auto-rotate, I knew we couldn't be far off the ground. As I peered through the dirty cloud, I was sure I could see the ground getting closer and closer and closer. To me it looked as if we were about six feet above the ground. That's when I decided to launch myself off the skid. Just before I let go, the pilot reversed the pitch on the blades—part of the process of auto-rotating a helicopter to the ground. The reverse in pitch momentarily raised the helicopter before settling it down on the ground. By the time I cleared the skid, we were a good ten or more feet in the air. I hit the ground and tumbled ass-over-elbows. As I was somewhere between dazed, stupefied, and pissed (but not hurt), the helicopter settled back down and the sensible ones—laughing so fucking hard at my Keystone cop antics that they could hardly walk—stepped out of the helicopter.

Then the chase was on. First we had to locate the Vietnamese suspects, but we had to let the dust settle so we could see. Just as we oriented ourselves in the quarry, the pilot headed back to Chu Lai—part of the plan. As the helicopter lifted off, the dust storm began anew. Our curses fell helplessly to the roar of the engine, the wind, and the flying dirt that again blinded us. The only redeeming aspect of what was quickly become a slapstick comedy was that the dust storms incapacitated the Vietnamese pushers as much as it did us. By the time the dust settled and we could continue our chase, it was as if time had stood still. Everyone in the rock quarry had been frozen in place waiting for the dust storm to pass. As soon as one of us could see, all of us could see, and the chase began from where it had stopped.

We quickly located and apprehended the three Vietnamese women, all in their late teens or early twenties. During the onslaught of the dust storms, Burney had climbed back into his truck. I got to him as quickly as I could to make sure he wasn't helping himself to any of the 135 vials the women sold him. He singled out the female who transacted the deal with him, but because the other two women were with her, we took all three into custody. Then we started looking for my money. It had disappeared. We searched the women as much as we dared. A strip search would have to wait until we got them back to post where a female nurse would search them. But a pat down of their bodies, a search under their hats, and so on, turned up nothing. We searched their path of intended escape and found nothing. We never found the $270 MPC. It had evaporated into the helicopter's swirling wind. I assumed that either there was a fourth member of the group who managed to abscond with the money during the dust storms or one of the women stashed it somewhere in the rock quarry and we simply couldn't find it.

I eventually received compensation for my lost $270, but it took three months of fighting with the CID office at Long Binh. The bureaucrats were upset because I hadn't gotten their approval before giving Burney the buy-money. For a time I resigned myself to my loss, but eventually someone up the chain relented and paid me the full $270.

Despite these problems, we counted our bust a success: we had 135 vials of heroin and three pushers. We loaded the women into the back of Burney's truck. The rest of us rode with Burney or in the tail vehicle that had joined us at the quarry. We went back to our office on Chu Lai and notified the national police. A strip search of the females didn't turn up my money or any more evidence. When the national police arrived, we released the women and the dope to them.

Whenever we apprehended Vietnamese nationals off post, as in this case, we turned them over to the national police. If we arrested them on post, we turned them over to the ARVN police. In either case, the circumstances of the transfer to Vietnamese control were the same. We always had the suspects in handcuffs. When the Vietnamese police arrived, we took off the handcuffs. and the policeman used a cord to tie the suspect's hands behind the back. Then they put a big, wide, black blindfold over the suspect's eyes. The blindfold covered the eyes, nose, and half the forehead. They then loaded the suspect into the back of a jeep and drove away. During the whole process, the suspects invariably resigned themselves to their fate. They were very humble and exceedingly differential to the police. They sat in the back of the jeep with their heads bowed, showing neither defiance nor fear, just resignation.

I heard rumors that the Vietnamese police took suspects out into the bush and shot them. I have no evidence that that ever happened, and personally I think the Vietnamese suspects were no different than the Turkish thief I'd caught years before. An official Army report concluded, "Many identified subjects that were arrested received little or no punishment and were subsequently released to continue their trade in narcotics. Enforcement efforts became counter-productive when the local population … saw offenders back on the street." Given the corruption rampant in the ARVN and national police, I suspect a pusher's chances of surviving an arrest depended on family connections, or for whom he or she worked, or the caprice of the policemen involved.

Although I'm not sure what happened to our suspects on this day, I'm confident that the dope went directly back into circulation. We believed that anytime we turned over heroin to the national police or ARVN, it went back on the street. We had no proof of that, but our suspicion ran high. "Evidence seized," an Army officer reported, "in most instances, was turned over to the local [Republic of Vietnam] law enforcement agency participating in the raid. Ultimate disposition of evidence retained by local authorities could not always be verified." That's a nice way of saying the drugs went back on the market.

One day Lt. Hargrove, our detachment commander, watched me as I chemically analyzed heroin from two hundred vials we'd confiscated in a raid. It's a process during which a chemical is added to the suspected heroin. If the heroin turned purple, we knew it was an opium-based drug, such as heroin, instead of powdered sugar or some other inert substance.

After watching me for a while, the Lieutenant asked, "Is this the stuff that we're giving to the national police?"

"Yes, Sir," I replied, continuing my work.

"Well, do you think it's possible that we can put a little chemical in each one of those vials before we give it to them so that all the heroin in the vials will be purple? That way it shouldn't end up back on the market."

I explained that although I thought it was a good idea, in fact we'd kicked it around among the agents as well, it would never happen. The Vietnamese police would get the equally corrupt Vietnamese politicians to protest such an action. First, they'd act indignant over our apparent lack of trust in them, our faithful allies. Then from a legal angle, they'd argue that we were tainting the evidence and, thus, jeopardizing chances of winning a conviction when the drug dealers went to trial—which, of course, wasn't going to happen anyway. The American officials would stumble all over themselves to apologize for this apparent lack of trust by explaining to the Vietnamese that some wrong-headed CID agent had taken it upon himself to concoct such a hare-brained idea, and had since then been properly reprimanded. Then the officials would rush to the defense of our allies' legal system that, they would say, was stemming the tide of drugs to American soldiers by aggressively prosecuting drug pushers. When all that was said and done, we in the CID would be told to never, ever taint the heroin again. So we would once again hand over confiscated vials full of untainted heroin to our trusted allies, the Vietnamese police, who would put it back on the street.

Nevertheless, our statistics continued to look good because we confiscated so many vials. And, the Vietnamese made money off the same vial two or three times before some dickhead GI used the heroin in it and discarded it under his barracks. Then his captain could add the vial to his collection growing on the shelf in his office. "So, LT," I concluded. "there's something for everybody. Why fuck with such a perfectly devised system by tainting good heroin?"

"It was just a thought," the lieutenant said, sounding more than a little hurt as he walked away.

And so, with the help of Private Burney, the drug addict, I had been the lead investigator on a good drug bust. We collared three Vietnamese drug dealers and confiscated $270 MPC worth of heroin. Dutifully, we wrote our reports and turned our suspects and evidence over to the national police. In short order, the drugs—and probably the dealers—were back in business. The national police lined their pockets, we filed our reports that made our body count look good, and Burney kept getting high. Yes, it was a system that offered so much to so many.

Burney was also instrumental in the largest drug bust I saw in Vietnam. Ted Keater, from whom I received my jeep and grease gun, was the lead investigator. He apprehended Burney and, of course, offered not to press charges against him if he provided good information to bust a dealer. True to form, Burney offered to turn in another female pusher. She lived in a small hamlet just outside the north gate. The plan was for him to buy three vials—$6 worth of heroin. (Keater wasn't nearly as ambitious in his plans as me.) Once Burney made the purchase, he was to come out of the hooch and remove his fatigue hat as he walked back to his jeep. That was the sign that she had taken the buy-money, and Burney had the heroin on him. We'd then swoop down on the hooch and bust the woman.

On the appointed day, we had eight agents and MPIs divided into three teams. Two teams went into the village ahead of Burney to stake out the house. At a safe distance, Keater and I followed Burney out the gate. Once into the village, we stopped fifty yards behind him as he made his way to an adobe-looking hooch with a thatch roof, shuttered windows, and a wattle sty adjoining it. Burney parked his jeep near the hooch—close, but far enough away so he had time to give the pre-arranged signal on his way back to the jeep. He knocked on the only door and someone inside let him in. A couple of minutes later he came out of the hooch, took off his cap, and walked toward his jeep.

Like flies swarming to a honey pot, we hit the hooch. There was only one person inside, a seventeen-year-old female. The one-room hooch was furnished with only a bed, a table, and a couple of stools.

But under a blanket along one wall, we found boxes containing thousands of empty vials and an old US Army ammo can with seventeen pounds of heroin! There are roughly 454 grams in a pound. A vial contained one-quarter of a gram. That means that if all the heroin in that hooch was intended for vials, which I'm sure it was, that seventeen-year-old girl had enough heroin to fill nearly 31,000 vials with a street value of $62,000. Given the amount of capital required to have that quantity of narcotics on hand, I have no doubt that the young woman was merely the employee of a local military officer or political leader. We did our duty and turned her and the untainted heroin over to the national police. She and her heroin (or rather, her employer's heroin) were back in business within days. But our body count looked good.

Twelve-year-old Giang Vo was one pusher who wouldn't go back into business. As I mentioned before, most Vietnamese pushers were female. When they were males, they tended to be quite young. Vo was one of them. In September 1971, the local Joint Task Force (a quasi-police force made up of ARVN and United States advisors) targeted Vo in his hamlet along QL1 south of Chu Lai. Once the American informants had purchased heroin from Vo, he was placed in a truck and driven north of the village. The task force was concerned that a local mob would interfere with his arrest. The plan was for him then to be transferred to an ARVN vehicle. On the way north, young Vo began throwing vials from the truck and eventually jumped out of the truck himself (or so the report states). The investigators determined that he'd struck his head on QL1's pavement, causing a fatal injury. Now an angry crowd of Vietnamese gathered, and it took American and Vietnamese officials hours to defuse the tense situation. Eventually, the Americans returned to Chu Lai and confiscated twenty-nine vials of heroin in the vehicle from which Vo had jumped. The drugs were turned over to the ARVN and, I suspect, sold again to GIs.

Not all pushers we busted were Vietnamese. There were, of course, GIs involved in the lucrative illegal trade as well. How successful we were against them depended in large measure on the quality of our police work. Some days the dickheads won.

On one such day, one of the MPIs busted a guy who sold a vial of heroin to an informant. The MPI recovered the one vial and the marked buy-money. When he got the GI pusher to our office, he went through the process of filling out the paperwork and conducting the interview. At one point during the interview, for an inexplicable reason, the MPI momentarily stepped out of his office. When he did he left the vial—the single piece of evidence—on his desk. I walked into the MPI's office just in time to see the pusher setting down an empty vial. He looked up at me and smiled. I saw a trace of white powder on his nostrils. He had snorted the evidence before the MPI had tested it to determine whether it was heroin. To protect the MPI, we turned the narcotics sales case into an under-the-influence case. We couldn't very well report that the pusher, whom was caught red-handed selling a vial of heroin, snorted the evidence while in police custody.

On other days, we won. On one such day, while driving toward the gate, I saw a GI walking through the gate from off post. He was carrying a gym bag that looked quite full and heavy. I stopped him and asked him where he'd been. He said he'd just been off base and was heading back to his company area. I asked him what was in the bag.

"Nothing," he said.

"OK," I said. "Let me see the nothing."

He set the bag on the hood of my jeep and reluctantly opened it. The bag was stuffed full of plastic packs each containing ten marijuana cigarettes. There were literally hundreds of marijuana cigarettes in his gym bag. I busted him, wrote the report, and turned him over to his unit. I don't recall the final disposition of the case, but by that stage of the war, a slap on the wrist for such an offense had become standard.

By mid-1971, drug offenses clogged the Army's legal apparatus. "During July 1971," according to one report, "the volume of drug offenses became so great that some cases took several months to come to trial. Therefore the Army changed its policy of court-martialing all drug offenders, and, as a result, it was able to handle drug offenses cases more quickly." Officially, the policy was to court-martial only GIs charged with selling drugs. But, as the same report concluded, "[I]t was difficult to prove that a man was a seller." As ludicrous as it sounds, the GI I busted could have argued that the gym bag full of marijuana was for his use, or he liked giving it away to his buddies. Without an actual buy, the kind we set up with Burney, proving sales of narcotics is very difficult. So, that bust at the gate probably resulted in little more than the loss of a stripe and a $100 fine for a couple of months.

With great ease, GIs and Vietnamese nationals smuggled marijuana and heroin on to Chu Lai. For the GIs traveling on official business off post, it involved neither effort nor ingenuity to stop at any of dozens of small villages along QL1, buy dope, stash it someplace on their vehicles, and bring it back on base. Then they sold it, shared it, or used it. The Vietnamese employees coming through the gates were searched, but pat down searches revealed little. Strip searches, particularly of the women, would prove more effective, but extremely cumbersome. With over five thousand nationals—most of them women—coming through the gate to work every day, five thousand strip searches would have been a virtual impossibility. So, for the Vietnamese man carrying bags of marijuana cigarettes or vials of heroin in his pants' pockets, the pat down searches were effective. But for the women carrying drugs inside bras or vaginas, the pat downs were a waste of time.

As the presence of empty vials around Chu Lai demonstrated, the flow of drugs on to the post continued unabated. As a last resort in stemming the tide of drug use on the post, the MPs would make unannounced searches of barracks or work areas, usually with dogs specially trained to find marijuana and narcotics. Such raids could net a laundry list of contraband: unauthorized firearms and ammunition, knives, bayonets, syringes, water pipes, ready-made marijuana cigarettes, bags of marijuana, cigarette papers, heroin-laced cigarettes, hundreds of assorted pills, and dozens, if not a hundred or more of vials, either empty or containing heroin. Seldom were these contraband items used as evidence against the soldiers. The theory, instead, was just to take it—drugs, weapons, and so on—out of circulation. This tactic, too, had little effect on the overall drug problem.

Getting drugs out of circulation, as well as abusers into treatment, was also the motivation behind the Army's amnesty program. Begun in 1969, but officially sanctioned the next year, the program allowed drug users to turn themselves in to their NCOs or officers with a promise of immunity from prosecution. The program established a number of stipulations to receive immunity. For example, an abuser couldn't be under investigation for drugs at the time he turned himself in. Additionally, he couldn't turn himself in more than once—although that stipulation quickly changed and the program became a revolving door through which some dickheads frequently traveled. Abusers turning themselves in for the amnesty program were assigned to rehabilitation programs, either unit-run or at larger rehabilitation centers.

Another aspect of the program was the placement of amnesty boxes at locations around the posts. Abusers could deposit their drugs in the boxes; the drugs were then destroyed with no attempt to identify who had turned them in. Because recidivism rates were so high for those who participated in the rehabilitation programs, and because a few vials thrown into an amnesty box couldn't counter the easy availability of drugs in Vietnam, the amnesty program negligibly affected the Army's drug problem.

By June 1971, President Nixon had enough. He had become convinced that the burgeoning drug problem in the States was being exacerbated by the return to the States of Vietnam veterans using or addicted to heroin. On June 17, the president announced that the military would identify all heroin users in Vietnam and provide them medical treatment before their return to the States.

The next day, the Army declared its drug counter-offensive and issued instructions on how it intended to enforce the presidential decree: everyone leaving Vietnam would be given a urinalysis. "If the sample proves negative," the message read, "the individual will continue normal processing procedures so as to depart as scheduled. If analysis shows that personnel have heroin in their system, they will enter a quarantine center where they will receive medical treatment." If, during this period of quarantine, the medical staff determined an individual was addicted to heroin or required more extensive medical treatment, he'd be medically evacuated to a major military hospital in the States. "Those individuals who are not determined to require more intensive medical treatment will remain in quarantine until their urine no longer shows positive (daily urine samples will be taken), or until medical authorities determine release is appropriate." The message informed users that they would not be subject to any punishment if their urine tested positive. After all, the purpose of the program was "to assist the individual who has a heroin problem." Finally, the message concluded by stating that everyone, regardless of rank or sex, would provide a urine sample before leaving Vietnam.

Therefore, in order to get out of Vietnam when it came time to rotate back to the World, everyone had to provide a urine specimen to determine whether there were opiates in his or her system. For the males, the vast majority of the GIs, that meant lining up to go into a room that was about eight feet wide and twenty or twenty-five feet long. The room was partitioned in half lengthwise with a four-foot wall. On each side of the partition ran a metal, trough urinal. Each urinal was about fifteen inches wide and ten inches deep. Two lines of GIs formed outside of the room. Each soldier was given a small bottle—a regular urine specimen bottle, not the cough syrup bottles we gave the dickheads—labeled with his name and social security number. About ten or fifteen guys walked into each half of the room and lined up in front of the urinals, each facing a guy on the other side of the partition. Sitting at one end of the partition on an elevated chair, like a tennis referee, was an observer. His job was to ensure that everybody was peeing in his own bottle, that no one was passing bottles back and forth, that someone wasn't pulling a different bottle of urine out of his pocket and filling his labeled bottle, or that some other subterfuge wasn't being used to make sure a GI had "clean" and not "dirty" urine. After all, dirty urine—that showing any opiate in the system—prevented his departure. GIs could be pretty creative in making sure their urine was clean when they peed in the bottles. The observer's job, then, was to make sure GIs were providing samples of their own urine for testing.

Eventually there were four facilities, called Urine Testing Laboratories, to conduct the urinalyses. In July the first opened at Cam Ranh Bay. Long Binh and Saigon opened next, and in October the last facility opened in Da Nang. Initially, testing included only those GIs heading back to the States after their year in the war. The Army, however, quickly added categories of troops requiring urinalyses until virtually anyone in-country more than thirty days provided a sample before leaving Vietnam for any reason. By the end of the first year of the program, the Army had tested nearly one million specimens at a cost of $1.9 million.

Of Army soldiers returning to the States after their year in Vietnam, 4.7 percent tested positive. What that figure really shows is that roughly 95 percent of the GIs abstained from using heroin in the seventy-two hours before being tested. If anyone used heroin over seventy-two hours before testing, it wouldn't show up in his system. Everyone knew about the testing, particularly the urinalysis required before leaving, and drug abusers certainly knew how long opiates remained in their systems. So what the 4.7 percent figure really shows is how incredibly stupid or hopelessly addicted were 4.7 percent of the GIs leaving Vietnam.

When someone peed dirty, the Army sent him to a rehabilitation center. It was a rehab center in name only. Everyone associated with the drug problem in Vietnam knew that rehabilitating the war's drug abusers in-country was a pipe dream. Recidivism rates were astronomical. Well over half of drug users identified through urinalysis were identified again by another urinalysis. The other forty-some percent had just gotten smarter.

On the surface the rehab centers looked like, well, rehabilitation centers. They had counselors who held "rap sessions" with the abusers. They had coffee shops where the users could get together "to work through" their problems. Instead of rehabilitating abusers, though, these rehabilitation methods merely set the national agenda for the "victim-veterans." The only positive thing to come out of the rehabilitation centers is that after being held there for a couple of days, a GI could pee clean and go home. Basically, all the GIs that had lined up at the trough urinals, peed in the bottles, and flunked the urine test went through detoxification that could take as much as seventy-two hours. Those hours would be pure hell for a heroin addict.

An addict absolutely fears withdrawal. He knows what's going to happen when his body isn't going to receive the drug it has become so dependent upon. About eight hours after ingesting his last dose of heroin, an addict will appear to be very tired, yawning uncontrollably. A few hours later, he'll develop the symptoms of the common cold: runny nose, watery eyes, chills, goose bumps, and sweats. Then comes the body ache—deep-to-the-bones body ache—followed by diarrhea and vomiting. Violent voiding of body contents will leave an addict weak and in great pain. By about seventy-two hours, all these symptoms will subside. In Vietnam, if a soldier was lucky, he could now pee clean and go home. Chances of him remaining clean after he got back to the World were slim.

The military wasn't treating any addiction. It was just waiting for the heroin to get out of an abuser's system. After seventy-two hours, his body would be functioning relatively normally and he could pee clean. But he still had the psychological addiction to heroin. It's like being an alcoholic: once an alcoholic, always an alcoholic. Once an addict, always an addict. But when he peed clean, he got on an airplane and flew back to the World. Consequently, this program met neither the spirit nor intent of President Nixon's decree.

The drug counter-offense, however, made politicians and generals feel good because they could demonstrate that they were doing something about the drug problem in Vietnam. Other than that, the programs cost millions of dollars, rehabilitated few soldiers, if any, and returned drug abusers to the States whose only accomplishment had been that they had not used heroin seventy-two hours before peeing in a bottle.

The real problem was a simple supply and demand equation. The Vietnamese possessed a nearly limitless supply of heroin. Demoralized

US troops created a nearly insatiable demand for the drug. There was really nothing anyone could do to stem the supply. A corrupt South Vietnamese government certainly wasn't going to inflict pain on its own people or jeopardize its own profits to fix what it saw as an American problem. The only fix to the problem, then, was to remove the demand, which the United States did in May 1973 when the last American troops (except those assigned to the US Embassy in Saigon) left Vietnam.

I left Vietnam over forty years ago. The heroin abusers I arrested in the years since then could be the same ones I apprehended back then. The war didn't create our national drug problem, and it didn't make our soldiers use heroin. After nearly thirty-five years of busting drug abusers, I can authoritatively say that I don't know what makes one, civilian or soldier, use drugs—then or now. But I do know that once they're on drugs, particularly opiates, they'll forsake all else to stay on drugs. At some point, if the drugs don't kill them, they may decide to get off drugs and, depending on their determination, they might make it. Nevertheless, it disturbs me that we, as a society, have been browbeaten by the mental health and social science communities into thinking it's our fault that someone uses drugs. If there's a legacy of the drug abuse in Vietnam that we're still living with today, it's that idea. Beginning in Vietnam, doctors and social workers began the process of telling society that an abuser isn't to blame for his addiction, rather we are.

I reject that conclusion. I was in Vietnam during the height of the heroin epidemic in 1971, and I was in Los Angeles for twenty-seven years while drugs ravished the streets. Society is not to blame for drug trafficking, drug abuse, or drug-related violence and other crimes. The dickheads are.

CHAPTER 6   DESIGNLESS DEATH

Death. I've always found it a simple topic. Call it Calvinistic determinism or fatalism if you wish, but I don't believe there's anything we can do to avoid the timing of our deaths. To use an old cliché, "When your number's up, it's up."

I've spent a lifetime as a policeman and I've never thought much about the danger of it. It's not that I'm not afraid of death. I think everyone has a degree of fear about the unknown, and death falls into that category. Even someone who commits suicide, I think, fears death. Once I watched a man jump to his death from the Golden Gate Bridge in San Francisco. For the first third of the way down he fell with his arms at his side, resigned to his impending fate. But then, fear gripped him. When it did he flailed like Icarus with the same results. He had invited death, but at the last moments he feared it more than he feared living under the burden that drove him to jump from the bridge. Similarly, I fear death, too. But I don't believe that anything we do or don't do in any way changes what Fate has determined for us: When it's your turn to leave this life, there's nothing you can do about it. That attitude about death came with me to Vietnam.

To Vietnam, too, came my view of the physical aspects of death: the whole, partial, or fragmented corpses, whether new or rotting. Early in my career, I learned that one must become hardened to the sight of death and accept life's most gruesome spectacles. One must emotionally deny the humanity of a pile of blood, bones, and flesh. One must do away with the idea that a dead body is that of a once-living, breathing, sensate human being. Frankly, a lifeless body becomes just a slab of meat. Obviously, such detachment isn't possible if the lifeless body is one's spouse or child or anyone else to whom one had an emotional tie. But, some stranger? Somebody that you've never seen before in your life? As cold and callous as it sounds, his or her body becomes a slab of meat. This attitude also came with me to Vietnam.

I suspect I was more fortunate—if that's the right term—than many soldiers in having been exposed to the emotional and physical aspects of death many times before coming to Vietnam. There is, I believe, something to be said for growing up on a farm, butchering livestock, and, in general, witnessing the life cycle of other living creatures. But my education for Vietnam also included witnessing dying and death, sometimes in the most grotesque ways, of fellow humans.

The first time I watched a man's life ebb from his body I had just turned sixteen. One evening after dark, a couple of high school buddies and I were traveling west on Highway 12 heading to Bowman, North Dakota. About twenty miles into our journey we came upon a truck accident. It had just occurred, and we were among the first to arrive on the scene. The trucker had been hauling leach-line pipes. Leach-line pipes are long pipes used to leach liquid from septic tanks. They're three or four inches in circumference and look like regular pipes except that along the length of each pipe is perforations. These holes allow the liquid from the septic tank to leach into the ground.

When the trucker drove off the highway and hit the far side of the ditch, his load of leach-line pipe shifted forward. One of the pipes hurled into the truck cab and drove itself through his back and out his chest. When we arrived at the accident, he was sitting in the cab with a pipe sticking about twelve inches out in front of him. His blood dripped out of the pipe's holes in a slow motion, grotesque cascade onto his lap. Although alive and coherent, he was going into shock. His flesh looked gray and pasty, and the cloudiness that accompanies death had already entered his eyes. Nevertheless, he sat there talking to another trucker who was assuring him that help was on its way.

When the rescue team arrived a short time later, someone used a hacksaw to cut the pipe at the backside of the driver. With the shortened pipe still stuck through him, the ambulance team loaded him on a gurney, laying him on his side. The trucker was still talking to those near him, but it was obvious to us gathered rubberneckers that he was already a dead man.

As we teenagers continued on our trip, adrenaline fueled our thoughts and words.

"Did you see that fucker?" one of the guys gushed. "His fucking blood was coming out of that fucking pipe!"

"Yeah, it was fucking awesome," I added. And it was. It was the first graphically gory human death that I ever witnessed. I believe it also began the process of making me dispassionate about the suffering of strangers.

My first military assignments in Turkey and Germany further exposed me to the gruesomeness of life. I'm not sure what the legalities were behind this practice in Turkey, but when somebody died along the side of the road, his or her body might lie for days where it fell. Eventually, authorities would cart the body off, but in the Turkish heat it didn't take long for bodies to start decaying, bloating, and smelling. Seeing such bodies lying along the sides of roads was very common and not for the squeamish. As an MP in Germany, too, I had witnessed death. I'll never forget the teenage girl at Lundstahl who committed suicide by using her father's pistol to shoot herself in the stomach. And, of course, there were many bloody and deadly automobile accidents that maimed, mangled, and killed American GIs.

As a CID agent at the Presidio in San Francisco, I worked dozens of cases during which I saw the victims of suicide and of homicide. My most memorable case involved a victim of California's infamous Zodiac Killer. On October 11, 1969, the Zodiac Killer shot taxicab driver Paul Stine at pointblank range in the back of the head. After shooting Stine, the Zodiac Killer opened the passenger's front door and pulled his victim toward the opening. He then ripped a piece of Stine's shirt off to mail later to authorities.

As the duty investigator that evening, I was at the MP station when someone called about a shooting immediately outside of one of our gates. I was dispatched with the MPs; we were the first cops at the scene since the San Francisco police had not yet arrived. The scene was stark. The front passenger door of the taxicab stood wide open like the mouth of a vomiting monster. The bloody vomitus caught in the mouth of the monster was the taxicab driver lying on his back across the seat with his arms extended over his head. The base of his neck rested on the edge of the seat, and his arms and head extended out the door. His head tilted grotesquely back. Blood covered everything: his face, his shirt, the car seat, steering wheel, front window, everything. Blood trickled down his arms to his fingertips. The blood dripped off his fingers and pooled on the street.

We had responded to this bloody scene only because we feared that the victim might be a GI because of the location of the killing. But once we determined that the victim was a San Francisco taxicab driver, we remained on scene only to wait for the civilian cops. After the San Francisco detectives arrived, we readied to leave the scene when someone decided that, because of the location of the murder, maybe the

Zodiac Killer was a GI. For the next several months, I worked closely with two San Francisco homicide detectives investigating the Zodiac killings. Our collaboration, however, got no one closer to solving the cases. To this day, the Zodiac killings remain unsolved.

By the time I arrived in Vietnam, then, I'd seen and smelled enough death to harden me emotionally against its most gruesome manifestations. Nothing I saw in the war shocked me. And I saw plenty of death.

The face of death I saw in the war, however, never resembled the images beamed into Americans' living rooms on the evening news. The rows and rows of shining caskets draped with flags that were being loaded into cargo airplanes aren't what I remember from the war. In fact, I don't remember seeing one casket my entire time in Vietnam. The bodies I saw were of young men who had died during homicides, accidents, suicides, and, of course, from drug overdoses. The bodies I saw were never entombed in a sterile casket shrouded in a flag. Instead, they were lifeless, lying in a pool of blood, zipped up in a black body bag, or lying on a gurney in the morgue or in the morgue's stainless steel refrigeration units. Wherever they were or however they died, my ability to detach myself from their humanity proved an invaluable asset to me.

Such detachment is common among those of us who deal with death in our professions. The most remarkable, if not bizarre, example of this detachment that I ever witnessed resided in the person of Chu Lai's medical examiner working at the morgue in the 91st Evac Hospital. He was in his late fifties, an ancient age by Chu Lai's standards. I don't know if he was a civilian or in the military. The only time I saw him, he wore hospital scrubs or a white smock, neither of which would have had rank insignia even if he was in the military. He conducted most of the autopsies I attended while at Chu Lai, our own veritable Dr. Death.

Fortunately, I had witnessed many autopsies before arriving in Vietnam. As an MP in Germany, I voluntarily attended autopsies, including that of the young girl who shot herself in the stomach. Because I had applied to the CID at the time, it made sense to me to show the agents that I could handle all aspects of the job as an investigator. And witnessing autopsies was a part of the job: an investigator must be present during an autopsy to collect any evidence that might be extracted from the body, such as bullet fragments or the tip of a knife that might have broken off. Once I became a CID agent, I also witnessed autopsies while in San Francisco. So by the time I'd arrived at Chu Lai, observing an autopsy had become rather routine for me.

Whenever investigators had to witness autopsies, Dr. Death would ask those of us attending if we'd ever seen an autopsy. Ostensibly, he asked the question so that if he had first-time viewers, he could make the experience as educational as possible. He'd explain the equipment he'd be using, and during the procedure he'd have a running monologue about what he was doing. But he had a much more sinister, hidden reason for determining if he had any greenhorns in attendance: he wanted to gross them out and make them ill. If he could get them to faint, he was happy. If he could make them vomit, he was ecstatic.

For the uninitiated observer, there are plenty of opportunities to be shocked during an autopsy. The procedure begins with the Y-cut: an incision in the pelvic area just above the genitals, to the bottom of the sternum, then to each shoulder. The incision looks like a "Y" the length of the trunk. Then the examiner uses bolt cutters to cut the rib cage along the incisions to the shoulders. A couple more minor incisions and the chest lifts out, leaving all the internal organs exposed. The organs are removed one at a time, weighed, dissected, and examined. The lungs, for example, are tested to see if a victim died from a lack of oxygen. A small piece of lung tissue is dropped into a glass of water to see if it floats. If it does, there was oxygen in the lungs at the time of death. In other words, the person didn't die from asphyxiation. Besides such easy and immediate tests, samples of each organ are saved for further analysis, if required. Other specimens, such as blood, stomach and bowel contents, urine from the bladder, and so on are collected and sent to a laboratory for toxicology analysis.

After the internal organs are examined and samples collected, the examiner begins the post-mortem of the brain. This is the procedure that can weaken the knees of the most seasoned observers. The medical examiner makes an incision above one ear, then around the back of the head to a point above the second ear. The skin is peeled away from the skull, pulled over the crown of the head, and down the face. It looks as if someone is removing a rubber Halloween mask. I've heard coroners refer to the loosened skin as a death mask. With a saw, a small V-notch is cut in the front of the skull right between and a little above the eyes. Then the skull is sawed along a line that runs from one side of the V-notch, completely circumnavigates the skull, and terminates at the other side of the V-notch. Once this cut is made, the examiner inserts a hook into the V-notch and pops off the top of the skull. The brain stem is cut, and the brain is removed, weighed, examined, and dissected in the same manner as the other internal organs.

Once the post-mortem examination is completed, the medical examiner begins the process of putting the body back together. The brain is put into the skull, the top of the skull set back in place, and the skin pulled over the head. Any other removed body parts are dumped into the body's cavity and the chest is put in place. Then all the incisions are sewn with a bold overcast stitch that gives the corpse a Frankenstein's monsteresque appearance.

If this unembellished procedure wasn't enough to test the fortitude of his observers, the macabre Dr. Death enjoyed playing freakish practical jokes. For example, about halfway through an autopsy, he'd announce that he was hungry. He'd walk to a nearby table, take a sandwich out of a lunch box, and begin eating it—bloody-gloved hand and all. After taking a few bites, he'd lay the sandwich on the face of the corpse, return to performing the autopsy, pause, pick up the sandwich, take another bite, set it back down, and so on. If the autopsy hadn't thus far made a greenhorn ill, this antic usually worked. We more callused observers just figured the old doctor was fucking nuts.

Another bizarre ruse of his required a magician's sleight of hand. Even though I'd come to expect his antic, I never could figure out how he did it. At some time during the autopsy, he'd hide a small container of tuna fish in the body cavity—how he did that was the mystery to me. As he continued the procedure, he'd reach into his jacket pocket, pull out a plastic fork, and poke into the body cavity. From there he'd retrieve a piece of tuna fish and eat it. I've seen greenhorns and the most experienced investigators alike lose their lunches over that trick. Dr. Death thought it was all pretty funny and took great pleasure in doing it. He had a ghoulish sense of humor, to say the least. While he represents the caricature of those of us who must deal with death, his oftentimes-cavalier attitude toward the death of others is characteristic of the attitudes of many of us. A psychologist might call it a defense mechanism. We called it getting by.

Fall is deer hunting season. The North Dakota prairie is brown and dry. Early mornings are crisp and chilly. For weeks before opening day,

Dad and I would drive the gravel roads and section lines looking for the best places to hunt. We'd search for the telltale signs of mule deer. Oftentimes we'd seen a mule buck studying us from a nearby rolling hill. Don't ask me how, but the deer seemed to sense they were safe until opening day. Then they could be harder than hell to find. But find them we would.

Before dawn on opening day, we'd load our hunting rifles and a couple of Mom's homemade lunches into the pickup, drive out of the farmyard and head to our predetermined hunting ground. As the sun's rays sliced into the chilly morning, we'd be walking the edges of a draw or sneaking over the crest of a hill hoping to find our trophy buck. Once we located him, Dad would give me the first shot. Peering through the telescope, I'd place the cross hairs on the center of his front shoulder. The idea was to kill him with the first shot.

Crack! The buck took two steps and dropped to the ground. Adrenaline fueled my sprint across the hundred or so yards to him. I slit the buck's throat and, under Dad's supervision, gutted my trophy. When one is done gutting a deer, the entrails steam, caused by exposure to the cool morning air. They are a mushy, smelly, crimson pile. Coyotes and other four-legged or winged scavengers of the plains appreciate the effortless meal.

Deer hunting. That's what I thought of as the medical examiner unzipped the black body bag in the morgue. The bag contained about thirty-five pounds of fresh, but mostly indistinguishable body parts— a mushy, smelly, crimson pile. The stench of death wafted out of the bag as he unzipped it.

When I arrived at the morgue I had told the examiner that I wanted to view the body.

"There's not much to see," he said.

"I've got to look at the body anyway. That's my job," I told him.

We walked over to the refrigeration unit. He opened one of the small stainless steel doors, rolled out the tray upon which the body bag lay, and unzipped the bag. That's when the images of deer hunting hit me. As I studied the mushy pile, I recognized a couple of teeth held together by a small fragment of bone adorned with a piece of human lip. That was all I could recognize that told me I wasn't looking at deer guts.

When the blob lying before me had been scraped up, a fully intact wallet—barely discernible because of a coating of blood and pieces of innards and flesh—had been tossed into the body bag, too. I used a large tweezers to pluck the wallet from the mire of mush and took it to a large sink to rinse it. It was a bi-fold, black, plastic souvenir wallet embossed with Americal's blue-field, Southern Cross insignia. Inside it were a couple of pictures, a few MPC (military payment certificate) bills, and his identification card. The ID confirmed what I'd earlier been told: the muck in the bag had once been the body of Private Jerry Burman. There would be no other way to identify him. There wasn't enough left of the former two hundred pound GI to identify him with fingerprints, dental records, or anything else (this was well before DNA testing). Eighty percent of him had disintegrated; his family would receive the 20 percent remaining in the bag.

The previous evening at approximately 9:45 p.m., Private Burman had assumed guard duty at a perimeter tower on a mountain six miles directly west of Chu Lai. The Americans called it Hill #270; the Vietnamese called it Núi Dá Ong. The tower wasn't really a tower. It was more like a bunker built on top of a bunker. It had railroad tie sides up about chest high piled with sandbags on the outside, a wooden roof also piled with sandbags, and a 360-degree view of the barren hilltop and the jungle below. Beneath the tower, more railroad ties, earth, and sandbags formed the outpost's Medic Bunker where the medic lived in a field clinic. That evening Private Burman relieved Sergeant Thomas who went into the Medic Bunker to visit. Thomas returned to the tower fifteen minutes later to retrieve an ammo can to sit on, chatted a moment with Burman, and then took the ammo can back into the Medic Bunker.

At around 10:20 p.m., Sgt. Thomas and the other twenty-two men on Hill #270 heard a large explosion. Men rushed to the tower above the Medic Bunker only to find bloody human remains plastered to the inside of the tower's walls and roof and scattered on the ground outside of it. The tower suffered little damage; the opening between the roof and sides had allowed the explosion to dissipate. Staff Sergeant Cummings mustered the other troops on the hill and after the roll call confirmed Burman was the missing man. At 11:35 p.m., Sergeant Cummings notified the MP desk sergeant of the incident. The desk sergeant called the on-duty CID investigator.

Next day, as a Dust Off—a medical evacuation helicopter—brought the body bag back to Chu Lai and the morgue, I caught a helicopter ride from Chu Lai East out to Hill #270. I examined the tower and interviewed all twenty-three soldiers on the hill. Within the bloody tower, I found white, glistening pieces of teeth and duller fragments of bone embedded in the wood. In the early morning hours before my arrival, the soldiers on Hill #270 had picked up Burman's remains and placed them in the body bag. Despite their best efforts to police up the vicinity of the tower, pieces of human remains and blood still coated the inside of the tower and mixed with the hilltop's barren soil outside of it. It was impossible to escape the putrid odor of decaying human remains on Hill #270.

What had happened was obvious: At approximately 10:20 p.m. the previous evening, Private Burman sat on an ammo can in the tower. He held a brick of C-4 explosive in his lap. C-4 is a common plastic explosive. It's malleable and can be formed into virtually any shape. It's exploded with a detonating device we called a "clacker"—a small, hand-held electrical generator connected by wires to a blasting cap. Squeezing a small lever on the clacker generates an electrical charge that activates the blasting cap. So when the blasting cap is inserted into the C-4 and the clacker is squeezed, the C-4 explodes. The soldiers on Hill #270 had a large, easily accessible quantity of C-4 to explode dud mortar rounds. As Private Burman sat on that ammo can, he squeezed the clacker and blew himself into smithereens. Yes, how Private Burman had died was obvious.

Why it had happened was far less evident. No one I talked to believed, or admitted to believing, that Burman had a drug problem. Therefore, I dismissed the idea that he'd gotten high and intentionally or unintentionally killed himself. He had been in trouble before, but certainly not enough to motivate him to commit suicide. The previous November he'd been court-martialed for failing to obey orders from both a commissioned officer and an NCO, offenses occurring the last week of October and first week of November, respectively. He pleaded guilty to both charges and received a sentence of three months at hard labor, a fine of $25 per month for three months, and a reduction in grade from Specialist Four (E-4) to Private (E-1). The military judge suspended his confinement that was then remitted—that is forgiven— in February. Such troubles with military authority didn't provide me with any answers to his death. I had to dig deeper.

Twenty-year-old Jerry Burman from Massachusetts entered the Army in August 1969. The Army made him an infantryman, an 11-Bush. At the end of January 1970, he arrived in Chu Lai. At the time of his death, he was beginning his fourteenth month in Vietnam. I don't recall checking into whether he'd voluntarily extended beyond the normal twelve-month tour or had been involuntarily extended in Vietnam by the Army. His military records today don't indicate why he was still there. Nevertheless, he'd already served a year in the war and was still in the bush at the time of his death. He'd told his closest buddies that he had a girlfriend; they believed she, too, was from Massachusetts. In March he would have celebrated his twenty-second birthday. A few days before his birthday, instead of a birthday card from his sweetheart, he received a Dear John letter. Only a couple of buddies knew about the letter. They thought he was handling it well. The explosion at 10:20 p.m. told them he hadn't.

Few events in the war could devastate a GI more than a Dear John letter, usually from a girlfriend but sometimes from a wife. For most GIs, even the best conditions in Vietnam were hellish compared to home. At nineteen or twenty years of age, a young man would find himself in Vietnam scared, homesick, and lonely. Thoughts of home and fantasies of his girlfriend or wife back in the World seemed to make the unbearable bearable. Then, usually without any forewarning, a Dear John letter would arrive.

For many guys, these were letters from their high school sweethearts. Like so many young couples, a man and woman, still in or barely out of their teens, were madly in love when he volunteered for or was drafted into the war. They had expressed their undying love and made promises to each other. While he was gone, she'd start college or a new job, but most importantly, she'd keep the home fires burning while waiting for him to return home when they'd marry and have 2.5 kids. Then while he was in Vietnam, he'd get the Dear John letter: "You remember Joe?" she'd write. "Well, Joe and I are in love, and we're going to get married. I'm sorry. I didn't want to hurt you but I've been so lonely." Or, "You remember the football player Sam? I'm going to have his baby." Whatever the excuse was, the letter was really saying "I'm dumping you, pal." The guys who stayed home and won the girls were usually those with money, political connections, or a family doctor who'd document an old football injury to make someone unfit for military service (never mind that he played racket ball and jogged five miles every day).

Unfortunately, a lot of GIs received Dear John letters while in Vietnam. Needless to say, these were traumatic to young men fighting for God, country, mom, and apple pie. After receiving such letters, some GIs would take leave—the military's vacation time—so they could return to the States for a short time to save their marriages, usually without success. But most of the time, troops just lived with the emotional pain or, as in Private Burman's case, they ended their lives.

There's certainly no way to document the latter. In fact, in Burman's case, despite what I knew about his situation, I concluded my official report, "There is nothing to indicate that [Burman] took his own life, however it is possible that he was playing with C-4, and it was accidentally detonated, killing him instantly." On the official tally of deaths in the war, his cause of death is given as "non-hostile—other accident." Despite the information I'd received from a couple of his buddies about the Dear John letter, I never found it. I don't know if he destroyed it, if it disintegrated along with him in the blast, or his buddies were lying—and I have no reason to believe they were. I didn't find a suicide note either. It would have been the irrefutable proof that he'd taken his life. So other than the testimony of his buddies, I had nothing to state positively that he'd committed suicide. The facts that he may have received the Dear John letter, that he had no reason to have C-4 in the tower with him, and that it's hard to conceive of anyone "accidentally" inserting a blasting cap into a brick of C-4 to detonate it were all irrelevant.

My gut told me he'd committed suicide. But in Vietnam, we operated under an unwritten rule that we reported a death as an accidental unless the evidence drove us to no other conclusion than suicide. In other words, if we could find a way to avoid a suicide determination, we did. Our reasoning was simple: parents and a wife would rather get notified by the government that a son or husband had died accidentally instead of by his own hands. That was the reasoning at our level, at any rate. However, I'm not sure whether the Army sanctioned such deception to protect the families or the Army. Nevertheless, in Burman's case I concluded he'd died accidentally, because to rule otherwise was speculation based on circumstantial, albeit convincing, evidence.

After I concluded my investigation on the hill, I planned to go to the morgue to view the body—what remained of it. I asked the radio operator to get me a ride back to Chu Lai. The normal procedure was for the radioman to use a universal call sign for any helicopter in the area and ask the pilot to stop by and pick up a passenger. Normally, in very short order my ride would arrive. On this day, however, I waited an extraordinarily long time for a ride—hours, in fact. I grew nervous as the sun began to set. I knew that if darkness shrouded the hilltop, no helicopter would risk flying at night just to give me a ride back to Chu Lai. Generally speaking, the helicopter fleet flew only during daylight hours. Nocturnal venturing ran against the grain of common sense. (This fact, of course, was before night-vision goggles and all the other technology that now allow US soldiers to "own the night.")

Because I'd convinced myself that the war wasn't my war and because I wasn't a combat soldier, I had no desire to remain overnight in the bush (and the bush, from my perspective, was any place off the installation of Chu Lai). After all, the only reason I was on Hill #270 was to investigate a crime, and I had completed that job. The darker it got, however, the closer the war came to being my war—not the war of drugs and dickheads, but the war of bugs, dirt, heat, and deprivation. I hadn't been in Vietnam very long, but I'd spent every night there in an air-conditioned room sleeping in a bed. I had no intention of breaking that routine. Now, as I waited for a helicopter, I was coming dangerously close to spending the night on a barren hilltop in the bush. Of course, I was the only guy on Hill #270, if not all of Vietnam, who gave a shit about my predicament.

At the last moment the radioman found a helicopter heading to Chu Lai that would stop to pick me up. It landed just long enough for me to climb aboard and took off before I'd even settled myself on the bare, metal floor. Except for two door gunners, a pilot and a copilot, the helicopter was completely empty. Moments after leaving the hilltop, the pilot started flying as if the devil were chasing him. It was the wildest helicopter ride I've ever had. The pilot had the helicopter going as fast as it would go, flying at treetop-level or below. Every time he came to a tree, he'd just hop over it. He'd fly straight at a hill and, at the last moment, bank one way or the other to skirt around it. What should have taken only a few minutes—Hill #270 lay only six miles west of Chu Lai—was lasting much longer. After many minutes of feeling like a steely in a pinball machine and a few minutes before we landed, one of the door gunners handed me a communications headset. Given the noise inside of a helicopter, the only way to communicate is through the headset. Because I usually had no reason to communicate with the crew, other than with hand signals and nods of the head, I generally didn't wear a headset.

But now I put on the headset and a voice said, "Do you remember me?" I was sitting with my back to the pilot's seat, so I looked at the two door gunners thinking that one of them was talking to me. Neither was, so I turned around and looked toward the front at the pilot and co-pilot. Across the back of the right-seater's helmet was stenciled the name "SNORKOWSKI." "Yeah, I remember you," I replied.

Three days before, I had helped one of the MPIs interrogate CW2 Snorkowski for what the Army calls "wrongful appropriation" and the rest of us call stealing. A full five years before Johnny Cash recorded "One Piece at a Time," a country song about an automobile assembly line worker who stole a car by sneaking it out of the factory in a lunch box one piece at a time, Snorkowski had devised a rather ingenious scheme to steal an Army jeep one piece at a time. He'd taken the parts from the motor pool and smuggled them off post, where he reassembled the jeep at a girlfriend's hooch. Eventually, he was driving around in a stolen jeep.

Someone had become jealous of his ingenuity, or indignant about his thievery, or jealous about his girlfriend, or whatever it is that makes friends snitch on each other. Whatever the reason, one of his friends informed the MPI that Snorkowski was driving a stolen jeep. He got apprehended and brought into our office, where the MPI and I interviewed him.

Snorkowski was a cocky, I'm-a-pilot/you're-nothing type of guy. During the interview he began to piss me off, so I got pretty aggressive. "The Army might recognize you as a warrant officer and you might be a pilot," I yelled at him, "but as far as I'm concerned you're nothing but a goddamn thief. You can call yourself whatever you want, but you're a thief. If I've got anything to say about it, you're going to Leavenworth."

I knew that he wouldn't be going to Leavenworth. I didn't know anyone who went to Leavenworth for stealing in Vietnam, especially something as abundant as jeeps. But he didn't know that. So I was just trying to adjust his attitude for the interview. And it worked. He quickly became contrite and confessed to the whole scheme. I suspect he later learned that no one was going to send him to Leavenworth for stealing a jeep, so the helicopter ride was his way of adjusting my attitude. In the interrogation room, I was in charge. In the helicopter, he was.

While Snorkowski skirted the trees and hills as we approached Chu Lai, he told me that I'd mistreated him during the interrogation. He said I'd not shown him the respect he deserved. This helicopter ride, he informed me, was but a sample of what he could do to me if he wanted to. He talked about people falling out of helicopters from three thousand feet in the air and that sometimes such accidents just happened. I certainly took his comments as threats.

So with the helicopter ride and by his words Snorkowski was trying to scare me as I'd scared him. The only problem was that I didn't know the capabilities of the helicopter, so I was oblivious to how dangerously he was flying. It was a thrilling ride, to say the least, but I wasn't terrified. However, he certainly scared his copilot and the two door gunners. They, of course, knew the capabilities of the helicopter and knew how dangerously close to crossing the limits of them he was. In this case, for me, ignorance was bliss.

When he landed in Chu Lai, I left the helicopter and headed to the morgue. I figured there wasn't much I could do about his bad flying. His copilot and gunners, however, reported his death-defying flight, and his commander grounded him. Now he had to answer for a stolen jeep he could no longer drive and for recklessness in a helicopter he could no longer fly. Mr. Snorkowski had not had a very good week.

When I got to the morgue, the medical examiner opened the body bag for me, and I thought of deer hunting. The wallet in the ooze of leftover human being inside the bag positively identified Burman. Despite what I knew about the Dear John letter, I followed the rule and declared his death accidental. On March 29 I closed the case.

Certainly, there were times when the evidence pointing to suicide was so overwhelming that an investigator had no choice but to conclude that a GI had killed himself. Commanders then had to make the difficult choice whether or not to inform a family that a soldier had committed suicide. Understandably, a family found it very difficult to accept such a fact. Frequently, when a family learned that suicide was the cause of its loved one's death, it contested that determination and asked the Army to overturn the finding, as I had found out while working at the Presidio. That was also the case in the death of Private First Class Robert Henry Lyster.

In July 1970, nineteen-year-old Robert Lyster, a white West Virginian, entered the Army. After basic and artillery training, he shipped to Vietnam where he arrived in November. Whether his addiction to heroin began before he came to Vietnam is unknown, but by February 1971, he was a full-blown addict. Those soldiers stationed with him at Fire Support Base A-2 would later testify to a CID investigator that he "appeared to be intoxicated constantly."

One evening in February, Lyster and a buddy drank beer as they waited to go on guard duty shortly after midnight—a fact that illustrates the joke Army rules had become by 1971; permitting someone to drink alcohol is not the Army's way of getting a soldier ready for guard duty. Although no one saw him snorting skag, he told one buddy that he had. After a number of beers, Lyster went to a separate room in a bunker to write a letter. In it he wrote, "I'm so fucked up right now that I can barely write, and it's not on beer."

Shortly he came out of the room acting irrational and irritated. Some shoving and grappling followed, during which he loaded a clip into his M-16 and threatened to shoot Private First Class John Signal. Lyster was restrained and received a bruised face. Despite his obvious intoxication and irrational conduct, his NCO sent him on guard duty. As he walked out of the bunker he said, "Ive [sic] still got the rifle and clip and I can still do what I want to do." At one point he was seen outside the bunker crying and saying he was going to kill someone.

A short time later, the soldiers in the bunkers heard a gunshot. No one bothered to investigate. Private Signal later said, "[W]hen we heard the shot…I didn't think anything of it. I was convinced that [Lyster] was trying to scare me by firing into the air." A full half an hour later, the NCO left the bunker and found Lyster's body about twenty-five feet from the bunker. He ran back into the bunker and told the other GIs. Signal ran out of the bunker. "I checked for a heartbeat but found none," he said. "I looked for the wound and found that his head was badly split open and most of his brain was laying [sic] a couple of feet away." Lyster had placed the muzzle of his M-16 under the right side of his chin and pulled the trigger. The bullet traveled upward through his head exiting on the left side of his skull, leaving a gaping hole on that side of his head and blowing out a large portion of his brain onto the ground.

A Dust Off transported Lyster's body to a nearby hospital, arriving around midnight. The doctor pronounced him dead on arrival from a "self-inflicted gunshot wound to the head." The medical examiner reported Lyster had died from a "perforating gunshot wound of head with avulsion of brain." A CID report came to the same conclusion: Private Lyster had killed himself. There would be no hiding this suicide. The commander wrote to Lyster's parents in West Virginia, "[Y]our son died instantly from a self-inflicted gunshot wound. It may be of some consolation for you to know that all members of my command were saddened by the untimely incident." (One wonders how such an incident could be "timely.")

The Army routinely investigated such deaths during what is called a line-of-duty investigation. If the investigating officer determined that a soldier died "not in the line-of duty," the family did not receive life insurance money. In deaths such as Lyster's, that determination was unavoidable.

Within days of being notified of her son's death, Lyster's mother wrote to his commander. She got right to the heart of the matter: "Insurance does not pay for suicide. The Army took him & left no one to help support us. Suicide is what the Army wants to insist on so it will look better on their part." The mother said that she heard on the radio that her son and others were caught in crossfire during an enemy attack on the base. She now believed the Army was covering up. In her emotionally tortured state, she also rambled into other possibilities: maybe her son accidentally shot himself; maybe someone else accidentally shot him. Anything but suicide. "We could of [sic] been spared great shock & anguish if it [the cause of her son's death] had been stated differently."

Lyster's parents also contacted the local Reserve Officers Training Corps (ROTC) commander and solicited his help. On their behalf, he wrote to their son's commander saying that the parents "do not feel that their son would have committed suicide and adamantly request substantiating evidence which would indicate that the death was caused by intent, or from the accidental discharge of his weapon."

The son's commander responded directly to the parents. His response brought them no consolation or insurance money: "A formal line of duty investigation and the report by the...CID substantiate that death was caused by a self inflicted gun shot wound to the head." He also informed them that their son's "fire base did not sustain any hostile attack" on the evening he died, so he could not have been the victim of crossfire. The commander now revealed to them that their son had been "despondent for at least four days preceeding [sic] his death, however he would not confide with them [officers and friends] as to the problems causing his depression."

It's worth noting that in none of the correspondence to Lyster's parents did Army officials even hint that their son's death involved alcohol and drug abuse. Although officials were unable to avoid the conclusion of suicide in his death and, as a result, caused "great shock & anguish" to his parents (and the loss of insurance money), the Army could avoid embarrassing itself by hiding the fact that another soldier had died because of the drug problem in Vietnam.

In not one extant record reviewed in the National Archives during the research for this book did Army officials inform families that a son or husband was under the influence of an intoxicant at the time of his suicide. That he was "despondent" or "depressed" for one, two, or three days before his suicide is the euphemism often used. If the Army sometimes felt compelled to inform families that their loved ones had committed suicide, why did it always avoid the equally shocking reality that drugs were involved in many of those deaths?

There were many suicides tied directly or indirectly to drug abuse, especially heroin. The availability of weapons (particularly the M-16) to soldiers coupled with heroin-induced despondency drove dozens (if not more) of soldiers in the early 1970s to make the choice to end their lives rather than deal with their addiction. "Self inflicted gunshot wound to the head," "self inflicted gunshot wound to the chest," or "self inflicted injuries" are phrases easily found in MP blotters, CID reports, medical records, and morning reports—a unit's daily status report. A true accounting of such deaths is impossible. The deception we practiced by avoiding the term "suicide"—when avoiding it was possible—as well as the Army's near black-out of information in letters to loved ones about the abuse of drugs or alcohol before soldiers killed themselves, have been and continue to be effective in covering up the true number of "self inflicted" deaths in Vietnam, particularly those caused by drug abuse.

Not all "self inflicted" deaths were suicide. In some cases the mix of youthful stupidity, rampant testosterone, and plain foolishness resulted in the death of someone with no intention of dying. Such was the case with PFC Johnny Korella.

Private Korella, a Pennsylvanian, entered the Army in February 1971, one month before his twentieth birthday. Six months later he arrived in Vietnam, an infantryman assigned to Chu Lai. On one of his first trips into the bush, he met Sgt. Baker Winters. Korella was a likable kid who impressed those who met him with his wit and intelligence. Sgt. Winters was no exception.

Winters owned and carried into the bush a Smith and Wesson, .38 caliber revolver. Although it was an unauthorized weapon, Winters grew to trust Korella and showed it to him. (As I've mentioned before, the carrying of unauthorized weapons was very common.) Korella liked the revolver. He and Winters made the deal that when Winters left Vietnam Korella would get the first chance to purchase it.

Winters's time to rotate back to the States came the first week of November. The day he was to leave, he took the revolver to Korella's hooch. Korella paid him $35 and received the gun loaded with five rounds, a black holster, and a black cartridge belt with twenty-four extra rounds. They shook hands and Winters headed to Chu Lai East to catch a helicopter ride to Da Nang.

A short time later, Korella and three buddies sat in the hooch as Korella admired his new purchase. One of the buddies later testified, "I got the impression that he was fascinated by the revolver, more or less like a child with a new toy."

In the midst of his fascination with the weapon Korella asked, "Anyone here a compulsive gambler?"

Someone said, "You mean like with cards?"

"No," he said, "to play Russian Roulette with my revolver?"

"We all laughed," testified one soldier, "because it was a joke."

Korella then spun the cylinder that his buddies testified had one round in it, pointed the gun at his stomach and pulled the trigger. The weapon didn't fire. He spun the chamber again and, as one soldier related, "He then pointed the weapon at me, —I told him not to do it. Finally he put the barrel to his head [his right temple] and pulled the trigger. The weapon fired. At the time it went off I was looking at [his] face and he looked completely surprised."

One of the other soldiers who had been lying on a nearby bunk testified, "I heard the shot. I jumped up and saw [him] shakeing [sic], and then slump against the wall. I ran out yelling for a medic." Korella was dead on arrival at the hospital.

There was no evidence of any drug or alcohol abuse by Korella. No one knew him to be depressed. One buddy called him a "mature and responsible individual" who was "happy." The line-of-duty investigator ruled his death as accidental; his family would get the insurance money and an honest letter from the commander saying that he was "playing" with his recently purchased revolver, when "[t]hinking the weapon to be unloaded, he spun the cylinder, placed the weapon to his head and pulled the trigger causing the weapon to discharge inflicting a fatal wound." (He really didn't think the weapon was unloaded, but from the commander's point of view that was a little, forgivable lie.)

According to Korella's releasable military records, he was posthumously awarded a Bronze Star for his three months of service in Vietnam. The cause of his death is listed as "non-hostile—accidental self destruction," the same cause given for many of the drug overdose deaths I researched for this book. Yet the Army listed the death of

Burnam, who, if he didn't commit suicide, did die from an accidental self-destruction, as "non-hostile—other accident." There appears to be little rhyme or reason to some of the classifying of deaths.

I don't know how many soldiers died under similar circumstances to Korella, but during my time at Chu Lai his "accidental" death wasn't the only one I investigated. I'd also investigated a similar incident involving a ranger at a small off-post bar. He'd been drinking beer with some fellow rangers. They were notorious for carrying an array of weapons, some authorized, many unauthorized. After drinking several beers, they decided to mess with the barmaid. One of them had a two-inch revolver that he carried concealed. He emptied the cylinder of all but one round, and the rangers began a game of "fake" Russian Roulette. Each of the rangers would take turns spinning the cylinder, holding the gun to his head, getting the barmaid's attention, and pulling the trigger.

Although the Rangers intended to frighten her into thinking each time that someone was about to blow his brains out in her bar, the reality is that the rangers knew which way the cylinder would turn when they pulled the trigger. Each ranger in his turn could see the one round and knew, when the cylinder stopped, whether the bullet was in a position to fire. If it was, he'd spin the cylinder again, with great drama, just to show the barmaid his bravery. When the bullet stopped in a position that the gun wouldn't fire, he'd place the gun against his temple and pull the trigger. With a click, the hammer would fall harmlessly on the firing pin, the barmaid would gasp, and the rangers would roar with laughter. Next guy's turn.

Unfortunately, one poor ranger forgot the basics of the weapon he and his friends used. The cylinders of revolvers do not all rotate in the same direction; some turn counter-clockwise, others turn clockwise. When he looked at the cylinder of the revolver he was holding and saw the location of the bullet, he calculated that it would rotate harmlessly in one direction. In fact, it rotated in the opposite direction, ending up directly under the firing pin. He placed the gun to his temple, got the barmaid's attention, pulled the trigger, and to the shock of his friends and the barmaid, he splattered his brains all over the wall of the bar. Another "accidental" death and another name on the Vietnam Memorial Wall.

Of course, not all accidental deaths were the result of immature stupidity. The military is a very dangerous profession, even in peacetime. Young troops working around dangerous machines can often result in horrendous accidents that maim or kill. Add to that reality the facts of war (the rush to execute missions, the need to get the machines back on the road or in the air as quickly as possible) and one has a formula for disaster. If one accepts the official death tally for the war, nearly eleven thousand of the deaths of the roughly fifty-eight thousand names on the Wall occurred in a non-hostile manner. Many of those were the results of accidents.

Specialist Five Jack Cavendish died in such an accident. The nineteen-year-old Floridian enlisted in the Army in early 1970 after having received his degree in aerospace maintenance from a Florida college. The Army made him a CH47 Chinook Helicopter repairman. At the end of May 1971, he arrived at Chu Lai and began working on the fleet of Chinooks. Two months later, at about 5:30 p.m., I got a call from the MP desk that there had been a death at Chu Lai East. I jumped into my jeep and drove down to the flightline. A crowd of soldiers had gathered quite some distance from a lineup of Chinooks. I walked over to where the men stood; they had to be standing there for a reason. In fact, they had gathered around a crumpled soldier lying on the concrete. He was dressed in greasy jungle fatigues—obviously a mechanic and obviously dead. I looked directly at his face. It was about twice as wide as it should have been. I looked at his head from the side. It was about half as thick as it should have been. Whatever had happened to him (and I had no idea at this point) had crushed his head like one would crush a grape between a finger and a thumb.

I found the warrant officer pilot who could tell me nothing about what had happened. He had been in the helicopter until someone ran up to tell him his mechanic had been thrown off the top. I found that only a repairman working on a nearby Chinook had witnessed the accident. He told me that at a little after 4 p.m. Cavendish stood on the stairs of a work platform at the side of the aircraft while working on one of the engines. At that point, the engines had been idling with the two huge blades slowly churning the thick Vietnamese air.

After the engines were shut down, Cavendish climbed farther up the stairs, probably to check the rotors directly under the blades. By now, according to the witness, the blades "were still turning very slowly." As Cavendish stood up, one of the front blades caught him on the back of the head. Instead of just knocking him off the helicopter, the blade embedded itself into the base of his skull, slid him the whole length of the blade, and then slung him as if from David's

PLACE CID, Office of the Provost Marshal Chu Lai, APO 96374	DATE 71	TIME 1900	FILE NUMBER 71-C10948-

LAST NAME, FIRST NAME, MIDDLE NAME 7C	SOCIAL SECURITY ACCOUNT NO. 6 6	GRADE SP

ORGANIZATION OR ADDRESS
132nd AVT Co, APO 96374

SWORN STATEMENT

I, _____ 7C _____ , WANT TO MAKE THE FOLLOWING STATEMENT UNDER OATH

About 1615, _____ 71, 7C was working on an air craft, when he was struck in the head with a rotor blade. Prior to this, He had been working on the engines Prior to the accident, the aircraft had been running at idle; however they had been shut down. I was in an air craft adjacent to the one that he was working on. When I dismounted the craft that I was in, I could see that the air craft that he was working on was almost stopped, however the blades were still turning very slowly. I observed _____ climbing up the side of the craft. One of the blades from the front rotor struck him and knocked him to the ground. After the blade struck him, the blade made approximately two revolutions. After he struck the ground, there was no movement from the body, and he appeared as though he had been killed instantly. One of the men that was in the aircraft that _____ was working on, arrived on the scene and he then called for medical aid. This a ir craft is a CH 47 B model (CHINOOK)

XXXXXXXXXXXXXXXXXXXXXX END OF STATEMENT XXXXXXXXXXXXXXXXX

EXHIBIT A	INITIALS OF PERSON MAKING STATEMENT	PAGE 1 OF 2 PAGES

This document is a representative sample from the files held by the National Archives and Records Administration on cases the author investigated during his time in Vietnam. Such documents supported and helped the author reconstruct cases described in this book. This witness statement describes the death of a Chinook helicopter mechanic accidentally killed by the rotating blades of a helicopter.

slingshot nearly thirty yards from the helicopter. Pronounced dead on arrival at the hospital, the medical examiner determined that he'd died from "acute fractures of the head and neck region." He most certainly died before he hit the ground. Inexplicably, his cause of death is listed as "non-hostile—air loss, crash on land (helicopter, non-crew)." Regardless, unlike the fools who died playing Russian Roulette or from drug overdoses or from suicides, Specialist Five Jack Cavendish died in the service of his country and we should remember him with honor. He deserves a wall with his name on it.

There were, of course, many such accidents. I remember the death of a young lieutenant near Quang Ngai City, about twenty-five miles southeast of Chu Lai. He'd been riding in the back of a deuce-and-a-half truck with ten or fifteen other GIs. As the driver maneuvered the truck down a narrow road, probably traveling too fast, one of the front wheels dropped off the side of the road. As the driver fought to get the truck back on to the road, he rolled the vehicle into a rice paddy, coming to rest upside down. The GIs in the back of the truck scrambled out of the paddy and everyone gathered together on the road's terra firma. One of the NCOs checked everyone over and found only a few minor bruises. At that point, only the driver's ego had suffered under a blistering cussing out from his passengers.

Then someone realized the lieutenant was missing. The murk and muck of the rice paddy made any search for him futile. Not until someone flagged down a heavy equipment operator and he righted the truck did the group find the lieutenant. The truck had trapped him under the water and he drowned—another victim of a dangerous profession.

To conduct my investigation of that accident, I caught a helicopter ride from Chu Lai to Quang Ngai City. I worked on the case until after dark and checked into the local billeting office—a military-run motel. The manager marked his establishment with a large Holiday Inn sign. The hooch I stayed in would never meet Holiday Inn standards, but compared to sleeping at a fire support base in the bush, it was as good as one came to expect in Vietnam. It wasn't my hooch, but it wasn't the bush either. Next morning I caught a ride with a forward air controller in his two-seater, single-propeller Piper Cub. As he flew at treetop level on the way to Chu Lai, he assured me that his airplane had an armored underbelly—"hundreds of extra pounds of protective steel," he said—keeping us safe from enemy small arms fire. Then he decided to show me what kind of aerobatics he and his airplane could do. He began doing barrel rolls and spins—vertical, horizontal; it didn't matter. I wonder what all that extra weight is doing for this little piece of shit airplane now, I thought to myself. By the time we landed at Chu Lai, I was glad to have both feet firmly back on the ground.

The lieutenant's drowning near Quang Ngai City represented a rather typical drowning incident for the 23rd Americal. Given all the rice paddies filled with water, the narrowness of many of the roads, and thousands of GIs coming and going in trucks, jeeps, and every sort of military conveyance imaginable, such accidents were unavoidable. That wasn't the case with Chu Lai's worst drowning incident.

In an early afternoon of October 1971, a dozen troops were playing football on the sandy beach east of the runways. Around 2:30 p.m., they decided to quit because some of them had to get ready for guard duty. During the game, they had all become coated with the beach's fine sand, so a number of them decided to rinse off in the water. On the best days, swimming at Chu Lai was not easy. An active surf and strong undercurrent challenged the strongest swimmers. During the winter monsoon season (roughly November through April, but coming as early as September and lasting through May), the water was downright dangerous. If that wasn't enough incentive to stay out of the water, just five days before this incident, Typhoon Hester had nearly destroyed Chu Lai (more about that later). Nevertheless, eight of the twelve soldiers who had been playing football decided to rinse off in the dangerous waters mauling Chu Lai's beach.

Very quickly the swimmers found themselves being pulled out to sea. Individually they struggled to get back to the beach—some made it, some didn't. One soldier, now about sixty meters out into the ocean, knew he was losing the struggle and began calling for help. A hue and cry along the beach brought another dozen or so soldiers who formed a human chain to try to reach the floundering swimmers. One of the football players managed to swim out to the struggling GI, the one whose cries had summoned help. The tragedy is told best in his own words: "I made it out to him and start[ed] to come back in with him and we got hit by a big wave and I lost him. I went down and ... I was hit pretty bad. I had a hard time getting my breath and I start[ed] looking around for [the other soldier] but I could[n't] find [him]. Then I saw [a sergeant] and he grab[bed] me and brought me to shore but I want[ed] to find [the other soldier] and start[ed] to go back out but they [wouldn't] let me so I had to sit and watch them try to help the guys who were still left."

He was one of the lucky ones. The surf and undercurrent kept ripping apart the human chain as the desperate soldiers tried to reach the other swimmers. Rescuers quickly became victims. Eventually a helicopter arrived overhead and dropped life preservers and lifelines to the struggling swimmers below. Five football players drowned, and one of the football players and two rescuers received treatment at the 91st Evac Hospital. Two days later, a helicopter crew found and fished out of the water the bodies of all five drowning victims. A friendly game of football and a poorly conceived idea to rinse off sand added five more names to the Wall.

Accidents and suicides, along with drug overdoses, took most of the young lives in the deaths that I investigated while at Chu Lai. But a number of deaths also occurred at the hands of other GIs. In combat, the military calls killing its own "friendly fire." I found that in a non-combat environment, such deaths are the result of "not so friendly fire."

CHAPTER 7   NOT SO FRIENDLY FIRE

Shortly after midnight, twenty-three-year-old Floridian Arnold Beckworth began crawling through the perimeter fence of the 23rd Administration (Admin) Company Motor Pool. What caused him to do something so stupid and, as it turned out, deadly we'll never know. The motor pool was well within the confines of Chu Lai, so he wasn't sneaking onto the post from off-base. If he had been sneaking on post, his actions would have made more sense. If he worked at the motor pool, he could have walked through the entry control point (its main gate), so that didn't make sense either. Nothing made sense. Try as I did, I never came up with a logical reason why Specialist Two Beckworth climbed through the fence at the motor pool, but he did.

As Beckworth maneuvered through the concertina wire, Specialist Four Harland Fike, working the midnight guard shift, saw what he believed to be a sapper coming through the perimeter wire. He chambered a round in his M-16, yelled "Halt!," and fired a warning shot. The "sapper" continued climbing through the fence. In quick succession, Fike squeezed off three more rounds. One, possibly two, of the rounds struck Beckworth in the chest. Fike and the other guard on duty saw the "sapper" crumble lifelessly in the concertina wire. The second guard cautiously approached the "sapper" while Fike, shaking almost uncontrollably by now, tried to keep his weapon trained on the enemy.

"It's a fucking American!" yelled the second guard. "It's a fucking American! You just shot a fucking American!" he yelled toward Fike. "The motherfucker, what the fuck was he doing?!" The second guard was now screaming at the lifeless body, "You fucker, what the fuck were you doing, you son-of-a-bitch?!"

Fike slumped against the wall of the main shop, slid down the wall until he was sitting on the ground. He began to cry—he'd gone from being scared shitless because he thought a sapper was attacking his post to realizing that he'd just killed a GI. "What the fuck was the son-of-a-bitch doing?" alternated with the thought, "What are they going to do to me? I just killed an American."

Someone had the presence of mind to call the 91st Evac Hospital, and an ambulance arrived to cart the body away. The medics had a hard time disentangling Beckworth from the concertina wire, but managed. There was no rush to get him to the hospital. When they got him there, the MOD (medical officer on duty) pronounced him dead. The death certificate said that Beckworth died of a gunshot wound to the chest. Back at the motor pool, an NCO assigned another soldier to Fike's post and sent him to his barracks.

The telephone in our hooch rang at around 1:30 a.m. I was the on-call agent, so the telephone was sitting on the table next to my bed. The MPI on the other end began telling me what had happened. I was his backup that night, so I was supposed to offer him guidance on major investigations. He told me that some guy had crawled through the perimeter wire at the motor pool, the guard challenged him, then shot and killed him.

"OK, let me get this straight," I said. "He's crawling through the wire. The guard is doing what he's supposed to do. The dickhead got shot and killed. Well, hell, he got what he deserved. Go ahead and handle it." I rolled over and started to drift back to sleep.

The conversation had lasted three, maybe four minutes. I might have offered some advice such as "Call it a justified homicide," but that was about it. I didn't see any reason to disrupt my sleep over it. After I hung up the telephone and rolled over, Darrell Ross's voice broke the silence in the hooch. He'd heard my side of the conversation and knew pretty much what had happened.

"I wouldn't do that," he said, "If I were you, I'd go in."

Just a little bit annoyed that someone was questioning my judgment, I said, "I think everything is fine. The MPI's got it well in hand." Ross had been at Chu Lai longer than me; he knew CW4 Strawberry better than me; he knew what we could and couldn't get away with; and, he knew that I shouldn't have rolled over to go back to sleep. I should have listened to him.

Next morning Strawberry met me at the door. I hadn't gotten four feet into the building. He was furious. His clenched fists trembled at his sides. In one hand he held a partially crumpled report. Buried in the stream of screaming, I made out "dumb son-of-a-bitch," "stupid motherfucker," "incompetent asshole." I was getting the impression that I should have gotten out of bed when the MPI called me. Standing across the room was the investigator who'd called, and he looked both afraid—I think Strawberry had chewed his ass before I got there—and sorry—sort of like he'd ratted on a fellow cop. He'd just told the truth so I didn't see any reason for him to feel that way. By now Strawberry's face and mine were inches apart. Every time he said "son-of-a-bitch," he sprayed me with saliva.

I tried to explain that it appeared to me that it was a justifiable homicide. "How the fuck do you know that," he screamed, "when you didn't even get your sorry ass out of bed to go to the fucking scene?" Well, he had me there. Nothing I could say was going to make him listen to me. Besides, by now I was beginning to think that I should have gotten out of bed; Strawberry certainly thought so, and he was in charge. And maybe he was right. I don't think anything would have ended any differently if I had gone to the scene at 1:30 in the morning, but at least I could have surveyed the area, interviewed the guards, and then concluded it was justifiable. That would have been the end of it. But that hadn't happened. Finally Strawberry thrust the report in my face, told me to take it, and "Get your fucking ass over to the motor pool and do what you should have done last night!"

Now I was pissed. As I drove away from our office I glanced at the report, saw what unit Fike was in, and headed to his company area. By the time I arrived at the barracks I'd made up my mind that whatever the facts were in this case, I'd prove it was a justifiable homicide. I could have gotten a confession of murder out of somebody and still determined the shooting was justified.

I quickly located Fike, a scared-to-death young kid. I didn't approach him with normal CID bravado. We talked. He told me he'd been in the bush, he'd shot at people, and he'd been shot at, but he never thought he'd kill a fellow GI. Not only did he feel great remorse for an American's death, but also he knew he'd be severely punished for it. "I didn't mean to kill him, I really didn't," he kept telling me. He'd look at me plaintively and ask, "What are they going to do to me?"

Nothing I said could assuage the remorse he felt over the incident. I wasn't a chaplain anyway, so I didn't really think it was my place to make his soul feel better. But I could keep his ass out of jail. I assured him that everything would be all right. I hadn't even been to the motor pool yet, but I told him that I thought that he was completely justified in what he did. After all, he was just doing his job, and it wasn't his fault that some dickhead had climbed through the perimeter wire. "If I have anything to say about it," I told him, "there ain't nothing going to happen to you for doing your job." My assurances to Fike would not have made CW4 Strawberry happy.

Fike and I then went to the motor pool. He showed me where he'd been standing when he fired. I found four expended casings on the ground. His M-16 was still leaning against the shop wall where he'd sat and cried when he learned the "sapper" was an American. Someone had taken the clip out of the rifle, but when I opened the chamber another live round ejected. The weapon had been leaning against the wall primed to fire. I confiscated the weapon, one bullet and the four empty casings. Fike also showed me the spot in the concertina wire where Beckworth had died. I saw the blood on the ground and on the wire where the medics had disentangled him.

I went back to the barracks with Fike and found the other soldiers who'd witnessed the shooting. By interviewing them, I confirmed everything that Fike had told me. Under normal circumstances, I probably had enough to close the case. But this was not a normal case—I was on a mission to prove beyond any doubt that Fike was justified in shooting Beckworth.

I spent the next few weeks investigating the case. I searched the 23rd Admin Company's files and found that it didn't have an SOP (standard operating procedure) for motor pool guards or an SOP for firing a weapon. In other words, the company had no published orders telling a motor pool guard how to do his job or when to fire or not to fire his weapon. I reviewed the SOP for Chu Lai and found that the job of motor pool guard wasn't singled out in it. So, a perimeter guard working at the motor pool which lay well within the confines of Chu Lai was governed by the same instructions for a guard posted on Chu Lai's perimeter fence.

Then came the clincher: I found the posting instruction read to all perimeter guards—motor pool included—the night Fike shot Beckworth. It read, "VC Agent Report Effective anytime thru 4 May 71. Chu Lai to be attacked by indirect fire and sappers. Individuals involved in attack on Chu Lai will wear ARVN uniforms, but will be bare foot for their own identification. Inform all personnel on guard force, anyone observed in wire will be fired upon. Targets need not be identified as hostile. If they are in or near the wire, fire to wound, if necessary fire to kill. Near is anything within 25 meters of the wire." As far as I could see, Fike had actually violated the order by challenging Beckworth and firing a warning shot. He should have shot the intruder on sight.

In my final report I quoted the VC Agent Report and its instructions, then wrote, "This order was designed for the personnel on the extreme perimeter, however this was not brought out in the briefing [to the guards]. So when the order was read, [i]t would have indicated all perimeter wire; ie, Motor Pool perimeter wire." I titled the case "Justifiable Homicide" and closed it. Today, the cause of Beckworth's death is listed as "non-hostile—accidental homicide."

With great contrition I gave my report to Strawberry. I apologized for having been so negligent in performing my job as the on-call agent and assured him that I would never again make such a stupid mistake. With a father's stern admonishment that the spanking hurt him more than it hurt me and that he was confident that my mistake had been only a momentary lapse in judgment, he accepted the report and its conclusion. With appropriate remorsefulness, I left his office to return to mine. As I passed Ross's office, I smiled and gave him a thumbs up. Victory can sometimes be the sweetest when the vanquished doesn't know he lost.

Today I still believe the shooting was justified. After I cooled down from Strawberry's ass chewing, I did a thorough investigation. If the facts had indicated otherwise I wouldn't have called it justified. But the facts led me to that conclusion. I believed then, as now, that the young troop shouldn't be punished because he was doing what he was told to do. Plain and simple. He wasn't the bad guy in this incident. The bad guy was shot crawling through the wire.

Not all GI-on-GI violence was accidental or deadly. In most cases, it was just a matter of young men, oftentimes driven by drink or drugs, in conflict over some minor issue that escalated to violence. I remember two troops in the medical battalion fighting over a pair of pajamas. Indignant because another GI had taken his pajamas, a medic ran into the Headquarters and A Company Orderly Room, grabbed an M-16 from the weapons rack, ran out of the room, and fired several rounds at the alleged pajama snatcher. I interviewed both the shooter and the pajama snatcher, but neither would make a statement. When they sobered up, both realized the stupidity in what they'd done and wanted to get it behind them. No one was ever punished for the incident.

Far more numerous were incidents of drunk and disorderly conduct at one of the clubs. In one such incident, a drunk private first class from Baton Rouge, Louisiana, climbed onto a club's stage and began to intimidate members of the band. The master-at-arms escorted him from the club, but he soon returned. A melee of sorts broke out, and the Louisiana troop brandished a knife. Another GI responded by pulling a Smith and Wesson .38 caliber pistol from a shoulder holster and threatening bystanders. Somehow, the club manager defused the situation and got everyone to leave his club, which he immediately closed for the evening. We later identified the GI with the pistol. A couple of MPs and I apprehended him. When we searched him, we found the pistol and about nine grams of marijuana.

As well, long before "drive-by shooting" entered America's vocabulary, we had similar incidents in Vietnam. In May 1971, a troop was hitchhiking on a side road when he saw an Army deuce-and-a-half truck approaching. He waved for the driver to stop, but the vehicle continued as if to drive by him. When the truck was just about to him, a passenger dressed in uniform pointed a handgun out the side window and shot him. The bullet hit the hitchhiker in the chest and exited out his back. He was later found by another GI, transported to the 91st Evac Hospital, and underwent surgery for his wound. When I investigated the shooting, he couldn't tell me anything more than that he was shot by the passenger in an Army truck. I never solved the case.

Not surprisingly, the presence of women—and the sexual overtones to that presence—oftentimes sparked violence between male GIs. One case I wasn't involved in, but I remember well, involved a "security violation" (a 50-piaster whore) being sneaked into an open bay hooch. A GI had smuggled her on the post in the back of a truck with the intent of keeping her in his hooch for the whole night. When he got her into the hooch, his roommates thought that they ought to be able to participate in the fun, too. He refused to even discuss the issue because, as far as he was concerned, the whore was his and his alone. As he and the woman partied, he got drunk, eventually passing out. When he regained consciousness some time later, he discovered he'd been far more generous with the whore's services while he was sleeping than when he'd been awake. After he'd passed out, the whore decided to make as much money as she could in as short a time as possible. By the time the drunken GI awakened, she'd made money from several of his hooch mates and was busily working on making more. He reached under his bunk and pulled out an AK-47 he was keeping as a war souvenir (an illegal war souvenir, at that). He opened fire on the people he felt were betraying him. He killed three GIs, wounded two or three others, and shot the woman, although I don't remember if her wounds were fatal. Although this is an extreme case because of the number of killed and wounded, violence among male GIs over Vietnamese women was common.

Violence caused by women, booze, drugs, or a combination of these took on a much more sinister face when race was mixed in. The racial tensions in the United States during the sixties and seventies were accentuated in Vietnam. By the early seventies, many of the black troops saw themselves trapped in a white man's war. They began drawing analogies between service in the war and the institution of slavery. With nothing more than black bootlaces, some black artisans began braiding "slave jewelry" (bracelets, rings, chokers and so on) that African-American GIs proudly wore to demonstrate their blackness, the idea of black power, and their opposition to the white man's war. Some of the bracelets were six or eight inches wide, covering an entire forearm. Or someone would have a bracelet around his wrist that had strands of braiding running down the back of his hand and a loop around his finger like a ring. Others wore a braided inch-high choker around their necks. Once in awhile, you'd see someone with slave bracelets on both wrists, wide enough to cover both forearms and straps running up to and around their biceps. When I was in Vietnam, many of the lower-ranking enlisted black soldiers wore this "slave jewelry," but I never saw one black officer or NCO wearing it. I doubt that Colin Powell wore any when he was in Vietnam.

"Dapping" had become popular in the States, and the black troops brought it to Vietnam. It involved an elaborate exchange of "handshakes," for lack of a better term, between two "black brothers." These ritualistic greetings could last anywhere from a couple of minutes up to twenty minutes. One-handed, two-handed, open palms slapping, back of hands tapping, closed fists meeting high, low, straight on, back-to-back, front-to-front, tapping, slapping, dapping. A few white guys tried it, looked silly, and quit. Dapping was through-and-through African-American. Dapping and slave jewelry set apart black troops from the other races on the military posts.

Such divisions engendered distrust, misunderstanding, and apprehension that in turn fueled antagonisms among the racial groups that often erupted into violence. Military police blotters and CID reports are full of such incidents. The stories that follow happened many, many times and are only illustrative of the racial violence that was always present at military installations during this time.

Early in March 1971, a Puerto Rican soldier by the name of Antonio Guerrero rushed into the Arms Room of Headquarters and A Company,

23d Medical Battalion, grabbed an M-16 from the rifle rack, slapped in a clip, chambered a round, and threatened to shoot the armorer and another soldier if they didn't leave the armory in three seconds. On their way out of the Arms Room, they heard Guerrero saying, "I'm gonna get the blacks." (That's a direct quote from a written statement. Guerrero probably said "I'm gonna get the niggers," but by the early seventies there was a growing sensitivity in the military against such pejorative words. I suspect that the author of the statement was reflecting that trend.) Guerrero left the armory and ran up a long, sloping hill to the Headquarters and A Company barracks.

On the front steps of the hooch sat five black troops. An investigator later learned that Guerrero was angry with the black soldiers for harassing (sexual harassment by today's standards) the hooch maid. I'm only speculating, but Guerrero, as so many young troops did, probably fell in love with his hooch maid. When the black soldiers harassed her, he felt honor-bound to defend the object of his affections. Whatever his reasoning, he began to fire at the five soldiers. Three of them ran for cover. A fourth one was hit in the lower left leg. The fifth soldier stayed with his wounded friend, looking for a place to pull him to safety. By now, Guerrero stood over them as they still sat on the steps. He could have killed them, but instead told them that he would kill them "next time," and then left the porch.

The wounded soldier was treated at the hospital. Guerrero was apprehended and charged with aggravated assault. I don't know if his commander punished him for the incident, although if he did I suspect he got off lightly considering the nature of the crime. Such incidents were common enough to create an impotent justice system. The death of Sergeant Rodney Stillwell demonstrates how lightly a soldier might be punished for an even much more serious crime.

By October 1971, SGT Stillwell, from Massachusetts, had proudly earned the label "lifer." He entered the Army in 1964, spent five of the next seven years overseas, and was on his second Vietnam tour. One morning in October, he had a confrontation with Private Frank James, Jr., a native of New Mexico, in the unit's supply room at LZ Rawhide on Hill #65 northwest of Chu Lai. Private James used his M-16 to shoot SGT Stillwell in the chest or stomach (there is conflicting information in the police blotter). A Dust Off transported Stillwell to Da Nang , where the doctor pronounced him dead at 9:50 a.m. James was apprehended for the shooting.

By the time he was court-martialed, the offense had been reduced to a violation of Article 134, Uniform Code of Military Justice (UCMJ). Article 134 is the catch-all article that allows the military to punish a troop for just about anything that doesn't fit neatly into one of the other offenses. One would think James would have been charged with homicide or, at least, manslaughter. But he wasn't. In February 1972, James pleaded guilty to unlawfully killing Stillwell. The judge sentenced him to "be confined at hard labor for six (6) months, to forfeit $150.00 pay per month for a period of six (6) months, and to be reduced to the grade of Private (E-1)." The reviewing judge, however, decided that only the portion of the sentence that did not include confinement would be carried out. In other words, Private James would serve no time in prison for Stillwell's death. In the final analysis, SGT Stillwell's life was worth a fine of $900. (In 1973 James was again tried by court-martial for being AWOL [absent without leave] from his organization at Fort Hood, Texas. He was found guilty and sentenced to "be confined at hard labor for three months and to forfeit $75.00 per month for three months." The reviewing judge once again suspended the confinement at hard labor. A few months later, James was discharged from the Army.)

Two final thoughts on Stillwell's death: This shooting may have been a variation of fragging, the killing of NCOs and officers by subordinates that had come to plague the Army by the early seventies. If it was, the leniency shown by the military justice system to James could only have exacerbated the decline of military discipline. Secondly, it is worth noting that the last entry on Stillwell's official military record is that he was "KIA," killed in action. However, in the Combat Area Casualty Figures database, his death is listed as "non-hostile—accidental homicide." Considering that James pleaded guilty that he'd unlawfully killed Stillwell, that Stillwell's official record says he was KIA, and that in the Combat Area Casualty Figures he's listed as an accidental homicide, one wonders what his family was told about his death.

All such deaths that the CID investigated in Vietnam were senseless, but the death of SGT Antonio Flores at the hands of SGT Rico Garcia epitomized the meaninglessness of them all. Both soldiers were decorated Vietnam War veterans. SGT Flores entered the Army in November 1967 and was on his fourth overseas tour by 1971. He'd spent two tours in Germany and was on his second tour in the war. He was an 11 Bush—an infantryman. He did not spend his time in

Vietnam in air-conditioned offices; he fought in the rice paddies and jungles and had been awarded two bronze stars (awarded to a soldier who distinguished himself by heroic or meritorious achievement or service while engaged in an action against an enemy of the United States) with "V"s for valor—medals earned for heroism. He'd been wounded four times and awarded a Purple Heart for each. He was a Malaysian from Guam instilled with the proud heritage of ancient Chamorros warriors. His military record reveals a man who'd met the enemy and relished the meeting. He was a scrapper. He liked the adrenaline rush of a good fight—with the enemy or one of his own. It would be his doom.

SGT Rico Garcia, too, joined the Army in 1967, became an 11 Bush, and was on his second tour in the war. During his first tour in 1968, he was a tunnel rat. His job was to go into the "spider holes" that led to labyrinthine underground tunnels where the VC lived, stored supplies, set up hospitals, and in general survived without benefit of sunlight and out of the sight of the Americans' most sophisticated surveillance equipment. The spider holes were small, so company commanders picked (or condemned) small men (Garcia stood just a fraction over 5'5" and weighed 127 pounds) to wiggle into the holes to carry out underground search-and-destroy missions. (Today, I know a couple of guys who were tunnel rats, and mentally they don't walk with the rest of us. I'm not a psychiatrist, but my guess is that many of them suffer from psychological issues related to the fear and confinement inherent in those spider holes.) After Garcia's first tour in the war, he returned to the States where he taught English to non-English speaking Latin American soldiers. He then received an assignment to the Canal Zone in Panama. From there he returned to Vietnam in October 1970. He'd been luckier or more careful than Flores; for all his time in the war, he had not earned any Purple Hearts or Bronze Stars. But he had been awarded an Army Commendation Medal with V for valorous actions that saved his and his buddies' lives while on patrol—a fact that would come to haunt him during his court-martial. Garcia was a Mexican-American from San Antonio, Texas, who was proud of his heritage and his service to his country.

Garcia and Flores were hardened war veterans and true American heroes when fate drew them together one night in March 1971. That evening the Division Combat Center's NCO Club had a floorshow. The attraction was a Filipino band. The adaptability of the Asian band members to their environment must be admired: they played a mix of country and western, soul, rock and roll, and Latino music. The place was packed. Thirty-some small tables cluttered the floor. Soldiers sat four or six to a table, others stood by the bar, some leaned against the ten support poles running in two parallel lines toward the stage. The overflowing crowd left some soldiers standing outside the club looking in through the doors and windows. Smoke hung heavy in the room. Vietnamese barmaids maneuvered through the crowd carrying trays laden with cans of beer and glasses of mixed drinks while enduring the groping of horny GIs just in from the bush or getting ready to leave the next day.

Garcia sat with a couple of other soldiers, one also a Mexican-American, at a table in the second row from the stage. He enjoyed the band. He had seen the same band at Da Nang while on R&R (rest and relaxation) and had befriended one of its members. As he tried to get into the mood of the evening, thoughts of his wife distracted him. He'd just returned from a leave in Texas. He had not heard from his wife, to whom he had been sending money, for some months. In February, he asked the Red Cross to check on her. The Red Cross volunteer found her living with another man. This information was bluntly delivered to Garcia who then flew back to the States to file for divorce. He had returned to Vietnam only days earlier. Now the evening before he was going out into the bush, he sat with his friends, spoke Spanish with his Mexican-American friend, listened to a band he liked, drank bourbon and Coke, and tried to forget his wife.

At a table directly across from Garcia's table sat Flores and his buddies. His was a close-knit group. One of the soldiers had gone to high school with him on Guam. The others knew him well—not as well, maybe, but they were friends, not just acquaintances. It was a rowdy group. They sang boisterously with the band; they banged their fists on their table; they laughed loudly. They were in the club to have a good time and everyone knew it.

At some point in the evening, Garcia approached his friend in the band and asked if the band would play "El Rancho Grande." The band readily agreed. While the band played and sang in Spanish, Garcia stood. The Flores table became rowdier, its soldiers yelling "Olè" wherever they felt it was needed in the song. After the song, Garcia sat down and Flores yelled over the din, "Hey Puerto Rican!" Garcia looked over at the smirking Flores but said nothing. Flores then walked over to Garcia. Now Garcia told him, "I'm not a Puerto Rican." Flores responded, "You

Mexicans cut up people. We crush them. I'll meet you after the show." (There was some uncorroborated evidence that Flores and Garcia had been feuding for a few days before this incident, but I found no evidence to prove that.) Soldiers at both tables began talking about the impending fight. Flores and his buddies were excited by the possibility of a good fight after the show; Garcia and his friends less so. At one point, Garcia showed his tablemates an eight-inch blade "Mexican hunting knife" he carried, although he didn't indicate that he intended to use it in the fight.

The band quit playing around 10 p.m. Those in attendance flooded out the two doors (a front door and a side door) that emptied on to a barren, hard dirt courtyard. About thirty yards from the front door, the courtyard turned into the soft, white sand beach that disappeared into the ocean. Garcia intended immediately to leave the area, but once outside, he remembered his hat left inside. He went back into the club, retrieved his hat, and came back out. By now a crowd, later estimated at fifty to seventy-five soldiers, had gathered. Flores and his buddies confronted Garcia. Flores had taken off his shirt and was standing in some sort of martial arts defensive stance as he and his buddies began taunting Garcia. Bystanders began joining in on the heckling of Garcia: "Come on coward!" "Come on chicken!" "Come on pussy!" Garcia looked at Flores and said, "Why should I fight you? I have no reason to fight you. We are fellow soldiers. We should be getting along together. I have no reason to fight you." He turned and tried to walk away, but the crowd pressed in. "Sir," Garcia would later testify, "I was afraid for my life."

After Garcia's repeated attempts to leave and taunts from the crowd and Flores, the crowd had completed encircled the two and was pressing them closer together. Flores and Garcia were just inches apart. Flores kept saying, "I'm ready for you man." Suddenly Flores lunged toward Garcia, then he staggered back. Some GIs in the crowd saw Garcia holding a knife. A couple witnesses testified later that Garcia then shouted, "Who's next?"

Someone in the crowd yelled, "[Flores] has been stabbed!" Attention quickly focused on the bleeding soldier staggering and holding his right side. "Wow, man," one of Garcia's buddies said to him. "You better go run and turn yourself in man 'cause those guys [Flores buddies] are going to get you." The crowd now parted, making room for the wild-eyed Garcia to escape.

He sprinted toward the beach and then nearly one mile to the company area. He ran into the orderly room looking like a troop in trouble. One of the clerks ran to the first sergeant's quarters to get help. The first sergeant testified, "[U]pon entering [the orderly room], I saw [Garcia] sitting on the edge of one of the clerks' bunks and upon seeing me, he got up off the bunk and approached me and said something to the effect, 'Top, I fucked up. I cut up a man down at the club.'"

An on-duty MPI received a call from the MP desk sergeant about the incident. Because it fell into the category of a major violation, the investigator called me at my hooch—I was his backup that night. He told me that there'd been an aggravated assault (an assault with a weapon) at one of the clubs, the victim was at the hospital, and there was a suspect. I went first to the hospital. When I arrived, a medic told me that Flores had died. The offense had changed from an aggravated assault to murder.

I went directly to the morgue to view the body. Flores was lying naked on a gurney. I could see that the doctor had made a surgical incision on the right side of Flores's torso, just below the rib cage. Under the incision, I could also see the puncture wound from the knife. The surgical incision looked like it'd been closed by a sail maker; black stitches looped about one inch apart held the cold, lifeless flesh together. The top half of his body took on a gray-yellowish color as gravity pulled the blood of the lifeless body down toward the gurney where it pooled, still encased in the skin, giving the bottom half of his body a dark, bruised look. His lips were blue. His dull, dry eyes with dilated pupils stared blankly toward the ceiling. No question about it: I had my corpus delicti.

A photographer arrived so we could get pictures of the body and the wound. The photographer had a hard time aiming the camera properly to get a good shot. Eventually we moved two more gurneys over to the one where Flores lay. We put one on each side of Flores's body and locked the wheels in place. The photographer got on top of one gurney, stepped one leg across the body so as to straddle Flores, looking straight down on him. He took a couple of photographs of the body from about the waistline up, to include the head, shoulders, and arms. (During research on this book, the only part of the court-martial record denied to me under the Freedom of Information Act were these photographs of the body.)

I left the hospital, climbed into my jeep and drove to Garcia's unit. He wasn't there. As I'd expected, he'd been apprehended and taken to the MP station. I talked to the company commander, first sergeant, clerks, and others who were around when Garcia came running in from the club or had talked to him shortly afterwards. Witnesses told me that he'd come in to the orderly room and told anyone that would listen that he had stabbed someone at the club—an act of self-defense, he told his commander. He also told them that he didn't have the knife anymore; he got rid of it while running down the beach.

I left the unit and went to the MP station where I attempted to interview Garcia. When I advised him of his rights, he said he wanted a lawyer. From that point on, any information I would obtain would have to come from someone besides the suspect. I had no power to get any information out of him.

My biggest problem on this case was trying to find the murder weapon. Because he wouldn't talk to me, I didn't know if he buried the knife on the beach, if he threw it in the water, or what he did with it. I had no idea at all. It was by now very early in the morning and still very dark. A search for the knife would have to wait until daylight.

After daybreak I asked the EOD (explosive ordinance) troops to meet me on the beach with their metal detectors. We combed the beach from the club all the way back to Garcia's unit. We found a lot of cans buried in the sand, a little bit of change, and some jewelry, but we never located the knife. Someone—and it wasn't me—concocted the idea that if we didn't have the knife, we could have a knife that might look like the murder weapon. We got a five-inch (three inches shorter than Garcia's knife) hunting knife somewhere, and the government submitted it as evidence during Garcia's court-martial. No one at the trial thought it was anywhere near in appearance to the murder weapon. The testimony about the knife ran like this:

Q. [Prosecution] I want to show you Prosecution Exhibit 5 for Identification and ask you if in any way is this the knife similiar [sic—consistently misspelled] to the one that you saw in the hands of Sergeant [Garcia]?

A. [Witness] (Witness examines the knife.) Not really.

Q. Basically the same type of design as to a hunting knife as opposed to a pocket knife?

A. No, not really.

Q. Was the knife that Sergeant [Garcia] was holding a pocket knife?

A. No.

Q. Was it a hunting knife—that type of knife?

A. Probably—yes.

Q. So in that respect, it was similiar to this exhibit?

A. It was similiar.

So we submitted as evidence a knife whose only similarity to the murder weapon was that neither was a pocketknife. Nevertheless, given Garcia's statements in the orderly room, the death of Flores, and numerous witness statements, the fact that we didn't have the murder weapon wasn't a fatal defect in the government's case against Garcia.

In May 1971, SGT Garcia stood trial for the unpremeditated murder of SGT Flores. Garcia chose a trial by military judge alone instead of a full panel of officers and enlisted to hear his case. It was a matter of choosing the known over the unknown. I'm reasonably sure that the defense attorney had practiced law in Vietnam and that the judge had presided over other courts-martial in Vietnam. So the defense attorney knew the judge, if not personally, at least by reputation. The defense counsel may have even appeared before this judge on other cases and had a sense for what the judge would do in a case like this. The counsel knew that Garcia's medals and the fact that he was a tunnel rat would be brought out in the trial, and he probably had a sense of how this judge would react to those issues. If he decided that Garcia was guilty of the charge, he would take those other issues into account before sentencing him (and there was little doubt that Garcia would be sentenced for something. The evidence was too overwhelming.) On the other hand, if Garcia opted for a full panel, it was anyone's guess who'd serve on that panel—and, anyone's guess how the panel would react to the evidence. So Garcia's defense counsel undoubtedly knew it would be easier to elicit some sort of sympathy for his client from one judge than from a whole panel.

The government's case against Garcia was straightforward: Flores was dead and Garcia was the cause of that death. The specification of the charge read, "In that Sergeant [Rico Garcia], US Army, Company D, 3d Battalion, 21st Infantry, did, at Chu Lai, Republic of Vietnam ... murder [Antonio Flores] by means of stabbing him with a knife." All the evidence pointed to Garcia's guilt.

The defense's job was much more formidable than the prosecution's. It had to prove that Garcia hadn't intended to murder Flores, but that the death was the result of circumstances surrounding the buildup to the fight and a terrible accident, all caused more by Flores's actions than Garcia's. The defense would try to prove that Flores fell on Garcia's knife. Garcia had only pulled the knife to protect himself because of his abnormal fear of crowds.

The hospital's pathologist testified first. His testimony didn't help the defense. Flores had died of "massive hemorrhage from an abdominal stab wound and this wound resulted in two lacerations of the liver. In addition, it resulted in the laceration of the right kidney and the right adrenal gland." Although the pathologist agreed with the defense that the force of a body falling on a knife could have resulted in these injuries, he also testified that he found two tracks of the blade in Flores's abdomen. In other words, the knife had been thrust into Flores, partially removed, and thrust in again, not the expected track marks if he'd fallen on the knife. Based on this evidence, the prosecutor sarcastically asked Garcia, "Now if Sergeant [Flores] came forward at you and you never took that knife away from your body, did that man run himself on that knife twice?"

"I don't know, sir," Garcia replied. The defense's argument that Flores had fallen on Garcia's knife was proving to be untenable.

The defense's second strategy was to pin its hopes on Garcia's "abnormal" fear of crowds that caused him to draw his knife in the first place. The prosecution would attack this defense just as vigorously. In the process, the fact that Garcia was a decorated war hero worked against him. The defense had presented his Army Commendation Medal with "V" as an exhibit demonstrating why Garcia carried a knife in the field—to help him disentangle himself from booby traps, for example. The medal citation read that while on patrol, SGT Garcia "became entangled in a well-concealed trip wire attached to an enemy booby trap. Halting instantly, Sergeant [Garcia] quickly directed his comrades clear of his area before attempting to disengage himself from the wire. Expertly clearing himself from the detonation system, he alertly detected the well-concealed explosive device and skillfully disarmed it. Through his timely actions, Sergeant [Garcia] was responsible for preventing friendly casualties and contributed significantly to the success of the operation. His personal heroism and devotion to duty are in keeping with the highest traditions of the military service and reflect great credit upon himself, the 23d Infantry Division, and the United States Army."

The prosecution wasn't about to let the defense claim that this decorated war hero, a former tunnel rat, no less, was now afraid of crowds. The trial transcript shows a decorated soldier having to defend his heroism and the prosecution using that heroism in an attempt to get him convicted for murder.

The prosecution argued that Garcia had been decorated because he "exercised very cool judgment...in a most highly dangerous position." However, Garcia said that he was scared when he became entangled in the booby trap. The prosecutor agreed that anyone would be scared in such a situation, but Garcia had kept his head precisely because he was scared. Then he managed to think his way through the situation and save himself and his buddies. Was the crowd pressing around him and Flores any different? "Why didn't you stop in the middle of the crowd," the prosecutor asked, "and remain cool and think of a way to get out of it the way you did when you were tangled up in that booby trap?" Garcia kept saying he was afraid of the crowd. "Were you more frightened than you were when you were tangled in that booby trap?"

Having to defend his heroic action in the bush, Garcia responded, "When I was tangled in the booby trap, sir, I only had one thing in mind, and that was to get myself together and I took a long time; believe me, it took me a long time to get myself together, to also get myself down there and get myself untangled, get myself out of the booby trap and stop that [safety] pin [on the explosive] from going off, sir, it took me a long time. And I can say this: They had to stop the operation that we were in because of the delay on my part. I was taking my time."

"But why couldn't you take the same time," the prosecutor asked, "the same degree of cool-headed thinking in the situation with Sergeant [Flores] where you could have used that same cool head and waited a long time before having to decide to pull the knife?"

The defense's introduction of Garcia's heroic action and medal had backfired.

Next the defense tried to use the division psychiatrist to prove Garcia's fear of crowds. In this courtroom, as in courtrooms all across

America then and today, the substance of psychological testimony is based on which side asked the psycho-expert to testify and on what that side wanted the testimony to contain. Because there is no scientific basis for any of the psychological testimony, there's no way to disprove it. The only defense against such testimony is to bring in one's own "experts" to testify about the inaccuracies of the earlier testimony and hope that the judge believes it and not the other side's, or to discredit the other side's expert. (For a very good discussion of psychological testimony in today's courts, read Margaret A. Hagen's *Whores of the Court: The Fraud of Psychiatric Testimony and the Rape of American Justice*.)

In this case the prosecution did a good job of discrediting the psychiatrist. Under questioning, the psychiatrist acknowledged that he'd only spent forty-five minutes interviewing Garcia upon the request of the defense counsel. And his conclusion based on that interview?

"I concluded," the psychiatrist authoritatively stated, "that Sergeant [Garcia] does have a bona fide phobia for being confined in small spaces which is usually called claustrophobia. What this means is that when a person becomes enclosed either in a very small room or in a small space, he feels very, very anxious. Depending on the circumstances, he can become very excited and tries in every way to extricate himself from this situation. This is sort of an unreasonable fear which he does not have any control of."

The psychiatrist was then asked to explain to the court how such a phobia developed. The answer was something that he remembered out of his college textbook and had nothing to do with SGT Garcia. In a 1973 review of this case by a staff judge advocate, the reviewer criticized the psychiatrist who "spoke only in the abstract without referring to the incident in question or the actions of the accused."

The prosecution asked the psychiatrist if he'd performed "any form of special technique or test or other fashion to test the accused as to the extent of his phobia?" Well, no, was the response, but the "story that he gave me fit everything the way that a phobia should fit and I didn't feel it necessary to push it any further." And why had he looked for such a phobia in the first place? Because the defense counsel drew "my attention to that area," he responded.

The judge was beside himself. The defense was supposed to be arguing that Garcia had an abnormal fear of crowds, and, for the last hour, the division psychiatrist had testified that Garcia was claustrophobic.

The judge decided to try his hand at it. "Doctor," he said, "is there a fear that is called a fear of crowds?"

"Well, I am sure that there is a name attached to it," responded the psychiatrist. "I just don't know what the name is."

Defense counsel tried to salvage something from the testimony. "Sir," the defense asked. "If a person were enclosed by a close crowd, if he had this phobia, could he suffer from it?"

"Yes."

During closing arguments, the prosecution mentioned the "phobia theory" only to dismiss it. The defense counsel didn't even bring the subject up.

There were many other witnesses (including me) during the three-day trial. The other testimony simply painted the picture of the evening when Flores, described as a "bully" by defense counsel, decided to pick a fight with Garcia and ended up dying on an operating table at Chu Lai's hospital. The prosecutor best summed up the whole event when, during closing arguments, he said, "It is unfortunate, indeed it is tragic that such a fine young soldier should be caught up in such a situation. But it is equally unfortunate that another young man is dead." What this "fine young soldier" would have to pay for the death of the "bully" resided in the hands of the military judge.

The defense's strategy in choosing court-martial by military judge alone may have worked. The judge found Garcia not guilty of murder, but guilty of the lesser charge of voluntary manslaughter. There is no way, of course, of knowing if a panel would have found otherwise, but with the overwhelming evidence that Garcia had killed Flores, it's possible that a panel would have found him guilty of murder. The military judge also mitigated the sentence. The judge could have sentenced Garcia to a dishonorable discharge, forfeiture of all pay and allowances, and confinement at hard labor for ten years. Instead the judge imposed a discharge from the Army with a bad conduct discharge, reduction to Private E-1, and confinement at hard labor for one year and three months. (During the sentencing phase, the defense counsel brought up Garcia's claustrophobia to try to convince the judge not to confine him—it didn't work.)

The true cost to Garcia for Flores's death is incalculable. By all testimony and as evidenced by his military record, Garcia was an outstanding soldier. Prior to Flores's death, he'd never been in trouble. But in one fateful night, his life was destroyed when he acted, perhaps inappropriately, to the threats and intimidation of another soldier who everyone agreed picked the fight. As a result of his response to those threats, Garcia served hard time at the United States Disciplinary Barracks, Fort Leavenworth, Kansas, and received a bad conduct discharge in 1972. Who knows what paths he traveled after his discharge? He was, after all, a convicted felon. But Flores, the "bully" who started the fight?—in death he's memorialized on the Vietnam Memorial Wall, one of America's fallen heroes.

There was a much more sinister homicide trend in Vietnam than the barroom brawl variety that took the life of Flores. That was the deliberate killing of officers and NCOs by subordinate soldiers driven by grievances, imagined or real, against the war and the Army. In the vernacular, such an attack was called "fragging" because initially the weapon of choice was a fragmentation hand grenade. Eventually, though, any attack on a superior with any weapon fell into this category.

How many officers and NCOs were killed or wounded by such attacks is impossible to know. One study puts the number of fraggings at "788 confirmed cases, resulting in 86 deaths." Another study raises the confirmed cases to over one thousand, including wounded and killed. For what it's worth, Wikipedia reports, "There are documented cases of at least 230 American officers killed by their own troops, and as many as 1,400 other officers' deaths could not be explained." None of these figures can be confirmed. The official record of the causes of deaths in the war sets the number of "Intentional Homicides" at 234, but there is no way of knowing how many of those deaths included fraggings. Moreover, friendly fire was often placed in a category call "misadventure," which accounted for 1,326 deaths. How many fraggings became "misadventures" is also impossible to tell. So, as is so often the case in ferreting out the truth in this war, the facts are elusive.

I investigated a case involving an attack on a young second lieutenant and have no idea if it is counted in the fragging figures. He was a wet-behind-the-ears, recently-commissioned officer, and he wasn't liked by his men. He was serving under the delusion that in the bush the Army was still military and soldiers would take orders. A young private decided to kill him. At close range, the private shot the lieutenant with an M-79 grenade launcher. An M-79 grenade is about the size of a golf ball. The round embedded itself into the lieutenant's neck, but didn't explode. A Dust Off transported the officer to Chu Lai's hospital.

When I got notified of the attack, I drove to Chu Lai East and hitched a helicopter ride to the fire support base where the attack occurred. Going into the bush always had a surreal aspect. Dressed in my sports pants, short-sleeved shirt and loafers, carrying a briefcase full of forms and armed with my grease gun and a few mini-frags, I looked out of place surrounded by soldiers in OD jungle fatigues, helmets, flak vests, and armed to the teeth with M-16s, M-60s, M-79s, M-148s, and an array of hand grenades. But going into the bush to apprehend someone who'd just shot his commander added another dimension to the whole affair. I never saw the Vietnamese soldiers (VC or North Vietnamese) as my enemy, and always knew that I had a greater chance of being killed by a GI. This reality became accentuated by the fact that now I was going into the bush to confront a soldier accused of trying to kill one of his officers. If he was crazy enough to shoot his lieutenant with an M-79 grenade launcher, what are the odds that he's crazy enough to shoot some guy wearing civilian clothes who gets off a helicopter carrying a briefcase?

When I arrived at the fire support base, I learned that the private alleged to have shot the lieutenant was out on patrol; a fact that struck me as rather odd. Here was a soldier who'd just tried to kill an officer. Instead of disarming him and confining him in some way to the base, his NCO sent him out on patrol. I interviewed the other soldiers and took statements from them. There was no doubt that the shooting was a deliberate act and that most of the soldiers thought the lieutenant got what he deserved. According to one study, an Army psychiatrist concluded "most fraggings were partially the officer's or superior's fault." That's akin to the old argument that a rape victim deserved what she got because of the way she dressed or acted—the rapist isn't at fault, he couldn't help himself; the victim caused the attack. This attitude among the soldiers (and of at least one psychiatrist) clearly demonstrates the decline of Army discipline by 1971.

When I got back to Chu Lai, I went directly to the hospital. I had no idea if the lieutenant had survived the attack. At the hospital I learned that he was alive and resting after what must have been a cliffhanger of a surgery. The doctor had cut open the lieutenant's neck to expose the grenade while an EOD (explosives) expert stood by. Once the grenade was accessible, the EOD troop removed it from the lieutenant and the operating room—much to the relief of the medical staff.

I then checked with the private's unit and learned when he'd be returning to Chu Lai. When he did, I had the MPs apprehend him for attempted murder. I don't remember the outcome of the case. According to one study, "[o]nly a tenth of the attempted fraggings ended in court." I don't know if this case was one of the tenth or if it's even counted in the fragging figures for the war. But I do know I never had to testify in court regarding this incident.

In many ways, this was an unusual case because it was reported to us as an attempted murder of an officer in the bush. Usually when there were thirty men in a platoon out in the bush and one of them killed or attempted to kill a lieutenant, I don't believe we were notified. No one was going to pull thirty guys out of the bush for the sake of investigating the death of one lieutenant that nobody gave a shit about, particularly the soldiers that worked for him. And if we were notified, we'd go out into the bush and repeatedly hear "I didn't see shit" or "I don't know a fucking thing." We'd leave the scene with very little information because no one was going to rat on his buddy. My opinion is that fraggings and shooting of officers and NCOs happened more than the Army admitted, but were most often dismissed as accidents. Who could say that the shooting of an officer in the bush wasn't an accident? Particularly when none of the witnesses saw anything. The code of silence in the Vietnamese bush could be as impregnable as that of the Sicilian Mafioso.

Another case that I remember on Chu Lai resulted in the killing of a captain. (Some studies suggest that fraggings occurred most often at large support bases where racial tensions and drug abuse were epidemic compared to in the bush where troops had to depend on each other for survival. I have only anecdotal information to back me up, but the way I remember it, far more fraggings occurred in the bush than on Chu Lai.) The captain was not liked. While he was away on R&R, somebody went to his hooch and set up an anti-personnel claymore mine pointed at the entrance with a tripwire directly inside of the door. (The foundation of a claymore mine is a curved piece of steel. The convex side is packed with C-4 plastic explosive impregnated with BBs. The concave back plate directs the blast, propelling all the BBs forward, spreading as they get farther from the mine itself.)

When the captain came home from his R&R, he was undoubtedly happy as he walked toward his hooch, probably engrossed in thoughts of the beautiful woman he'd laid. He grabbed the handle of the door to his hooch, swung the door open, and stepped into the room. The claymore had been rigged to hit him at about mid-section and it did. The BBs hadn't traveled far enough to begin to spread, so he was hit with the full force of hundreds, if not thousands, of BBs grouped in a swath about three feet wide and one foot high. The blast cut him completely in half. I didn't investigate this case and don't know if anyone was ever held accountable for it.

Just to give one a sense of the frequency of these fragging incidents, while researching this book I found three fraggings that I investigated in March 1971 alone. That's just the ones I investigated and just the ones with records I could identify and obtain through the Freedom of Information Act. It is possible that, in fact, I investigated more such cases that month, and surely other agents investigated fraggings at the same rate as I did.

The first one I investigated that month occurred on March 8 when someone detonated an M-26 fragmentation grenade approximately fifty feet from a commanding officer's hooch on LZ Dottie. The next day the suspect struck the commanding officer and knocked him to the ground and also hit one of the NCOs. There never was enough evidence to pin the fragging on him, but he was charged with assaulting a superior commissioned officer and assaulting an NCO.

In another case, on March 21 a Chief Warrant Officer (CWO) found his locker booby-trapped with a grenade. A string had been tied to the safety pin of an M-61 baseball-type fragmentation grenade, the pin had been pulled out halfway, and then the string was tied to his locker door handle. The intent was that when he opened the door the safety pin would pull out, the spoon would fly off, and the grenade would explode. Fortunately for the CWO, he saw the device when the safety pin was only pulled halfway out. A few days before this incident, the CWO had a confrontation with Specialist Four Enrique Rodriguez, an Hispanic troop from Pueblo, Colorado. Rodriguez asked the CWO if he was "short," meaning his time in the war was about over. When the CWO replied, "Yes," Rodriguez responded, "You are shorter than you think." I apprehended Rodriguez and there the official record stops. It doesn't show that he made any statements or received any punishment for the incident. Based on the one comment that he made to the CWO, however, it's doubtful that there was enough evidence to punish him for the incident. In July 1971 he left Vietnam, had a short stint AWOL from his next unit in Washington State, and was discharged from the Army in December 1971.

On March 22, the day after the CWO had found his locker booby-trapped, the commander of Headquarters and Headquarters Company,

39th Engineering Battalion, was awakened when something hit the plywood wall of his hooch. "I heard something hit the side of my quarters," he wrote in a statement for me. "As soon as I heard this sound, I heard what sounded like a spoon releasing from a grenade." "I then started to get up," he continued. "When I raised my feet, there was an explosion, and I felt something hit my right foot. I jumped up and ran to my door to see if I could hear or see someone." He heard someone running, but couldn't see anyone. He checked to see if anyone living in the vicinity of his hooch had been hurt. None had. He was later transported to the hospital and treated for a shrapnel wound to his right foot.

I investigated the incident and identified a suspect. The captain had pointed a finger at him, and there were a couple of guys in the company that also fingered him as the perpetrator. A couple of hours prior to the incident, they'd seen him in a hooch playing with a hand grenade. After the explosion, he no longer had one. He, of course, denied detonating the grenade and then requested legal counsel. Two months later, I loaded him on a C-130 and flew with him to Saigon for a polygraph at the 8th Military Police Group (Criminal Investigation) headquarters in Long Binh. He flunked the polygraph, but it wasn't admissible. I then closed the case with a comment that I believed insufficient evidence existed to charge the suspect with a crime.

The reality of such fraggings is best summed up by Gabriel Kolko in *Anatomy of a War*. He writes, "When officers were strong leaders, one general complained in 1972, they 'commanded oftentimes at the risk of their lives due to the possibility of grenade incidents.' Where new officers attempted to impose discipline in units with racial and drug problems, 'there will in all probability be one or more grenade incidents in the first four weeks directed against the commander and the First Sergeant.' By the end of the war, fragging had intimidated a large number of officers, whose relationship with their men was shaped accordingly."

During 1971, fraggings, accidental shootings, barroom brawls, and other GI-on-GI violence seemed to threaten more harm to American troops than did the Vietnamese enemy. Add to that fact the deaths of GIs from drug overdoses, suicides, and accidents and Vietnam shaped up to be a pretty dangerous place for Americans in the waning years of the war. Of course, it was no picnic for our Vietnamese allies either—military and civilian—who were caught in a landscape marked by civil war and a declining, retreating American military.

CHAPTER 8   BEYOND THE PALE

This is the soldier brave enough to tell
The glory-dazzled world that "war is hell."

—Henry van Dyke (1852-1933)

On the Augustus Saint-Gaudens Statue of
William Tecumseh Sherman (1820–1891)

I drove out the south gate of Chu Lai and turned on to QL1. There I
saw a crowd of Vietnamese gathered at a wide spot in the road where
a couple of shanties (constructed from illegally obtained Army materials) gave the appearance of a small village. The sizable crowd of
young and old Vietnamese listened attentively to the haranguing of
a beautiful woman dressed in combat fatigues. I recognized her as a
cocktail waitress at one of the clubs on base—and not just any club.
She worked at the main club where they held USO shows and entertained visiting senior officers and other dignitaries. The scene piqued
my curiosity. I maneuvered my jeep onto the side of the road, avoiding an assortment of two-, three-, and four-wheeled motor-powered,
pedaled, or animal-drawn conveyances that one only sees assembled
in a poor, third world country.

As I walked across the road toward the gathering, I saw that the
woman had blood, a lot of blood, on her uniform and hands. A machete
hung in a scabbard on her right side. She'd been butchering something. I pushed my way through the crowd. Then I saw her handiwork.

At her feet lay two terribly dismembered male bodies. Both had
been decapitated and the hands and feet chopped off. Lying on the
ground off to the side, two lidless, wooden ammunition boxes contained the dismembered parts of each corpse. On one end of each box,
a pair of bloodied, bare feet protruded out of the box looking like a
surfer "hanging ten." At the other end of each box lay a decapitated
head: coal black hair matted with syrupy, still-glistening, dark blood,
eyes and mouth half open, splotches of dark blood and dirt covering

the face. Between the head and feet, bloody hands, cut off just above the wrists, formed the "body" of each grotesque figure. An artist painting the worst scenes in hell could not have envisioned such a picture.

The two dismembered bodies belonged to two VC sympathizers who'd been hauling a truckload of rice on QL1 when the local militia caught them. The cocktail waitress-cum-militia-officer personally carried out the execution of her nation's enemies. Although one could argue the ethics of such summary executions, they frequently occurred between the two Vietnams—perpetrated by uniformed and civilian Vietnamese—locked in civil war. That much I understood. What happened next baffled me.

When she finished her speech to the assembled villagers, she ordered her militia minions to pour diesel fuel over the truckload of rice and set it ablaze. Black smoke roiled from the back of the truck as the rice and diesel went up in flames. Why they destroyed perfectly good rice was beyond my understanding. That truckload could have fed everyone in the village for a year. The executions, the dismembered bodies, even the grotesque displays made from the body parts didn't shock me. After all, there was a war going on, and Vietnamese killing Vietnamese didn't surprise me. But I'll never understand the destruction of all that food. I'm sure the executions, the dismembered bodies and the destroyed food all sent a clear message about what would happen to VC or VC sympathizers, but it still rankled me to see all that rice go up in flames.

Such an event reminded me that I was in a war. In the excitement of investigating crimes, chasing dickheads, putting criminals in jail, and fighting a losing battle against drugs, I could have forgotten that there was another war going on around us—not the war of drugs and violence among American soldiers, but the war between North and South Vietnam.

Not all reminders of the war were as stark as the two mutilated bodies. For example, with great regularity the VC lobbed mortars and rockets into Chu Lai, usually targeting the airfield. Almost every evening, we'd hear the thud, thud of rounds walking up the length of a runway trying to hit the helicopters and airplanes parked in hangars or behind revetments. The first round sounded a long ways off. The next sounded closer; the next even closer. Each thud got closer as the VC used old-fashioned trial and error aiming. They'd see where the last round landed, adjust their mortar a few clicks, drop another round in, make another adjustment, and so on. With our hooch located north of the airfield, my hooch mates and I never considered these attacks a serious threat to us. Most of the time we didn't even leave the hooch for the safety of our culvert and sandbag bunker.

There were, however, exceptions. One night we were drinking heavily when shortly after midnight the rounds started hitting south of us. We didn't pay much attention until we realized the thuds sounded much closer than usual. We could tell that the rounds were falling north of the airfield. "Suppose we should go to the bunker?" someone asked. "What are you, a fucking pussy?" someone else drunkenly retorted. Just then one of the mortar rounds landed in an ammunition storage area located between our hooch and the airfields. The explosion was deafening, and a series of the secondary explosions scared the shit out of us. Seven of us scrambled, stumbled, fell, and climbed over the top of each other to get to the bunker. To enter the bunker, a tall person had to duck to avoid hitting the edge of the culvert, an opening just a little under six feet high. In our drunken scramble to get to the bunker, an MPI caught the top edge of the culvert right at the bridge of his nose. The force of the blow peeled the skin off half of his forehead. Once the secondary explosions stopped and tranquility returned to Chu Lai, we loaded him into my jeep, and I drove him to the hospital where he received treatment for his injury. Our MPI hero later received a Purple Heart for an injury sustained while under enemy fire—an injury really caused by his own drunken stupidity.

Besides the rockets and mortars, VC sappers—commandos who attacked American bases usually armed with explosives—also hit Chu Lai, but with much less frequency. They, too, never posed a threat to us in our hooch. Because the hooch sat on a bluff overlooking the South China Sea, more than a mile of sand, hills, and trees stood between us and the perimeter fence through which the sappers attacked. And, sitting on the north end of Chu Lai away from the airfield meant that we were nowhere near anything of interest to VC sappers. So, although during the evening we would hear the firefight and satchel explosions signaling a sapper attack, we never worried about getting hit by sappers in our hooch. They would have been wasting their time coming to our neighborhood—unless they were on a beer run.

Nevertheless, sappers did occasionally hit the base. On one such night we heard a firefight on Chu Lai's perimeter. As always, defenders beat back the attack. After the smoke cleared, the GIs counting the dead VC found a base barber who'd been killed coming through the wire. By day he cut the hair of Americans at the main Post Exchange; by night he was a VC soldier. During the day he had full access to the base and the trust of his American customers, when, in reality, he was reconnoitering the post for VC attacks. I don't know how many of the five thousand Vietnamese nationals who worked on the post were also VC, but I guess many. It would be difficult, I think, to be neutral in a civil war. One of the most insidious aspects of that war (and there were many) is represented by the machete-wielding cocktail waitress and the midnight-raiding barber. They both worked on Chu Lai for part of their day and fought each other for the remainder—each a warrior on opposing sides of a very long, bloody war and each making a living off the Americans.

Sapper attacks against Chu Lai, at least during the year I spent there, were ineffectual. Soldiers at Fire Support Base (FSB) Mary Ann were not so lucky. Mary Ann was the Americal Division's most westerly outpost, situated on a hill approximately thirty-six miles inland from Chu Lai and thirty-one miles from Laos. There in the early morning hours of March 28, 1971, sappers delivered a devastating, costly blow to the 231 men of 1st Battalion, 46th Infantry (1/46). In *Sappers in the Wire: The Life and Death of Firebase Mary Ann*, Keith William Nolan has written a thorough study of the sapper attack. His description is succinct and insightful:

> What happened on the night of March 27-28, 1971, at a
> remote hilltop fire support base named Mary Ann was the
> U. S. Army's most blatant and humiliating defeat in Vietnam.
> What happened, precisely, was that an enemy sapper com-
> pany slipped and snipped its way through the defensive
> wire around FSB Mary Ann without alerting a single guard
> on a single perimeter bunker. The sappers tripped not one
> of the claymore mines in the wire, nor did they ignite any
> trip flares. Moving with catlike nimbleness, they caught
> the defenders of FSB Mary Ann asleep at the switch. In the
> ensuing chaos [that lasted forty-five to sixty minutes], thirty
> U. S. soldiers were killed and eighty-two wounded. The
> sappers left behind only fifteen of their own dead as they
> disappeared back into the night. What happened at FSB

Mary Ann was as demoralizing as it was unexpected. The war was all but over. The troops were coming home from Vietnam, and the ones who soldiered on knew there were no more reasons to die.

The next day, survivors of the attack began the process of cleaning up: placing the dead in body bags, getting the wounded and dead onto Dust Offs for the journey back to Chu Lai, trying to regain some semblance of control over the hilltop, and disposing of the fifteen dead sappers, five of whom were burned on the post's trash heap—a war crime. At the same time, senior officers in Americal Division Headquarters and at the Military Assistance Command, Vietnam (MACV) began asking how anything like this could happen and who should be held responsible.

On April 1, an infantry captain completed the first report on the attack. In "Informal Investigation—LZ Mary Ann," his conclusions were not much different from the findings of two subsequent reports released over the next few months. He wrote that the attack was a "complete surprise" to Mary Ann's soldiers who were caught "not alert and quite possibly asleep." He said nothing about the burned enemy bodies or the use of drugs by Mary Ann's defenders. The first of those issues came to plague Americal's leadership; the second issue caused my short-lived involvement with the disaster.

Between March 30 and April 30, Americal's inspector general (IG) conducted a more thorough investigation of the attack. He gave his report to the commanding general on May 12. In it he discussed a number of tactical issues regarding perimeter defenses, weather conditions, intelligence reports, and so on. He concluded that the "attack was obviously well planned and quickly executed. In contrast, this was matched by general unpreparedness on the part of the defenders." He, too, never mentioned the burned dead sappers or the possible use of drugs on Mary Ann. He then recommended that the case be closed. In late May, his report was sent to the MACV IG for "information and action deemed necessary."

On June 5, the MACV IG recommended that MACV investigators conduct a more thorough investigation. The next day General Creighton W. Abrams, MACV commander, approved that recommendation. So during the rest of June, MACV IG investigators made three trips to Chu Lai conducting their own inquiry into the disaster. They did not avoid the issue of the burned enemy bodies or of the possible use of drugs on the fire support base.

In the meantime, however, FSB Mary Ann no longer existed. Before the attack, plans had been laid for the 1/46 to abandon Mary Ann and move north to Da Nang. Some of the equipment had already been removed from Mary Ann. The sapper attack had virtually no effect on the decision to close the outpost. On April 24, six days before Americal's IG concluded his investigation and six weeks before MACV IG began his, the flag was hauled down for the last time and Mary Ann remained nothing but a badly scarred hilltop.

MACV investigators focused their inquiry on three areas. First, they were concerned not only that dead enemy soldiers had been burned contrary to the Geneva Convention, but that the Americal officers tended to see the incident as an expedient way to dispose of the dead enemy bodies. Even at that, the investigators concluded that the burning of the bodies could have been "a relatively minor matter which could have been satisfactorily resolved by proper command action." Instead, Americal's leadership had completely ignored the incident, including the IG who didn't even mention it in his report. But that it had occurred was indisputable; the MACV investigators had pictures of the grotesquely deformed, charred bodies. And MACV was in no mood to let Americal leadership slide on this one. After all, on March 29, the day after the burning of the enemy bodies at Mary Ann, Lt William Calley, Americal's most infamous member, had been found guilty of premeditated murder for the My Lai massacre. Publicity on one war crime and a subsequent cover-up by senior officers had been damaging enough; MACV was not about to gift wrap another Americal fuck-up for the news media.

Secondly, the MACV investigators focused on the tactical and leadership problems that resulted in Mary Ann's inadequate defense. Coming to basically the same conclusions as had been found in the two previous reports, they wrote that the sappers had surprised the post "because the FSB was neither prepared for an attack nor alert." But they went further: "The success of the enemy in attacking FSB Mary Ann was a result of a combination of conditions and attitudes on the part of personnel involved, a failure to follow established doctrine for defense and lack of effective functioning of command." The disaster, then, wasn't just the result of common soldiers, the grunts, not doing their jobs, but also of the lack of leadership in the command. As a result of the MACV investigation into these first two issues, a number of Americal officers, including the commanding general of Americal down to the FSB commander and a few staff officers, paid with their careers for the burning of the enemy soldiers' bodies and their "lack of leadership" that allowed the sappers to overrun Mary Ann.

Finally, the MACV investigators looked into the use of drugs on Mary Ann, thinking that drug use by the defenders may have contributed to the disaster. Ultimately, not one word about drugs made it into their final report—and that's probably my fault. What did make it into the report was an unexplained reference to "the growth of permissiveness within the military establishment," but there is no way to know if that is a veiled reference to suspected drug use at Mary Ann.

Whether the MACV investigators heard during their inquiry that soldiers on Mary Ann were using drugs the evening of the attack, or they suspected such use because of the rampant drug problem in the Army in 1971, is not clear. Nevertheless, interrogators focused on drugs when questioning Americal's IG on June 9. "Were there drug problems?" he was asked. He replied, "I know of no drug problem in the 1st of the 46th." It was, at best, a naïve answer or a lie, and the MACV investigators zeroed in on it. Did you even "approach that problem" during the investigation? they asked him. He repeatedly said that although he never specifically asked any of the survivors about drug use at Mary Ann, he had offered to "all soldiers an opportunity to provide me any information they wanted to. I don't remember of any soldier bringing up drugs in relation to Mary Ann." In other words, he didn't ask for and no one voluntarily offered him information about drug use at the outpost.

The MACV investigators were incredulous. Their questioning of the Americal IG indicates that they suspected a cover-up. After all, had not the same man failed to mention the burned enemy bodies? They asked him pointedly if he'd purposefully left out of his report information about drug use at Mary Ann. No, he answered, because no such information had been provided to him. They asked him if he knew that the Army had a drug problem and, if so, how could he ignore it in his investigation? Yes, he knew there was a drug problem in Vietnam, but he didn't see a reason to ask about it. Had he "been remiss to not ask specific questions concerning the drug problems?" He responded, "No," again and again. Finally, the interrogators received an admission of sorts: "Well the drug problem as such never came up," he said, "until

I had just about completed the report." But then it had come by way of an inquiry from higher headquarters (he couldn't remember if it was "a congressional or just an IG inquiry"), and he'd decided that it was related to the drug problem in all of Vietnam, not particularly to Mary Ann. Remarkably, the inquiry had been instigated by information about drug use in Vietnam provided by one of the soldiers later killed during the sapper attack. America's IG deemed that fact a mere coincidence and decided not to pursue the topic. He then closed his report. (An investigator is admittedly under-the-gun to get a report to his commander for action in a timely manner. This fact would be especially true under the circumstances of one of the Army's greatest disasters in the war. America's IG would have incurred sharp criticism if he'd chosen to keep the case open and pursue the drug allegations that came to light just as he was completing his report.)

MACV investigators also questioned Mary Ann's operations officer about drug use at the post. He candidly answered them, "I would be naïve if I said that there was [sic] no drugs or marijuana on the base." However, he said he didn't see it as "a problem at the time." Today because of research by Nolan and others, we know that there were drugs on Mary Ann and that on the night of the attack, many defenders were in drug-induced states of euphoria that were shattered by the sappers. In 1992, one of the survivors told Nolan, "Thirty percent of the guys on the hill were heads. Marijuana, heroin, whatever you wanted." But in 1971, survivors would have been more reticent about Mary Ann's drug problem. The MACV investigators, to their credit, tried to determine to what degree that problem contributed to the disaster at the outpost. But they wanted tangible evidence if they were going to include drug use in their report along with the burning of the bodies, the unpreparedness of the defenders of the FSB, and the lack of leadership. To get that evidence, they asked for a criminal investigation of Mary Ann.

That fact alone must be unique in the annals of American military history. At what other time had military leaders asked a criminal investigator to determine the level of criminal activity that may have contributed to an American base being overrun by the enemy with a resulting 50 percent casualty rate?

One morning in June while the MACV IG was at Chu Lai conducting the investigation, Strawberry called me into his office around 7 or 8 a.m. He told me that sappers had overrun a landing zone (it was really a fire support base) called Mary Ann and that there were 130 or 140 casualties—

he thought, incorrectly I later learned, that all casualties were fatalities. That was the first time I'd heard about an outpost named Mary Ann, and, as far as I knew, the attack there had occurred the night before. As testament to the isolation of those of us in the CID to the rest of the military on Chu Lai, none of us had heard anything about an outpost being overrun until that morning in June. The incident had been a major disaster to Americal, and over two months later we were just hearing about it for the first time. In fact, not until I was researching information for this book did I learn that my trip to Mary Ann occurred well after the attack and more than a month after the outpost had been abandoned.

I don't know why Strawberry picked me for this assignment, but then we never knew how he assigned cases to us. He just did. He told me that there were indications that everyone was stoned when they got overrun and that I needed to go see if I could find any drugs at the site. He said some brass—important brass, not the garden-variety brass that we dealt with every day—would be out there waiting to talk to me. "Get whatever information you can from them," he told me, "then give them a good outbrief when you're done." That was the extent of my briefing from him.

I don't know where he got the information that everyone was stoned, or what he expected me to do with any drugs I might find. However, I knew that the case had generated some high-level interest: in addition to the important brass that I'd meet, he also told me that a helicopter was waiting to fly me out to Mary Ann, and its crew would wait for me to complete my investigation and fly me back to Chu Lai. That was extraordinarily unusual. Whenever we flew to remote sites and back to Chu Lai, we had to beg for a helicopter; we were nothing but hitchhikers. I had a designated helicopter only once during my time in the war and that was on the day I flew to Mary Ann. I knew then that this was not an ordinary case.

I grabbed my briefcase full of blank forms, drug test kits, minifrags, and my grease gun, jumped into my jeep, and drove to the helipad. An idle Huey sat on the pad, its crew obviously waiting on someone. I got out of my jeep, briefcase in hand, and approached one of the door gunners. "I'm Special Agent Skogen," I told him. "I'm supposed to go to Mary Ann. Are you my ride?" "Yes," he said. Then he leaned toward the front where the pilot and co-pilot sat and said, "Our ride's here." Looking back toward me he said, "Crawl in," as he handed me a headset. The engines whined as they wound up to speed.

I knew so little about Mary Ann that I decided to start my investigation right here. I slipped on a headset, adjusted the microphone and asked to no one in particular, "What's going on?" "Don't know," one of the crew members responded. He went on to explain that they'd heard that morning that Mary Ann had been overrun and that they were supposed to give a CID agent a ride out there. "Have any of you been there before?" I asked. None had. If I was relatively clueless about what had happened at Mary Ann, the crew was completely in the dark. Questioning them, even if it was only small talk, wasn't gaining me any information. I settled back for the ride, busying myself getting my grease gun out of the briefcase and jamming two mini-frags into my front pockets, motions that had by now become routine.

It was a beautiful day. A haze blanketed everything below us giving the countryside a gray hue. Green foliage was gray-green; blue water was gray-blue. The morning sun would eventually chase the haze away, but in the meantime Vietnam looked like a beautiful woman photographed by a *Playboy* photographer using a special filter lens—her blemishes were all safely hidden from view.

Leaving Chu Lai we flew over low, undulating sand dunes, leaving the ocean to our rear. Directly off Chu Lai, rice paddies checkered the countryside. Song (River) Trau, a broad, flat, muddy stream, meandered out of the hills to the west, around rice paddies, and dumped into Song An Tan. Fishing weirs—quite literally, fish-catching fences, looking from the air like large Vs—sat in the middle of both rivers. The weirs and paddies represented the basic native diet of the area: fish and rice. Eventually, the waters of these two rivers and dozens of tiny tributaries that likewise meanered around rice paddies and through the flooded lowlands of the coastal area, emptied into An Hoa Bay on the north end of Chu Lai where naval vessels supplied the post with the materiels of war.

Upon leaving Chu Lai by helicopter, we quickly traveled over the lowlands and entered the mountainous region. These were not fresh, young mountains with rugged, raw, naked rock edges like I'd seen in the Rocky Mountains. Instead we flew over old, rounded mountain tops covered with lush vegetation: a green jungle canopy blanketed Vietnam's mountains. Slow, muddy rivers meandered their way through the mountains toward the ocean. We generally flew lower than the mountains on each side of us as the pilot followed the rivers and valleys. At times, he turned the helicopter toward a mountain—

a hill, really—flew over it, then dropped back down to a new river or valley below and began to follow it.

The zig-zag flying, a pattern that made a helicopter a less inviting target, made the thirty-six miles seem much farther and gave me time to think about the case. All I knew is what Strawberry had told me, and none of that made any sense. From an investigator's point of view, there didn't appear to be an obvious reason to go to Mary Ann. If a base was overrun, that sounded like a tactical military problem to me. On the other hand, if everyone was stoned, as Strawberry had said, I could see why someone might ask for a criminal investigation. But if everyone died during the attack, what good would it do? And, to my knowledge, nobody was in custody, no drugs had been found, and no informant had ratted on his buddies. "Go out there and see if you can find some drugs" seemed like a pretty strange thing to be doing at an overrun military outpost. Of course, whether this assignment made any sense to me didn't really matter, so I told myself to stop analyzing the case, enjoy the trip out to Mary Ann, and see what I found when I got there.

"There she is," a crew member said. I slid along the floor toward the open door to get a better look. Mary Ann was nothing but a scarred mountain top. The oblong scar ran five hundred meters (about five-and-a-half football fields) across the mountain top from northwest to southeast and was nearly 150 meters wide. It looked like an old swaybacked horse. The northwest and southeast sides loomed over the depressed center. The north side of Mary Ann overlooked the Song Tranh, a river running near the base of the mountain. The north side also was very steep and rocky. The south side, however, sloped gradually down to a treed valley. Skeletal fingers of denuded trees—the result of Agent Orange, I thought—formed a ghostly Army surrounding the base about one hundred meters from the perimeter line—a trench that almost completely circumnavigated the hilltop (according to the IG report, the trench connected 80 percent of the perimeter). A large resupply helipad dominated the center of the post; a smaller helipad lay on the far east end. As we approached the base, I saw two Hueys orbiting in a pattern that put them straight across from each other at the same altitude over the base perimeter. They were offering protection for those who were on Mary Ann. Two more Hueys sat on the small helipad. We landed on the large resupply pad in the middle of the swayback.

As we did, I saw a small group of men standing directly north of the resupply pad. They were looking down the steep embankment to the river and seemed to be uninterested in our landing. I picked up my briefcase and grease gun and stepped out of the Huey. The door gunner said, "We'll be right here," as the pilot shut down the engine. I felt a bit like a dignitary having my own helicopter.

A junior officer left the group near the north edge and walked to meet me. There was nothing cordial about our meeting at the edge of the helipad, no handshakes, no good mornings. He simply asked me if I was a CID agent. I said yes. "Come with me," he ordered and led me to the group. I now saw that they were all brass. As I walked up, they were talking in hushed tones, but by the time I got to them, they stopped talking. The mood was palpably serious. Everyone deferred to one of the colonels, so I showed him my credentials and said, "I'm Special Agent Skogen, CID detachment at Chu Lai." He never identified himself to me, but I'd been told he was the MACV IG. He did almost all the talking for the group. In fact, the only other officers I spoke to in that group were the junior officer that met me at the helipad and an Australian officer.

The Australian officer is memorable because he was, well, so Australian. He wore combat fatigues, sleeves characteristically rolled up, and a bush hat with one side of the brim pinned up. In typical law enforcement efficiency, I wrote a field interview card on him (name, birthdate, description)—why on him, I don't know; his was the only card I wrote that day. He gave me his weight in stones and then converted that to pounds for me. Most peculiar though was what he said when I asked him, "Who made the discovery that this site had been overrun?" He said he had. Today I know that was a lie. The attack had been a pitched battle, and a Nighthawk gunship and artillery from a nearby fire support base had helped fend off the attackers. There was no "discovery" to be made. Everyone that needed to know was well aware that the base had been overrun. Nevertheless, I dutifully wrote on his field interview card that he'd discovered the disaster.

The colonel told me the firebase had been overrun by VC sappers and that the defenders had suffered heavy casualties. He also said he'd received information that the soldiers had been under the influence of drugs at the time of the attack. Specifically, he said he had heard rumors that a number of the perimeter guards had been smoking marijuana. Then he said, "We have looked around here and we don't see any drugs, but then we're not the experts, you are. Take a look around and see if you can find any drugs."

"OK, sir," I said, "but first I'd like to talk to someone who was here when the base was overrun to see where I should start my search."

"There isn't anyone here to talk to," the colonel retorted.

"Well, then," I asked. "Could you tell me where you got your information about drug use here?"

"Just search," he responded impatiently, "and let me know if you find any drugs."

I turned and walked fifteen yards away from the group and looked around. The place was obviously abandoned. The only people on the site were the gaggle of brass, the crews of three helicopters on the ground, two helicopters orbiting overhead, and me. Gaping holes marked the locations of where there would have been dug-in CONEX containers, but they were all now gone. Bunkers scattered around the base and on the perimeter remained intact. But, there wasn't a flagpole or a piece of artillery. There weren't any clothes, ruck sacks, or bunks. It looked as if someone had taken a giant vacuum cleaner and gone over the top of the place sucking off everything loose or manmade. The bunkers and sandbags that remained would, in time, become part of the natural contour of the hilltop. Other than that, the place was clean.

By now the apprehension about this case that had been bothering me since leaving Strawberry's office became vividly real. Here I stood on an overrun fire support base, obviously stripped of anything that had made it a fire support base, and I was supposed to conduct a narcotics investigation. No witnesses, no subjects, no suspects, no contraband. "This kind of investigation might make sense to the IG," I thought, "but this ain't making any fucking sense to me."

I walked to the trench at the perimeter. The only thing I had to go on was the colonel's comment that he'd heard that the perimeter guards were high. So I stepped down into the trench and began following it. The trench was only broken in a couple of locations on the south side where roads led off the site. At some spots, the trench was only knee high; at others it came up to my chest. The trench connected twenty-two bunkers constructed of planks and logs and protected with sandbags. Most of the bunkers were still intact. I walked into each one and looked around. After I finished walking the trench, I started walking around the fire support base, looking at the ground, looking into bunkers, following obvious trails leading to and fro. I walked all over that base.

During my search I saw drug paraphernalia: discarded, empty heroin vials (not in the quantities I saw on Chu Lai, but vials nevertheless) and a few hash pipes for smoking marijuana or hash. The most common type of hash pipe in Vietnam, and the kind I found on Mary Ann, was a commercially-made pipe, hand carved from some sort of soft stone. They were about three inches long, one inch wide, and shaped like wedges. A pipe had an airhole on one end and a small pipe bowl, about the size of half a small marble, on the other.

All the pipes I found on Mary Ann had charcoal and residue in their bowls, and they would have tested positive for drugs if I'd tested them. I found the paraphernalia lying on the ground and shoved into cracks or crevices between sandbags or planks. In a couple of cases, I found paraphernalia lying on a shelf in a bunker. By the time I'd finished, I'd found enough drug paraphernalia to be sure that some troops on Mary Ann used drugs; how much they used or how many of them used drugs, I couldn't say. Nevertheless, that wasn't what the IG had asked me to do. Rather, he asked me to find dope, and I hadn't found any. My impression was that he wanted to see hard dope, a bag of weed, a joint, a vial of heroin, an opium button. But I didn't find any vials with heroin in them; I didn't find any bags of marijuana or marijuana cigarettes; I didn't find any opium buttons.

To me, it was pretty black and white: he asked me to find drugs and I didn't find any. I didn't pick up one piece of paraphernalia because I had no way to connect it to anyone. I would be confiscating contraband for no good purpose other than to clutter our evidence locker, and I could do that at Chu Lai, if that's what I wanted to do. If I had found dope, the consequences of finding it would have been the same: What would I do with it? To whom would I connect it for a criminal prosecution? That, too, I thought was ridiculous, but at least I would give it to the IG, because that's what he'd asked for.

My inspection—for lack of a better term, because this certainly wasn't an investigation—of the base lasted about forty-five minutes. When done, I walked back over to the cadre of officers that had remained clustered at the same location north of the resupply pad. The IG said, "Well, did you find any drugs?"

"No, I didn't find any," I said. He didn't ask about my finding any paraphernalia, so that subject didn't come up. Then he asked me if I'd be writing a report. "No," I said, "there's nothing to write about."

"Thank you very much," he said as he turned to converse in hushed tones with his group.

The same junior officer who'd escorted me to the IG now pointed back to the helipad and walked in silence with me back to the helicopter. I climbed into the Huey and said to the pilot, "I'm ready." As the crew started up the helicopter, I watched the junior officer walk back to the IG's group. As we lifted off from the helipad, the gaggle of officers on the ground started making its way toward the two waiting helicopters on the east end of the base.

The silence on the ride back to Chu Lai was only interrupted when the crew talked to each other about the flight—there was no small talk. No one asked me what I'd accomplished, and I didn't offer any information to them. We landed around 1 p.m. I drove straight to the CID building and walked into Strawberry's office. He looked up from his desk and asked, "Did you find anything out there?"

"Nope," I said shaking my head, "nothing out there at all." I wanted to ask him what the hell was going on, but decided not to. I figured he knew as little about the whole thing as I did, and I'd actually been at the scene. So I never asked any questions, none were asked of me. I never wrote a report, and Strawberry never asked for one. I could have confiscated all the paraphernalia I found and written a report on it, but that would have served no purpose. So other than having a designated helicopter for a day trip to the scene of one of America's major disasters, I'd accomplished nothing that day.

In retrospect, I still find the whole case amazingly strange. I think that if the IG really wanted to know if Mary Ann's defenders used drugs and if that drug use contributed to the disaster, he would have cooperated more with my investigation. To begin with, he offered me no useful information about the attack on the base. The morning I flew out there, I didn't know when the attack had occurred, the number of casualties, or the location of any witnesses. And I was not given any of this information by the IG. When I asked for witnesses, he told me there weren't any; just go search for drugs, he'd ordered me. When I tried to find out what had happened, the Australian officer simply lied to me. More importantly, when the IG told me to look for drugs, he didn't tell me that the base had been deactivated a month before and that all equipment had been relocated to Da Nang and elsewhere. If he'd told me that, I don't know what I would have done, but at least I would have known that my part in this affair was meaningless: why look for drugs at a stripped site? Given all these facts, it certainly didn't make sense for the IG to ask for a criminal investigation at the site of a military disaster, and then obstruct that investigation. If I had found drugs there two months after the attack, what was the IG going to do with them? How could he possibly draw a conclusion about what happened on the night of the attack if I'd found drugs on the site two months after the attack and a month after the site had been abandoned?

Was I negligent in not telling the IG that I found drug paraphernalia? I don't know, but I can't see that anyone could draw any conclusions from such a discovery either. After all, the presence of drugs or drug paraphernalia found so long after the attack wouldn't prove that anyone was high that night. The only conclusive evidence of drug use on that night would have been toxicology reports from the dead defenders' autopsies and blood and urine from survivors. But because the MACV IG got involved in the case so long after the attack had occurred, the bodies were all shipped back to the States and most were already buried. There wasn't anyone at that point that would exhume the country's fallen soldiers to find out if they were high the night they died. Moreover, all the survivors were dispersed around Vietnam, if not back to the States.

The more relevant question is whether the IG really wanted to know the truth about drug use on Mary Ann. Was my presence at the site and his obstruction of my investigation simply a ruse? My visit there would allow him, after all, to say that he'd had an "expert" search for drugs at Mary Ann and had, therefore, thoroughly investigated allegations that drugs were involved in the disaster. Because the outpost had been deactivated and stripped long before I arrived, I strongly suspect I didn't tell the IG anything he didn't already know.

I went into the bush dozens of times during my year in Vietnam, but the trip to Mary Ann is among the most memorable. Standing at the site of a military disaster—never mind the circumstances of my visit—was a sobering reminder of what happens in combat. I took other trips into the bush however that were far more dangerous and put me much closer to the shooting war.

I didn't particularly like going into the bush. Sleeping in my air-conditioned hooch and showering every morning were important to me. I also knew it was idiotic for somebody to go out there in civilian clothes, no protective gear, and untrained in combat. However, I told Strawberry, "If you need somebody to go out into the bush, I'll go." I volunteered because I knew nobody else liked going either. But, more importantly, I knew that someone had to go; that was unavoidable. I will admit, though, that going into the bush did add another dimension to the adrenaline rush that comes with police work. So when a case required someone to go into the field, I'd step forward.

I normally went into the bush if that was the only place I could interview a witness in a serious case. (I never interviewed suspects in the bush. I wanted them on my turf, not theirs.) I didn't go into the field to investigate someone for petty theft and certainly not for narcotics violations. Instead, when I flew into the bush I was investigating a murder, an attempted murder, or maybe even assault with a deadly weapon. So when I was working such a case and learned that a witness was in the bush, I would find out how long it would be before I could interview him without going into the field. If he was scheduled to return to Chu Lai within a day or two, I made a note to myself to go to his unit when he got back. But if it would be more than a few days before his return, I made plans to go out to the bush to interview him.

That was a two-part process. First I made arrangements with the unit to interview the soldier on a given day, say a day or so in the future, at a specific location. The unit ensured that he would be available at that day and place. I have no idea how the unit did that, but it did. When I showed up in the bush, my witnesses were always there for me to interview.

After making arrangements with the unit, I contacted the helicopter operations center. As I've mentioned before, I hitchhiked to get out to the bush (other than to Mary Ann when I had a dedicated helicopter). So once I knew when and where the unit would give me access to a soldier, I gave that information to the helicopter planners who'd let me know if they could provide me a ride. Oftentimes I'd find out I couldn't get a ride on the date and to the location I needed, so I would go back to the unit and come up with an alternate plan. Sometimes it would take me two or three contacts between the unit and the helicopter planners before we all agreed on a time and place for me to fly out to interview a witness.

I usually rode on helicopters ferrying supplies out to a fire support base or a landing zone. That meant that I'd ride out with nothing but supplies, a few new cherries, and me in the back of the Huey. While the helicopter crew unloaded the supplies, I'd conduct my interview. If I was lucky, I'd be done and ready to go back to Chu Lai in the same helicopter. If I wasn't so lucky, I'd hitch a ride on another helicopter heading back later.

Occasionally, a witness was literally in the bush, away from even the fire support base or landing zone. In that event, I'd find a helicopter scheduled to fly approximately over the location I needed to go to as it traveled from one point to the other. If I found such a flight, that helicopter crew literally dropped me off, rotors still churning, at some grid coordinates where I'd find the witness waiting to be interviewed. Sometimes the pilot would tell me, "We'll be back in forty-five minutes. If you're ready then, let us know." I'd conduct my interview and take a statement or two, keeping an eye on my wristwatch. In forty-five minutes I'd be ready to go. If I didn't have such an arrangement with the pilot that dropped me off, getting back to Chu Lai became pretty chancy. I needed to find a helicopter crew whose flight path took them near my location so they could pick me up on their way back to Chu Lai.

Frankly, getting picked up out in the bush, away from any sort of base, could be pretty exciting. It started when I asked the radioman to call in a helicopter for me. Once he found one, a couple of grunts would go with me to a treeless clearing that served as the patrol's landing zone. The clearing usually contained four- or five-foot elephant grass, waving slightly in the breeze. We'd crouch together at the edge of the clearing waiting on the helicopter. The grunts would, of course, be dressed for war: camouflaged jungle fatigues, flak vests, boots, helmets, and M-16s. I was decidedly out of place in my colonial administrator garb, but the grease gun made me feel less vulnerable than I really was. Usually after a short wait, I'd hear the whop, whop of a helicopter off in the distance. Sometimes it would come in high and drop straight down on to the landing zone. Other times, it came in low, following a valley or stream nearby. Regardless, they weren't staying long so I had to be ready to get in. As the helicopter got close to the ground, I'd sprint from our hiding place toward it. When I reached the helicopter, I threw my briefcase in, and put my foot on the skid. The door gunner would reach out, grab me by the arm, and yank me in. Seconds later we were in the air, leaving behind the grunts shaking their heads, "Stupid motherfucker."

That a CID agent's visit to the bush engendered the ire of the troops is an understatement. The antagonism ran deep and was always near the surface. Few soldiers bothered to hide their disdain for me on any of the visits to their sites in the bush. After all, once in the bush, soldiers were beyond the pale of acceptable conduct expected of them on the large bases such as Chu Lai. From their point of view, the Army's attempt to impose discipline over them only applied on the large support bases. In the bush, different rules applied. Survival overshadowed military courtesies; common sense trumped military protocol. In such an environment, it's not surprising that a CID agent in civilian clothes carrying a briefcase full of forms on a mission to interview a witness to a crime that a fellow soldier might pay for didn't receive a warm welcome.

When I stepped out of the Huey, I stepped into a hostile environment. The deeper into the bush, the deeper the hostility. A helicopter landing at a large fire support base, for example, was not an unusual occurrence. If I stepped out of a helicopter ferrying supplies to that base, soldiers saw me as just an annoyance. However, if I caught a ride on a helicopter that made a stop at a temporary landing zone near a patrol's jungle camp out in the middle of God-knows-where for the sole purpose of dropping me off, I was more than an annoyance; I was a threat—not directly because of my job, but because the helicopter brought unnecessary attention to the patrol's location. That attention might attract VC or NVA patrols that, under normal circumstances, passed by. The troops believed—and in retrospect, probably correctly—that I endangered all their lives by coming out into the bush and having a helicopter drop me off in an elephant-grassed clearing. But because I was investigating serious crimes, I believed—and Army leadership believed—that such risks were acceptable.

The irony in this is that while I had absolutely nothing to offer these troops—I represented, after all, nothing more than the imposition of Army rules over them when they didn't think Army rules should apply—I completely depended upon them for my personal safety from the moment I arrived in the bush until I headed back to Chu Lai. A less reciprocal relationship could not have existed.

Usually, I arrived in the bush with relatively little excitement: the helicopter would land, I'd disembark, the helicopter would take off, and a lieutenant or a senior non-commissioned officer would meet me at the landing site. Regardless of what the troops thought of me, the cooperation of the patrol's senior leader was absolutely vital for me to get access to and, I hoped, cooperation from the witness. Although the senior leader of a patrol could help me with those issues, he couldn't stop the open animosity.

As we walked into the patrol's camp, lounging troops—dirty, grungy, sweaty, tired, and patrol-weary troops bristled at my arrival.

"What's the fucking pig want, Top?" a soldier sneered, glaring right at me.

"None of your fucking business," the senior NCO invariably responded.

"Hey, Smitty," another soldier said. "The fucking pigs finally caught up to you."

"Yeh," Smitty responded grabbing his own crotch. "Motherfucker can suck my dick!"

And the lounging GIs laughed. I heard the same jokes, the same comments, and the same barbs so many times. The patrol leader and I continued threading our way deeper into the jungle, past poncho and foliage lean-tos, past the radioman and his equipment that would be my ticket back home, and, occasionally, past a small field kitchen. Finally, the patrol leader pointed out a troop, said, "Here's your guy," and turned and walked away.

If the other troops had been hostile toward me, the witness—the reason I was out there in the first place—made them look friendly. The normal antagonism that a soldier about to be made to "rat" on a buddy might feel toward an investigator was multiplied ten-fold sitting out in a jungle in the middle of a war. Whatever I wanted to question a witness about was, in his mind, pure chicken shit. So the first obstacle I had to overcome was his attitude. I learned very early in the war that being kind and reasonable with a witness in the bush garnered no cooperation. I also learned early on that troops in the bush possessed a remarkable degree of camaraderie. No one I ever interviewed in the bush wanted me to drag him away from his buddies while they were still out on patrol. So once I identified myself and told the soldier why I was there (he usually knew, of course), I told him, "You either talk to me here and cooperate with me now or you're going back to Chu Lai with me today. Right now, I'll walk back to the radioman and ask for a helicopter for the two of us. So which is it: here or back at Chu Lai?"

"I'm not going to be some fucking pussy and leave, so let's get it over with," was the usual response.

The witness would then settle down to answer questions and write a statement for me. In thirty minutes to an hour, I would be done. I then asked the radioman for a helicopter ride back to Chu Lai.

Of the patrol members, the radioman harbored the least hostility toward me. He, too, considered me a liability in the bush and wanted to get rid of me as much as the others. But he could become a folk hero of sorts by getting rid of me as quickly as possible. The longer he took to get me a ride, the more he suffered the barbs of his own buddies. Getting rid of me quickly made him a hero for the day.

Only rarely did I take a witness back with me. If I did, I relied on the senior officer or enlisted man to get him to cooperate with me on the trip back to Chu Lai. Fortunately, that didn't occur often; when it did, the tension was palpable. That I didn't get fragged trying to do it is a testament to the senior patrol leaders who kept everything under control when the potential for violence lay just beneath the surface.

I usually returned to Chu Lai with nothing more than a statement or two and some field notes. I'd combine those with the physical evidence already at the CID office and maybe the results of a crime lab analysis. As with any criminal investigation, sometimes the trips into the bush were productive and helped solve crimes; other times the crimes remained unsolved. But productive or not, by and large, going into the field, conducting interviews there, returning to Chu Lai, and compiling the reports was uneventful. Other times, however, quite the opposite was true.

Helicopters were the VC's and NVA's favorite targets. They flew relatively slowly and close to the ground; they could be shot down with small arms ground fire; and, when they landed or took off, they were sitting ducks. So it's not surprising that the VC and NVA shot at them at every chance. To counter the small arms ground fire, helicopter pilots landed and took off quickly—no idling around in the bush for those boys. Each pilot also had a sliding, steel shield that he could pulled into place on his vulnerable side—the one closest to the outside of the helicopter. The shields were high enough to offer some protection, but low enough so pilots could peer over them and see where they were flying. Helicopters also carried their own firepower. As a deterrent to ground fire, two flak-vested, helmeted door gunners armed with M-60s strafed in the direction of any small arms fire coming up from the jungle below.

What all this meant to me is that I expected we might be shot at landing or taking off from a remote site (ground fire was not as common at larger fire support bases or landing zones). If there would be shooting, I also expected it to be sporadic, maybe only a few shots from a single sniper, not a full-fledged firefight—the "mad minutes" Vietnam veterans talk about. Getting shot at normally didn't happen, but the possibility for it existed. Although I didn't dwell on the chance of taking hostile fire—I was too busy thinking about my investigation—I prepared myself for it.

So when landing, I mentally prepared myself to jump out of the helicopter, aim in the general direction of the enemy fire, and burp my grease gun a few times as I ran for cover. I wasn't trained for any of this, but I knew that if I had the grease gun and if I stood there with it draped over my back doing nothing, somebody would be screaming at me, "What the fuck are you standing there for?" So even though I wasn't a combat soldier, I knew enough that if I had a weapon and someone was shooting at me, I ought to shoot back. I never saw an enemy while landing; I never got hit. During the one time I did have to fire during a landing, I doubt that I hit anyone; and, to my knowledge, no other Americans ever got wounded during one of these landings I was on. For the most part, it certainly wasn't very glamorous.

One time, however, stands out in my mind as an exception to my normal arrival in the bush.

It began when Strawberry assigned me an assault with a deadly weapon case. I called a witness's unit and learned he was out on patrol and wouldn't be standing down for a couple of weeks. We went through the normal procedure of finding out when and where I could meet his patrol. Luck smiled on me: a Huey was heading out the next day with a load of supplies for his unit. Next morning I drove to the helipad. By the time the crew chief finished loading the Huey, there remained barely room on the floor of the aircraft for me. I squeezed myself in between stacks of boxes full of rations and eight ten-gallon, clear plastic bladders full of water. Thirty minutes later we were descending toward an elephant-grassed clearing in a small valley.

Just before we landed, the right-side door gunner opened up with a salvo of rounds aimed at a treed rise off his side of the helicopter. I looked out at the rise and saw a couple of muzzle flashes just inside the tree line. By then the wind from the rotors had pushed the tall grass down, and I saw ten soldiers crouched down on the ground, all of them firing toward the same tree line. When the helicopter landed, the crew chief started feverishly tossing the boxes and bladders out the left door.

I grabbed my briefcase and grease gun and jumped out the left door, too. As I'd practiced mentally many times before, I crouched down and shot in the same direction as everyone else. Just then a lieutenant, the platoon leader, walked over to me and began screaming at me. At first I remained crouched on the ground looking up at him in disbelief. He wasn't the least bit interested in the shooting, but continued to scream at me. I couldn't hear him, so I too stood up. Now the two of us stood face-to-face, wind from the churning rotor blades tearing at our hair and clothes, completely oblivious to the din of the weapons firing near us.

"We've been out here thirty fucking days," the lieutenant screamed at me, "and this is all the goddamn water you've brought us!" I had that look on my face that universally says, "What the fuck are you talking about?" He screamed again about the thirty days and so little water, adding, "You better get me some more water or your ass is mine!"

"Just a minute, lieutenant," I yelled back over the noise. "Wait a goddamn minute! I didn't have a fucking thing to do with these supplies you're getting."

"I want more fucking water!" the lieutenant screamed again.

"Lieutenant," I yelled. "I ain't got nothing to do with your fucking water!" The lieutenant was pissing me off. I could have been standing on Any Street in Anywhere USA: gone were the gunfire, the elephant grass, and the other troops. It was just this shithead and I arguing about how much water the helicopter had delivered to him.

"All I did was catch a ride on this fucking helicopter," I indignantly yelled. "I wasn't there when it was loaded. When I got to the helicopter, all this shit was on it. I didn't have anything to do with any of this," I said gesturing toward the supplies being thrown onto the ground. But he wasn't listening, just screaming. All this time he had his M-16 in his right hand, hanging at a forty-five degree angle pointed toward the ground. At one point he started leveling his M-16 and I thought, "This son-of-a-bitch is going to shoot me!" About that time, the helicopter lifted off and the elephant grass sprang back up. The lieutenant lowered his rifle, stopped screaming, and just looked at me.

We now both stood in chest-high grass; the sounds of the helicopter faded away and the shooting stopped. Whoever had been in the trees up on the rise was now dead or gone. Soldiers all around us stood up and began slinging their rifles. The lieutenant turned away from me, looked over his troops—counting to make sure everyone was on his feet, and said, "Let's get the shit picked up and get it back to camp." Soldiers grabbed boxes and bladders, and I followed them from the clearing to their jungle camp.

With the help of the lieutenant, I completed my interview of the witness. Not once during my stay at his camp did the lieutenant mention the water or his haranguing of me about it, and I decided not to bring it up, fearing that I might set him off again. Only later did I suspect that he knew all along that I had nothing to do with the water, but he needed someone to vent his frustration on. I was just a target of opportunity. He and his troops were tired, and he believed he'd been let down by some support puke who'd short-changed him on the amount of water he received that day. And, in turn, I think he felt that he'd let his troops down, too: he didn't have the water he'd promised them. Under such circumstances, why not take out your frustrations on the guy in civilian clothes that just climbed out of the helicopter that was supposed to bring you so much more water? In some bizarre way, it made sense. This strange trip into the bush ended with the lieutenant telling his radioman to get me a helicopter. I climbed into the helicopter and returned to Chu Lai without any of the excitement that had marked my arrival in the bush that morning.

Dismembered corpses, mortar bombardments, sapper attacks, and trips into the bush always reminded me that the war I waged against drugs and other crime in Vietnam was but a small part of a much larger picture: Vietnam's civil war. The GIs who violated the laws that we in the CID enforced were also the soldiers on the ground sent to Vietnam to fight an Asian army that their president had decided was an enemy to the United States and, of course, all freedom loving people of the world. The most sobering reminder of that fact occurred as I climbed into Hueys heading back to Chu Lai and found myself sitting on the floor next to one or two dead GIs. Sometimes they were zipped up in body bags; sometimes, when there hadn't been time to put them into bags after snatching their bodies out of the jungle, they weren't. There were times when, aside from the crew, I was the only living soul in a helicopter full of soldiers.

Those bodies not in the bags were, of course, the most haunting. I've seen these young men (most deaths in Vietnam occurred to soldiers between the ages of nineteen and twenty-one) when it didn't even look as if they should be dead because there was nothing wrong with them. I couldn't see any physical trauma on them. There were no bullet holes, no blood. They'd died from concussions. Other times, the corpses were terribly bloodied and disfigured.

Regardless, the same emotional detachment that served me well when working around the dead victims of violent crimes assisted me in the back of those helicopters, too. I could as easily detach myself from the dead young GIs taking up space with me in a Huey as I could from the suffering of a victim of some terrible crime. As I sat with those dead men, I never became philosophical about the obvious loss to our country, about the meaninglessness of the war, about the inhumanity we were perpetuating upon these people and them upon us, or about the tears that would be shed back in the States over these lost lives. I figured we, these dead GIs and I, were soldiers, and all of us did the job Uncle Sam paid us to do. On this particular day, the dead GIs' numbers had come up; it was their day to die. My number might come up the next time I jumped off a helicopter in the bush somewhere, or the next time I entered a hooch full of dickheads and one fired a full clip from his M-16 at me, or the next time I drove my jeep up QL1 and hit a land mine buried inches below the surface. But I never dwelt on those possibilities, because if it happened to me, as it had happened to them that day, someone else would be riding in the back of a helicopter with some dead guy dressed in civilian clothes. No, I didn't dwell on it. After all, I was having too much fun.

CHAPTER 9   YOU NUMBER 10 GI!

The 1958 bestselling novel *The Ugly American* portrayed America's dip-
lomats and military leaders as grotesquely arrogant and morally bank-
rupt representatives to Southeast Asia. Their attitudes and values—or
lack thereof—scuttled America's attempts to cultivate goodwill and
friendship in a fictionalized Asian country (an only thinly veiled
Vietnam) threatened by communist insurgents. The communists were
far better attuned to the needs and desires of the people of this country. The winner in this contest, of course, would be the communists.
As history showed, *The Ugly American* foresaw the fate of the region
with incredible accuracy.

The ugly American attitudes in the real Vietnam reflected hubris
at the highest levels in government. President Lyndon Johnson could
not accept the idea that his soldiers might lose to an enemy in "that
raggedy-ass little fourth-rate country." Consequently, contempt for
the Vietnamese flowed from the highest office in Washington down to
the country's representatives in Vietnam. And, as every good soldier
knows, shit rolls downhill to where the common soldier stands. There
the shit splats on his boots, putrefies, and petrifies. The result was
an attitude toward the Vietnamese that permeated the rank and file
and defined the character of interaction between American GIs and
the Vietnamese people. At that lowest level of Vietnamese-American
interaction, however, we were no longer "ugly Americans"; we were
simply "number 10 GIs."

At the GI level, the most common interplay between Vietnamese and
Americans was sexual. Therefore, most interaction occurred between
GIs and Vietnamese women. Other than our ARVN interpreter, a few
ARVN policemen, and a village chief now and then, I rarely came into
contact with Vietnamese men. Although I saw them driving around on
the post, working at the exchange, and doing menial labor, I had few real
contacts with them. For the military advisor in the field, the experience
would be different. However, for most GIs and for me, interaction with
Vietnamese was limited to women.

Our sexual drive was the root of our desire to be with Vietnamese women. We were young men with raging hormones. Vietnamese women were the way, then, to satisfy our sexual urges. It was a pure and simple case of sexual exploitation. What these women wanted in return from the soldiers had nothing to do with sexual gratification. It wasn't even a desire to be needed, some sort of psychological satisfaction. No, it was much more practical than that. While GIs exploited Vietnamese women sexually, the women exploited the GIs financially.

The women operated on an economic hierarchy based on what each woman wanted out of her sexual relations with a soldier. At the bottom of that hierarchy resided the 50-piaster (spoken of as "50P") whores. For the equivalent of thirty-three cents per customer, they performed fellatio, had sexual intercourse, or participated in whatever acts they had in their sexual repertoire. Next up the hierarchy were the women who hoped to entice soldiers to buy them material goods— black market goods—from the post exchange, or to order something for them from a mail-order catalog. Daily sex for a week might get them a new refrigerator, a stereo, maybe some new clothes. Sears. Roebuck and Company would be amazed to learn that so many sexual encounters in Vietnam began when a Vietnamese woman asked a GI, "You have Sears Roebuck?" They never asked about Montgomery Ward or any other mail-order company, just Sears Roebuck.

In response to that question, I always said, "No, but I tell you what, I can order one. I can have one sent from the States and you can order anything you want." That would work for a while, but I never did order a catalog or buy anything out of the exchange for one of them. My method was to promise them anything and enjoy the sex. Once a woman figured out that I'd lied to her, she'd yell, "You number 10 GI!"— the worst insult a Vietnamese woman could hurl at a GI, an insult with unknown origins in the misty past. The closest translation would be "You're an asshole." If she called someone a "Number 1 GI," it meant he was a great guy. No one ever called me a Number 1 GI, but many girls called me a Number 10 GI. When they said it, it came out sounding like "You Number 10 Quadi" because, I think, they tried to pronounce GI as a word. Anyway, after a girl figured out that I wasn't going to get her a Sears Roebuck catalog, she'd yell, "You Number 10 Quadi!" stomp out of my hooch, find another GI and say, "You have Sears Roebuck?"

The brass ring for the Vietnamese woman who pleasured the GIs— the woman at the top of the hierarchy—was to find a soldier who'd take her back to America as a war bride. She'd have a sexual union with the right GI, get him to fall in love with her, marry him, then head for the United States, leaving a life of war and poverty behind. Phrases such as "You marry me GI? Take me home? Take me to OOSA? Oh, I love you too much," meant she was looking for the brass ring. "Yeah baby, I'll marry you," I'd tell her. "I love you too much, too." Of course, I never married or intended to marry any of them. "You number 10 Quadi," each would yell at me as she stomped out of my hooch, only to find another soldier: "You marry me GI?"

My perception was that a woman did not remain in only one level of the hierarchy, but moved up or down it depending upon her age, the men she met, or her own personal ambitions. So while we were exploiting the Vietnamese women only for the sex they provided us, they were trying to use us for any financial gain that sex would garner them.

The majority of GIs found themselves confined to Chu Lai for most of their tour in the war. The 50P whore who had a job as a hooch maid might accommodate one of these soldiers. However, if a GI was lucky enough to be allowed off post—for example, a truck driver delivering supplies, he could pick up a 50P whore, have her crawl into the back of his truck, cover her with a tarp, and drive back onto Chu Lai. That's how he'd smuggle her on base. The driver would get first-customer rights with her, and then he'd pass her to his buddies or keep her for himself for however long she chose to remain on post.

There was a risk involved in this undertaking because to bring an unauthorized Vietnamese on the post was a security violation. If caught, he could be punished. But the rewards were so great and the chance of being caught so slim that soldiers never minded providing local women to their buddies. There were over five thousand Vietnamese day laborers on Chu Lai, but at any given time, there were dozens of 50P whores circulating through the barracks and hooches. Some of these women went undetected for weeks at a time while they had sex with troops.

Some GIs weren't so lucky. Seventeen-year-old Lat Thi Truong, known as "Tina" by the troops of 39th Engineering Battalion at Quang Ngai City south of Chu Lai, had been sneaked onto one of the battalion's sites. She apparently was doing a robust business when, during a lull in activity, two soldiers decided to show her a claymore mine. The weapon, particularly the clacker-triggering device, intrigued her. As she leaned over to place the clacker on the ground, she squeezed it, sending an electrical charge to the mine. Fortunately, the anti-personnel pellets in the claymore blew harmlessly away from her and the two GIs, but rocks and other ground debris kicked up by the explosion struck the two Americans. While they were dusted off by helicopter to the hospital at Chu Lai to be treated for lacerations, the MPs escorted the uninjured Tina off the military installation.

A more common means for GIs to obtain sexual gratification than sneaking 50P whores on the post was to go to one of the massage parlors. At these parlors, one got a massage or anything else piasters could buy. The girls who worked there charged a set rate for a massage, and then added on sexual acts for a few piasters more. The parlors had the official sanction of the Army; the prostitution did not. But a senior officer had to be an idiot to think that he could put pretty Vietnamese girls in a massage parlor, send in horny GIs who stripped down stark-naked to get a massage, and then not have sex acts take place. The French who preceded us in that part of the world opened brothels and gave soldiers chits redeemable for sexual pleasures at those establishments. In typical American fashion, however, the US Army refused to sanction such whorehouses and instead opened massage parlors and pretended that the women working at them offered the soldiers massages and nothing more. Nevertheless, massage parlors lacked the risks of sneaking a whore onto the post. So soldiers frequenting the massage parlors didn't have to worry about being punished for security violations or the unexpected detonation of a claymore mine.

Not surprisingly, with all this sexual activity on or off post, venereal diseases were rampant. I have no figures to back this up, but certainly far more GIs in the war contracted a venereal disease than were ever wounded by the enemy or injured by other military activities. Gonorrhea—clap—was the most prevalent VD. At sick call in the mornings, GIs lined up in droves to get penicillin shots. (I had my turn also to get these shots, but because I was a CID special agent, I never had to stand in line to get them.) Although Army training always emphasized the use of condoms, the idea of safe sex, popularized decades later by AIDS, ranked low on most GIs' lists of concerns.

The one thing that could get a soldier's attention—and undoubtedly kept some of them celibate for their year in the war—was a persistent rumor about a form of syphilis called black syph. It was thought to be incurable. Once a GI got black syph, the stories went, doom followed. There were no known antibiotics to fight the disease. Rumors swirled around alleged cases in which GIs had been diagnosed with black syph and the medics had whisked them away to some secret location where they'd suffer terrible deaths. According to the rumors, the Army placed these troops on the rolls of the missing-in-action soldiers (the MIAs). The government couldn't very well send the disease-ridden body of such a soldier home. Morticians would know the truth, and pretty soon the whole country would know the truth about black syph. No, it made more sense to take black syph's victims to some secluded location, sort of a leper colony, where they'd inevitably die; then list them as missing in action.

The rumormongers even had a theory about the origins of the dreaded disease. As with all rumors, an element of truth lurked somewhere in the shadows. Syphilis was a problem in Vietnam, and regulations required women working on post to be tested for it. The 50P whores from off-post, though, never got tested, and the disease made its way through the troops. Then from the troops to the women working on-post. So, Vietnamese women, both on and off post, contracted regular, garden-variety syphilis. They had no means to get penicillin to fight the disease, so they wheedled their GI boyfriends to get the medication from the hospital. By hook or by crook, the GIs would get the penicillin and give it to their girlfriends. The women would self-medicate in doses insufficient to cure them. The parasites that cause syphilis built up a resistance to the antibiotics and mutated the syphilis into a disease immune to conventional treatments, called black syph. So, the story went, when a soldier had sex with one of the women carrying this disease, he'd contract the disease and, shortly thereafter, be wasting away at a hidden black syph colony.

That's what the rumors were. I never knew anyone diagnosed with this incurable disease, and no one I knew disappeared to a black syph colony. I knew a lot of guys having a lot of sex, but not one of them became a black syph victim. So I had no substantiation of any rumors regarding the alleged disease. James Ebert, a student of the Vietnam War, believes all these rumors served a cause. "The purpose of the rumor [about black syph]," he wrote, "which seems to have been officially sanctioned, was to help give abstinence a boost. It apparently worked." It might have worked in some crowds, but not with my crowd.

During my year in the war, I never paid a 50P whore being passed around a unit on post, and I didn't frequent the massage parlors. I didn't have to. Wearing civilian clothes, driving my own jeep, and having a hooch with a great view overlooking the South China Sea endowed me with things that attracted Vietnamese women. They didn't know a lot about the Army's structure and virtually nothing about what I did on the job, but they quickly realized that I had my own transportation and unlimited access to the post. I drove on and off Chu Lai at will. And, I always had plenty of money and a hooch—not a barracks—to take them to. So Vietnamese women that met me learned one thing quickly: I had privileges that most of the GIs didn't have, and those privileges could, or they hoped would, equate into financial rewards for them.

Shortly after arriving at Chu Lai, I began meeting cocktail waitresses at the clubs. It wasn't long before they started inviting me to their off-post residences. (In all the times I went to waitresses' off-post hooches, I never once saw a man at any of them. It's as if the Vietnamese men knew an American was coming and made themselves scarce. If I'd been a Vietnamese, I would have hated the American GIs, and I'm sure they did.) Typically, that meant going out to a waitress's hooch a couple of hours before she went to work on post. We'd have sex and then I'd drive her to base. I could travel freely through the gate, but she couldn't. So I'd drop her off at the Civilian Processing Gate. She'd have to show her identification card and be searched before being allowed on post. I'd drive through the gate and wait for her on the other side. Eventually, she'd be allowed on base, climb into my jeep, and we'd drive to her club.

However, one of the reasons—probably the main reason—Ross, McSwain, Thompson, and I moved into a hooch shortly after my arrival in Chu Lai was to give us privacy so we'd have somewhere to take girls for sex. After moving into the hooch, I usually invited women to my place instead of going to theirs. If I did go off-post to a waitress's hooch, it was just to pick her up, bring her back to post; then we'd go to my hooch to have sex. Afterwards, I'd give her a ride to her club.

The scheduling of all this sexual activity can only be appreciated by four college guys sharing an apartment. How do you prevent one of life's most embarrassing moments? If you have four horny guys bringing women to the same location for sexual activity, you might think that someone is going to walk in on someone else at the most inopportune time. But we had a system of reserving the hooch for ourselves so that didn't happen. If one of us knew that he'd be bringing a woman to the hooch at, say, two o'clock on a given day, he told the other three hooch mates that the hooch would be occupied from two to four that afternoon. The system worked flawlessly. We were, after all, honorable men.

Well, almost honorable. The other side of protecting each other's privacy is that we never knew who the other guy was having sex with. And, a couple of times I did take advantage of that loophole in our arrangement.

Tom McSwain was the only monogamous sex fiend I've known. He had one girlfriend the entire time we were together at Chu Lai. We called her Kathy. She was a cocktail waitress at the main NCO Club— the same club of the machete-wielding militia officer. McSwain would let the rest of us know the hooch would be busy, and then he'd meet Kathy at the Civilian Processing Gate and take her to the hooch.

One day I was at Kathy's club having a couple of drinks, and she and I started talking and flirting. I decided that my friendship with McSwain could interfere only so much in my life, so I made arrangements to meet Kathy the next day at the gate at about two in the afternoon. I went back to the office, and when I saw McSwain and the other guys, I said, "I'll be needing the hooch tomorrow afternoon." Everyone understood.

The next day, just before two o'clock, I said, "I'm going to run up to the hooch for about an hour." I didn't have to say any more; my privacy was assured. I drove to the gate, picked up Kathy, and drove to the hooch. There were no preliminaries. We both knew why we were there. Only then did I find out that our interest levels in our present sexual activity were decidedly different. Kathy turned out to be the most disinterested sex partner I'd ever or have ever been with. While I was humping on her like a rutting deer, she was lying on her back, chewing gum and blowing bubbles. All this time I'd thought she and McSwain had a sexy, torrid affair. Now all I could think was, "I wonder how many bubbles she's blown for McSwain."

I'm not sure if it was Kathy's lack of interest or her bubbles that inspired me, but at some point during our tryst I decided that I would pull a trick on McSwain. I knew he wouldn't be upset that I'd had sex with Kathy. None of us ever had serious emotional feelings about the women we brought to the hooch. Although he'd maintained a monogamous relationship with Kathy, it wasn't because he had any affection for her. It was only that, despite her bubble blowing, she provided him the sexual gratification he wanted. So I knew to mess with his head would require more than simply telling him that it was Kathy I'd brought to the hooch that day.

As Kathy and I walked out to my jeep, I was struggling with figuring out a way to really upset McSwain. Kathy climbed into my jeep and just as I was about to, it struck me. "I'll be right back," I told Kathy as I sprinted back up the steps into the hooch. I went into the back bedroom and walked over to McSwain's bunk. I'd had sex with Kathy on my bunk, but McSwain wouldn't know that. On a small table next to his bed, he kept a bottle of hand lotion. I picked up the bottle and squirted some of the lotion on to the center of his bunk. Quite satisfied with myself, I went back out to the jeep and drove Kathy to work.

When I got back the office, I found Ross and Thompson and told them about Kathy and McSwain's bunk. Like two teenagers about to watch someone turn live frogs loose in the girls' locker room, they followed me to McSwain's office.

"Tom," I said, "ya' got a second?"

"Sure," McSwain looked up from his desk. "What's going on?"

"Well, I'm feeling a little guilty about this so I've got to tell you," I said as contritely as the circumstances would allow. Ross and Thompson looked on seriously—cops are good actors; it comes with the territory. I said, "I had Kathy up at the hooch this afternoon."

McSwain looked at me just a bit puzzled and said, "OK." With his countenance he asked, "So why are you telling me?"

"Yeah," I said, "but there was one problem with it."

"What's that?" he asked, his voice reflecting a growing irritation.

"Well, she'd been up to the hooch so many times with you," I explained, "that when I got her into the bedroom, the only place that she'd fuck me was on your bunk."

McSwain flew into a rage. He jumped up from his desk screaming at me. He didn't give a shit that I'd had sex with Kathy, but that we'd used his bed was inexcusable. He pushed me against the wall, mauled his way past Ross and Thompson, and ran out the door. He jumped into his jeep and headed toward our hooch. Ross, Thompson, and I followed him in my jeep. At the hooch, McSwain slammed on his brakes and slid to a stop right outside the door. As he ran into the hooch and back to the bedroom, we were close on his heels. When he got to his bunk, he put his hand down on the middle of it. With a jerk he pulled his hand back, dripping with white goo. He ripped all the bedding off the bunk, ran over to the door, and threw it all on the ground. Then he turned to attack me. Ross and Thompson grabbed him. Now the three of us convulsed with laughter.

"What's so fucking funny?" McSwain demanded.

I walked over to his bunk, picked up the lotion bottle off the table, tossed it to him, and said, "That's what you've got on your hand, you stupid shithead."

Ross, Thompson, and I sure enjoyed the moment. McSwain was still pissed, and it took him a couple of days to get over it. When he did, he asked, "Did you really have Kathy up here?"

"Yeah," I said nodding. "I did."

"Did she blow bubbles?" he asked sheepishly.

"Yes," I told him, "She blew big-ass bubbles."

He nodded and seemed relieved to hear that Kathy blew bubbles for me, too.

Although the hooch served all of us well in providing a secluded place to take women for sex, we still found plenty of opportunities for sexual activity off Chu Lai as well. And it seemed as if Darrell Ross always masterminded these events. He had an uncanny knack for finding bizarre sexual pleasures in the strangest places. About a month after I'd arrived at Chu Lai, he and I were off post investigating a crime. By now, I'd been off post a number of times and, with my personal arsenal close at hand, I no longer felt any anxiety about traveling in the countryside around Chu Lai. After we had completed our business at a nearby fire support base, we headed back toward Chu Lai when Ross said, "You know, I need a blowjob." That's all he said. He drove along a bit farther and turned off QL1 onto a dirt road leading into a hamlet.

There were twelve to fifteen mud-and-wattle hooches along the main route through the village. Ross pulled off the side of the road and parked in front of one of them. He got out of the jeep and disappeared into the open door. Some minutes later, he came out, jumped back into the jeep, and said, "You're next. It's already been taken care of." I said, "OK." I never thought for a second to question what he'd taken care of. Ross had, after all, introduced me to the pleasures of Vietnamese women.

I jumped out of the jeep and walked into the hooch. Inside an old woman sat on a stool at a table in the middle of the room. When I entered, she got up and walked over to a sheet of plywood propped against the back wall. She slid the plywood to one side (it screeched on the concrete floor) revealing a door behind it. The door led into a pitch black, windowless room. When the plywood was moved, a small amount of light penetrated the darkness of the room. With the aid of that weak light, I could see a naked woman sitting on a bed. I couldn't see her features enough to tell her age or physical condition. Afterwards, I often thought that she may have been old or disfigured. Why else would her place of business be such a room? But in the darkness I couldn't tell. The old woman who'd moved the plywood now put her hand in the small of my back and gently pushed me into the dark room. The plywood made the screeching sound again as she moved it back in place over the door.

Pitch black enveloped me. I couldn't see shit. A hand grabbed my hand and pulled me forward. I didn't resist. From then on, everything that happened was a repeat of my first visit to a hooch, except for the darkness. I could feel everything happening to me, but could see nothing. After she was through, she simply disappeared. In the darkness, I sat on the edge of the bed waiting to see what would happen next. Then I heard a knock on the plywood. It was the woman with me signaling the old woman in the outer room. Screech, the plywood slid back. I squinted as I walked into the light of the next room. Screech, the plywood covered the door again. I walked out of the hooch, got in the jeep, and we continued on to Chu Lai.

"Ross," I said, "you're a sick motherfucker."

"You don't seem to mind," he laughed. No, I guess I didn't.

Not surprisingly, in this environment where young, testosterone-driven men considered every Vietnamese woman a 50P whore masquerading as a maid or waitress, there were going to be sexual assaults against women who didn't want sex. However, a report of sexual assault was rare. After all, there wasn't much that would happen to a young GI who sexually assaulted a Vietnamese woman such as a hooch maid. Besides, she and her family depended on the money she made working on the post. To report an assault could, she believed, jeopardize her employment. So a simple sexual assault was, for these women, a small price to pay for their jobs. However, on rare occasion a woman would be courageous enough to report that she'd been raped.

In one such case, I apprehended a supply sergeant for raping an eighteen-year-old young woman. He was originally from Pennsylvania and was on his second tour in the war. He served as an infantryman on his first eighteen-month tour that lasted from October 1968 through April 1970. He returned to the States for a few months to attend school to become a stock control and accounting specialist. At supply school, he volunteered to return to Vietnam. By August 1970—just four months after he'd left—he was back in Vietnam. On July 12, 1971, when he had a little over thirty days left in the war, he raped eighteen-year-old Trang Thi Hung, a club waitress. She reported the crime and I apprehended him. The charges didn't stick, and he received no punishment for the crime of rape or a lesser offense of sexual assault. On August 15, 1971, he returned to the States. Almost exactly one year later he received a General Discharge under honorable conditions (most troops receive an Honorable Discharge), four years before his enlistment would have expired. A note on his official records reads, "Not recommended for further service." He'd been a problem to someone upon his return to the States, but for sexually assaulting the young Vietnamese woman at Chu Lai he'd received no punishment. The women who chose not to report sex crimes were undoubtedly right in believing that little would be done to the soldiers who assaulted them.

Some of these women were just lucky to survive the attacks; not all of them did. Early one morning in August 1971, for example, an MP patrol found the nude body of a Vietnamese woman dumped along QL1, north of Chu Lai. The woman, estimated to be twenty years old, had been beaten, sexually molested, and murdered. Her body was placed into a clear plastic bag, then stuffed into a wooden footlocker. Her murderer nailed the lid shut. He had driven about eighteen feet off QL1, where he threw the footlocker from his vehicle. The box smashed when it hit the road, dumping the plastic-shrouded woman on to the ground. Lying near the body, MPs also found bloodied sheets stuffed inside a pillowcase. Inside the broken box, they found a man's bloody white handkerchief. The blood inside the plastic bag with the body was still fresh when they found her. She had not been dead long. The woman—she might have been a 50P whore sneaked on to Chu Lai, or a waitress at a club, or hooch maid, or a luckless woman not associated with the post at all—was never identified and no one was ever charged with her murder.

Not all deaths of innocent Vietnamese were connected to sex crimes. In March 1971, an eight-year-old boy was scavenging on the trash dump at Landing Zone Liz, southwest of Chu Lai. The young boy, as so many Vietnamese children, had honed his skills in the art of retrieving treasures in these piles of trash belonging to rich American soldiers. Specialist Four (SPEC4) John Burkett and SPEC4 Charles

Gardenauer started shooting their M-16s at the young boy just so they could watch him scramble over the trash. He slipped and fell, rose again, fell again, as he struggled to get over the pile of garbage to the side opposite from the gunfire. One of the bullets struck him in the lower left side of his back. He fell, sliding a few feet down the trash heap, then rolled to a stop.

Lieutenant Rollins, the LZ's commander, ran toward Burkett's and Gardenauer's post when he heard the firing. He arrived in time to see the young boy fall for the last time. He relieved the two soldiers and ordered a medic out to the trash heap to check on the boy. A short time later, a DustOff helicopter transported the boy to Chu Lai where a doctor pronounced him dead on arrival. Burkett and Gardenauer were also taken back to Chu Lai and ordered into confinement on the charge of murder. They were shortly released back to their unit. Once the wheels of military justice began turning, the charge was reduced to manslaughter—after all, they hadn't intended to kill the child, had they? Then the charges were dismissed altogether. Five months later, Burkett had been promoted to sergeant and sent to Fort Polk in his home state of Louisiana where he trained troops in the art of war. Six months after the killing, Gardenauer, a native Californian, had fulfilled his two-year draft commitment, received his appropriate decorations for fighting in his nation's war, and left the Army. The Army never made either man answer for the death of that little boy. The Army's failure to hold GIs accountable for crimes against the Vietnamese reflected an American attitude about Asians and the Asian view of life.

One of the oft-repeated myths about fighting a war in Asia was that Asians didn't value life. Americans had, and probably still have, the perception that an individual's life in Asia is unimportant. During the Korean War, hordes of Chinese and North Korean troops with only enough rifles for every fourth soldier attacked directly into the scathing firepower of the United Nations' forces. As an armed communist soldier fell wounded or dead, a comrade picked up his weapon and continued the attack. If those soldiers had valued their own lives or their superiors had valued life, such suicide attacks would not have occurred—or so Americans thought. In Vietnam, visions of the self-immolating Buddhist monks and stories of sappers on suicide missions convinced Americans even more that Asians placed little value on life. Pictures of the summary execution of a Viet Cong by a Saigon police official during Tet in 1968 presented irrefutable proof of this fact. As popular support for the war waned in the early seventies, Middle Americans convinced themselves that, because there were "so damn many Asians," killing one or hundreds or thousands was meaningless. "They just don't value life like we do" was repeated in every Main Street café in the country.

That very notion is absurd. Anyone who's ever seen news footage of the wailing Vietnamese mother holding her dead child, or the old woman crying over the bodies of young dead soldiers, or the grieving grandfather sitting on the ground by his dead wife knows that the Vietnamese value life. However, the American penchant for believing that Asians valued life less than Americans, or even other Europeans, permeated the views of GIs toward the Vietnamese, and even the military justice system that should have held men such as Burkett and Gardenauer responsible for the death of the Vietnamese child.

Although the military justice system seldom held GIs accountable for such actions, the Army assuaged its conscience by instituting a system of solatium payments made to Vietnamese who lost property or loved ones to any American's actions. An official report published in 1975 explained: "In South Vietnam it was the custom for a representative of the United States to pay a visit of condolence to a Vietnamese injured by military activities or to the survivors of a deceased victim, and for a small amount of money or goods such as rice, cooking oils, or food stuffs to be given. The visit and payment took place when US personnel were involved in the incident that caused injury, regardless of who was at fault, and even if the incident was technically caused by combat. The donation was not an admission of fault, but was intended to show compassion."

Figures I have for a military law office in Da Nang show that in one six-month period, the military paid solatium payments totaling $17,735.83 (2,660,374 piasters) to one hundred twenty-two claimants. That comes to an average of $145.38 (21,800 piasters) per claim. A review of the MP blotters, however, shows that most victims received far less than the average.

For example, in September 1971, two young boys were seen running from the perimeter wire around the ammunition storage area at Landing Zone Aspen, twelve miles northwest of Chu Lai. The officer on duty ordered the guard to fire warning shots over the boys' heads. Unknown to the officer and the guard, a third boy was running ahead of the two observed youngsters. One round from the guard's M-16 struck the nine-year-old in the head. For his death, his father received a solatium payment of 1,500 piasters ($10). In another case, a four-year-old girl was run over by the trailer of a 1969 Kaiser five-ton truck when she tried to dart through a military convoy heading south on QL1. The wheels of the trailer crushed her. Her parents received a solatium payment of 70,000 piasters ($467) for her death. By far, though, payments ranged in the area of 4,000 to 7,000 piasters ($27-$47) for injuries or death.

Those of us in law enforcement tried to make the military justice system hold culprits responsible, but usually a solatium payment became the only acknowledgment that an American had caused an injury. However, that was not an acknowledgment of guilt, but a demonstration of "compassion." Such was the case in a hit-and-run accident I investigated.

On April 21, 1971, an Army two-and-a-half ton truck was traveling south on QL1 when it came upon a civilian passenger bus heading the same direction. In Vietnam a thirty-five-passenger bus might easily carry upwards to sixty or more passengers. Taking a bus didn't mean sitting on one of the bench seats. Those were the lucky riders. The other passengers sat on the roof, stood on a bumper, or clung to the side holding onto a mirror. The truck driver passed the commuter-laden bus, but as he turned back into his lane of traffic, the right side of the truck hit the front left corner of the bus, throwing the bus out of control. It careened off the road, coming to rest in a watery rice paddy. The jolt from hitting the truck and the wild ride into the rice paddy left one man dead, two passengers seriously hurt, and five more with minor injuries. The truck driver never stopped, but continued on his way south.

The MP desk sergeant notified me that there'd been a traffic accident involving a fatality between a US Army truck and a civilian bus, and that the American driver had fled the scene. The only other information he had was that a Vietnamese witness told the responding MP patrolmen that the truck carried beer or soda. I knew of only one place where one could get beer and soda, and that was Chu Lai's Post Exchange (PX). I went to the PX and asked the manager to pull all the invoices that would show where beer or soda was being delivered that morning. I took those invoices and sat down with a map of the outlying landing zones and support bases and eliminated any invoices for shipments that would have gone north or west of Chu Lai. That left only one invoice. A truck had picked up a load of beer for Landing Zone Bronco, south of Chu Lai.

Then I drove to the accident scene. The passenger bus had been moved from the rice paddy to a piece of dry ground off the side of the road. A G-5* officer had already been there and made solatium payments to the deceased's family and families of the injured passengers. American "compassion" had been amply demonstrated. I walked around to the front of the bus and saw OD green paint scraped along the front left corner of the blue bus, and I could tell where blue paint had been scraped off the bus. "Now," I told myself, "all I have to do is find the OD truck at LZ Bronco with blue paint scrapings on it."

The next day I hitched a helicopter ride to LZ Bronco. Once there, I found what passed for a PX, a small hooch-style warehouse containing beer, soda, snacks, cigarettes, and *Playboy* magazines. The NCO running the small concession told me he'd gotten a delivery of beer the previous day, and, if he remembered correctly, the driver and shotgun rider had been members of the 59th Infantry Platoon (Scout Dog) (IPSD). I went to the 59th IPSD's motor pool and started checking the right side of every truck there. Along the entire edge of the bed on a two-and-a-half ton truck ran an OD-colored steel-reinforcing band about six inches high. I hoped that I'd find blue paint on that metal band on one of the trucks. After checking about ten trucks, I found it: blue paint scrapings along the right rear side of the bed. I set my briefcase on the ground, opened it, and took out two small envelopes. I marked one envelope "blue paint/truck" and the other "OD paint/ truck." Using my pocketknife, I scraped off samples of each color paint into the appropriate envelope.

A check of the motor pool's records showed that SPEC4 Allen Stalworth had signed the truck out of the motor pool. I contacted the IPSD's first sergeant, and he told me that Stalworth had driven to Chu Lai the day before to pick up a load of beer. He also told me that SPEC4 John Snell had ridden shotgun. I first located Snell and talked to him. When I asked him about the accident, he said, "Yeah, we may have had an accident, but we didn't stop. We really didn't know for sure, ya' know." In his written statement he was more forthcoming, saying he believed Stalworth knew that he'd hit the bus while passing it. That made more sense than "we really didn't know for sure." I then found Stalworth and told him that I suspected him of being guilty of manslaughter and hit-and-run. When I advised him of his rights, he

---

An army headquarters is divided functionally into "G" offices, G-1, G-2, and so on. Officers in the G-5 office, the political/community affairs office, made solatium payments.

refused to make a statement and wanted a lawyer. By now it was getting late, and I caught the last helicopter heading back to Chu Lai.

The next day I drove back to the bus. I got a couple more envelopes out of my briefcase. I marked one "blue paint/bus" and the other "OD paint/bus." Using my pocketknife, I scraped paint into the new envelopes as I'd done at Bronco the day before. I returned to my office where I packaged the four paint samples and sent them to the crime lab in Long Binh.

The middle of May I received the results back from the lab. The report said that it was impossible to tell if the OD paint on the bus was the same OD paint off the truck. That part of the test made sense. Every Army vehicle in Vietnam had OD paint on it. For the lab analyst to say that the OD paint from one Army truck was the only possible match to the OD paint left on the bus was an impossibility. On the other hand, the blue paint that I scraped off the truck match exactly the blue paint that I took off the bus. The lab report gave me the conclusive evidence that Stalworth's truck had collided with the blue passenger bus. In my opinion, Stalworth had committed a hit-and-run resulting in the death of the Vietnamese man. As it turned out, however, that was irrelevant.

A little over a week after I'd read Stalworth his rights, he returned to the States at Fort Lewis, Washington, and was discharged from the Army on May 5, 1971—roughly ten days before I'd received the lab report confirming his hit-and-run crime. No one would recall him to active duty to charge him with the death of a Vietnamese man in a vehicle accident, even if it was a hit-and-run. Moreover, the National Police had never finished its investigation of the accident. For months I left the case open waiting on the Vietnamese police accident report. It never did show up. Finally, in August, a full four months after the accident, Strawberry told me to close the case, just to get it off our books. On August 27, I signed my final report on the case with a note that I'd submit a supplemental report, if "deemed appropriate," once the National Police completed its investigation. For my part, I was pretty proud of my investigation. I figured I'd worked hard on the case and solved it. If the system didn't punish the dickhead, that wasn't my concern as an investigator. I'd done what I was supposed to do; it was the system that let him get away with it. So in the end, a solatium payment showing the Army's compassion remained the only satisfaction a Vietnamese family received for the death of a loved one.

Most solatium payments were not related to the death or injury of family members. Usually, a Vietnamese receiving a payment had lost a few chickens, a pig, or a water buffalo. Sometimes such a payment might mean that a convoy of trucks ran over an animal—an accident. Other times, however, GIs had maliciously killed farmers' animals. I remember many times sitting in clubs listening to Huey door gunners talking about how many water buffaloes they'd shot that day. They'd be flying over an area and, out of pure boredom, start shooting at water buffaloes below them. One door gunner bragged about how he'd blown four water buffaloes right out of a rice paddy. Other troops talked about lighting books of matches and throwing the incendiaries onto passing wagons full of straw just to watch them burn. I never personally witnessed any of this, but I saw enough farmers showing up at the front gate seeking solatium payments for their losses to make me believe the stories were true.

It would be wrong, however, to use these anecdotes as a basis of thinking the Vietnamese were always victims. They quickly learned the nuances of the American system they had to deal with and used that knowledge to their advantage. Some solatium payments, for example, soon evolved into simple pay-offs.

One payment that particularly aggravated me involved one of the MPs at the main gate and a ten-year-old boy. The kid approached the gate and tried to get the guard to let him on base. The MP wouldn't let him on, remained adamant about it, and kept chasing the boy away. The kid spoke only vulgar English and yelled obscenities at the guard, but the MP just ignored him. The boy left for a couple of minutes and returned with a good-sized rock and threw it at the MP. The rock hit the guard in the face and broke his jaw. The MP grabbed the kid by the scruff of the neck, slapped him a couple of times, and turned him loose. The MP's partner called for an ambulance that took the injured man to the hospital.

A short time later, the boy returned to the gate with his mother and father. They berated the remaining MP. A crowd started gathering. Taunts and jeers were hurled at the guard. He got on the telephone to the desk sergeant to get some back up. The Desk Sergeant called G-5. Soon a jeep arrived, and the G-5 officer counted out piasters to the parents until they received payment satisfying their outrage at their child being slapped by the MP. Clearly, the boy should have been turned over to the local police for aggravated assault. Instead, the parents profited from the system that had been set up to show "compassion" to the Vietnamese.

Such payments, however, represented only the more innocuous exploitation of the solatium system by the Vietnamese. In other cases, such payments resulted from out-and-out extortion. The most memorable incident of this kind involved an old ARVN veteran. Monthly he created such a scene at the front gate that the Army paid him just to get rid of him.

He'd lost both of his legs, presumably in combat. He still wore his ARVN uniform as he traveled around in an old wheelchair. When I first arrived at Chu Lai in February, at least once a month he'd show up at the front gate and wheel himself into the walkway that went through the gate. He raised himself up to reach a hand grenade he was sitting on. Then he'd pull the pin on the grenade, holding the spoon so it wouldn't explode, and just sit there. The gate guard would call the G-5 office, and an officer would soon arrive with a briefcase. The officer would count out a stack of piasters to the ARVN veteran. When the vet got what he thought he deserved that day, he'd put the pin back in the hand grenade, slip it back under him, stuff the piasters in his shirt pocket, and wheel himself away. The whole scene became routine.

By early October, however, the extortion grew more brazen. Convoys left from or arrived at Chu Lai's gate on a regular basis. Vietnamese would sit on the side of the road watching for one of these convoys. As the lead vehicle arrived at a pre-determined location, a couple of Vietnamese men would grab a strap tied to a string of concertina wire and run it across the road. The convoy would come to a halt at the wire. Someone would radio G-5, and soon a jeep with a lieutenant would show up. The officer would count out a stack of money to the extortionists—that's all they were—until they'd agree to drag the concertina wire out of the way and let the convoy proceed. A couple of hours later, another convoy would show up, the wire would come out, the jeep would arrive, and so on. One of men orchestrating this whole scheme from the side of the road was the wheelchair-bound ARVN vet. He'd shelved his hand grenade routine for the more lucrative business of stopping convoys.

As this new scheme become more rewarding for the ARVN vet and his friends, they grew bolder. As their boldness grew, so, too, did the dangers of the extortion. For example, in early November, I was at the gate on another incident when a single two-and-a-half ton truck came down the road. A gathering of Vietnamese on the side of the road started pelting the truck with stones. One large stone hit the driver on the head and knocked him out. The truck lurched to a dead stop. Two Vietnamese men dragged the concertina wire across the road in front of the truck. I figured that someone would call G-5 and these sons-of-a-bitch would get their money.

The shotgun rider in the truck, however, had other ideas. He pushed the unconscious driver out of the way and started the truck's engine. The ARVN veteran wheeled himself onto the road behind the truck. I saw that he had an M-16 lying across his lap. The truck started moving forward, directly toward the concertina wire. I heard the driver shifting the truck into second gear just as he hit the wire. The wire caught on the front and rear differentials and the drive shaft. Now as the truck continued forward, the wire did, too. A teenage girl and a small boy and girl walking with her got tangled in the wire as the truck dragged it by them. Now the truck, the wire, and three young Vietnamese entangled in the wire continued toward the gate. The ARVN veteran shouldered the M-16 and fired. He had the weapon set on automatic. An M-16 doesn't recoil much, but on automatic it drifts upwards. The small stature of the veteran allowed the weapon to lurch upwards and pushed him back into his seat. In the process, his wheelchair tipped over backwards while he was still firing on full automatic. His co-conspirators scrambled for cover. Had it not been for the injured driver and the dragging of the three young Vietnamese, the scene would have been hilarious.

By the time the truck got to the gate and all the excitement had died down, the guard called an ambulance for the injured driver and the three Vietnamese. Hospital personnel stitched up the cuts on the Vietnamese, and their parents received solatium payments for their injuries. The driver had received such an injury to his head that he was returned to the States early and eventually received a discharge three months before his two-year enlistment ended. Nothing ever happened to the ARVN veteran, and extortion of funds through the Army's solatium payment program continued.

Besides devising schemes to profit from the Army's "compassionate" program, there were other ways that the Vietnamese demonstrated their entrepreneurship. The black market was just one of them. There were places one could go in the hinterlands miles from Chu Lai and find stacks and stacks of black market goods—it looked like a truckload sale at a Kmart. Cartons of cigarettes, cases of beer, stereo equipment, two-cubic foot refrigerators, toothpaste, Zippo lighters. Did I mention beer? I rarely went to a Vietnamese hooch where I didn't get offered a can of Budweiser beer.

My trips to Vietnamese hooches off post—not including the houses of waitresses—resulted from investigations involving Vietnamese nationals as subjects, witnesses, or victims. The ARVN interpreter and I would go to the local police headquarters in a nearby village to get or to deliver reports or simply to exchange information. While at the police station, usually the village chief would show up and chat with the interpreter. Before long I'd learn that the chief had invited us to his home where his wife and maybe a daughter or two would serve us a meal. These invitations reflected the genuine kindness of the Vietnamese people and exposed me to intimate details of their culture that, had I had a different job, I would never had seen. We always accepted the invitations. To do otherwise, the interpreter informed me, would be insulting the chief.

Their homes were remarkably similar: small mud-and-wattle huts; thatch or tin roofs; glassless windows with shutters; one main door with a latch instead of a doorknob; concrete, brick, or dirt floor; modestly furnished. In the middle of the main room usually sat a low, round table. Around the table sat small, three-legged stools. I'm not exceptionally tall, but I towered over my hosts. Anyone who, as an adult, has sat at a children's table in a kindergarten class can imagine what it's like to sit at a Vietnamese dining table. Once the handshaking was over, we'd sit at the table, and the women would serve the meal. I learned not to ask what I was eating, even if it was unrecognizable. If I didn't ask what it was and didn't spend too much time trying to figure it out, it generally tasted pretty good.

However, there were two things that the village chiefs' wives tried to serve that I absolutely refused to eat, and that was because they looked like what they were. One was a pickled slug. It looked like a slug, felt like a slug, and I could not bring myself to eat it. The second dish that I refused to eat was a chicken embryo. The first time a chief's wife offered it to me, it looked like she was serving me a hard-boiled egg. I watched my hosts to see how to eat it. They cracked the shell on it. I cracked the shell on mine. If one cracked the egg just right, the top half of the shell would lift off, leaving the bottom half of the shell whole. And sitting right there in the bottom part of the shell would be a little chick with its eyes closed. It looked as if the chick was about to hatch. If they had incubated the egg a day longer, they would have had a chicken. That view was startling enough, but the smell was worse. It smelled like a rotten egg. My hosts and the interpreter gobbled down the delicacy. I'm sure that I insulted many village chiefs because I wouldn't eat those chicks.

The interpreter told me that this delicacy had quite an elaborate preparation. A woman would have to know almost to the day when a brood of chicks would be hatching. A day or so before that time, she'd boil the eggs, place the boiled eggs into a container, and bury the container in the ground. Thirty days later, she dug up the container. The eggs were now ready to be served to her family and guests. The day that they were served, she boiled the eggs again. When served, they were steaming hot. Now one only had to crack open the egg, devour the chick, and drink the fluid that remained at the bottom half of the shell once the chick was gone. I could eat about anything in Vietnam, but I drew the line on the slugs and baby chicks on a half shell.

I do know that on one occasion at a village chief's home, I ate testicles. I'm not sure what species of unfortunate animal made the sacrifice for me to be eating its nuts that day, but I'd heard that Vietnamese ate the testicles from dogs and monkeys. Whatever animal contributed to our meal on this day, there were many of them. The chief's wife set a large wooden bowl, roughly fifteen inches across and six inches deep, in the middle of the table, and it was full of testicles, obvious testicles—I didn't have to guess what they were. There were dozens of them. They were a little on the chewy side, but they didn't taste half bad. She served the testicles with rice and a side of vegetables, a well-balanced meal.

I found these visits to the village chiefs' homes interesting and fun. We'd sit around the table and there'd be a lot of conversation, with the interpreter translating for me. There was always lots of giggling, too, and I'm sure much of it was at my expense, especially when I turned up my nose at slugs or baby chicks. They offered me black market American cigarettes to smoke and black market Budweiser beer to drink.

Except for a two-cubic foot refrigerator—another black market item—sitting in the corner of the main room, the Vietnamese had no way to keep their beer cold. And, for reasons beyond my comprehension, the refrigerator was never used for the beer. So any beer they offered would be warm—but not for long. Every hooch I visited had a block of ice—a product of Chu Lai's ice plant—sitting under a tarp in the corner of the main room. After the chief would offer a beer and I accepted it, he'd take a few cans to the block of ice. The block would have a groove on it the exact size of a can of beer. He'd lay the beer can in the groove, spin it for about thirty seconds, and then hand me an ice cold beer. I've tried it without success. It might have been black market beer, but it tasted great. The food (usually), the conversation and laughing, and the ice cold, black market Budweiser beer made these visits enjoyable and unforgettable.

Another big black market item was the $100 bill. Americans received pay in MPC. That and piasters bought whatever one wanted to buy. US currency was illegal. The Vietnamese, however, wanted US dollars and would exchange piasters at two or three times the going rate just to get their hands on it. Seeing the potential, GIs would have family and friends from the States send currency, usually in $100 bills, to them. Because it was illegal, however, someone couldn't send a box of $100 bills into country, but would hide the bills between the pages of magazines or books or any other creative way to get the bills past customs officials in the post offices. I'd heard that wealthy Vietnamese were sending the $100 bills to foreign banks, building a nest egg for when they'd have to flee and the communists would inevitably take over the South. I'd guess that by 1975, most of the Vietnamese who'd participated in the black marketing of $100 bills had safely fled Vietnam. What a way to fight a war: the rich positioning themselves for the day when their side loses.

Prostitution, extortion, black marketing, and, of course, trafficking in drugs all provided a means for Vietnamese to make a living off the Americans. Another means was simply thievery. MP blotters are full of accounts of Vietnamese stealing everything from food to electronics equipment to weapons and trying to smuggle it off post. I was fortunate, however, to be the investigator on one of Chu Lai's largest capers, nearly $60,000 worth of watches and jewelry stolen from the main exchange.

On the evening of May 20, 1971, a Vietnamese employee of the post exchange barbershop hid himself and two accomplices in the barbershop after the exchange closed. At 10:00 that evening, the three tore a hole through the wall of the barbershop into a connecting warehouse that contained the Gold Room, the storage location for rings and watches sold by the exchange. The three thieves loaded bags with jewelry totaling nearly $6,600. Then they broke out of the warehouse into the main exchange itself. Within the main building was the Caribe Diamond Works concession, a privately owned shop. The three Vietnamese busied themselves loading more bags with watches and jewelry totaling nearly $51,000. In less than two hours, the three thieves had stolen jewelry worth more money than most Vietnamese would expect to make in a lifetime. From the Caribe Diamond Works concession, they climbed over a wall on the north side of the exchange, made another hole in the wall to get into the appropriately named Beer and Soda Store, walked through it to the main entrance of the exchange, and walked out the front door.

Burdened by their load of jewelry, the three walked to the nearby 23rd Infantry Division, Administration Company Motor Pool. Inside the motor pool they found a sleeping American soldier. They woke him and brazenly offered him two Rolex watches and two gold rings if he'd give them a ride to the landing docks on the north side of the post. The soldier figured he had nothing to lose, so he climbed into a jeep with the thieves and their loot and drove them to the docks. They gave him the watches and rings, and he returned to the motor pool.

The thieves now tried for a couple of hours to hail a passing boat. Eventually, the crew of a South Vietnamese Navy patrol boat saw them on the dock and stopped. The thieves offered each of the four crewmen a watch for transportation to a nearby island where the mastermind of the plot lived with his family in a small fishing village. The Vietnamese sailors agreed to the deal and transported the three men to the island. Early in the morning of May 21, the thieves sat in a hooch in the village of Ky Hoa admiring nearly $60,000 in loot. For the price of eight watches and two rings, they had made their escape from the largest American military installation in the area. On the black market, their treasures would bring them more piasters than any of them had ever imagined earning.

There is an old saying that there is no honor among thieves. If there were, I would never have solved the crime. However, on May 25, one of the thieves came to me when the mastermind had given him only 160,000 piasters ($582 based on the official exchange rate of 275P per dollar) for his part in the robbery. Although a significant amount of money to him, he knew that his partner stood to make many times that selling the jewelry. He also told me how the robbery had been executed.

My interest was in recovering the stolen property, returning it to the post exchange and Caribe Diamond Works, and in identifying the American soldier who'd abetted the thieves by driving them to the northern docks. My informant could only tell me that the soldier was black and his first name began with the letter M. I snooped around the 23rd Admin Company until I came up with only one soldier who fit that description. As luck would have it, I found the duty roster that put him in the motor pool on the evening of May 20. I apprehended him, searched his hooch, and found the two watches and two rings, all identified by serial numbers. Now I needed to find the rest of the loot.

My Vietnamese informant and I went to the ARVN CID office where he provided the names of the four sailors who'd transported the three erstwhile friends to the village of Ky Hoa. On May 29, the ARVN CID questioned the sailors and recovered four more watches. On June 3, the ARVN CID apprehended the informant's two accomplices and recovered two more watches. Then all cooperation between the ARVN CID and myself ceased. The ARVN investigator refused to provide me any more information on his investigation or to turn over the jewelry he had confiscated. Every one of my inquiries on the case to ARVN CID office was stonewalled.

Altogether, we'd recovered less than a dozen pieces of jewelry valued at a few thousand dollars. To my knowledge, none of the rest of the jewelry was ever recovered and nothing happened to the perpetrators. Chances are very good, though, that the informant's life wasn't worth a bowl of rice, and that the ARVN CID investigator and his commander pocketed any profits from the sale of the looted jewelry. I never saw the three thieves after the ARVN investigation into their crime, nor did I see any more of the stolen jewelry. The post exchange and Caribe Diamond Works got back a grand total of two watches and two rings that I'd confiscated from the soldier driver.

None of this surprised me. After all, I'd already been exposed a number of times to the return of confiscated heroin back to the open market after we'd worked so hard to get it and nab the drug traffickers. Why should these same police be any more honest when it came to investigating a case involving stolen property? Especially when that property was valued at nearly $60,000? Nevertheless, I was proud of my investigation, even if the corrupt ARVN CID had prevented me from recovering all the stolen property.

From start to finish, the case had lasted less than two weeks. My final report, however, is dated August 25, reflecting the two months of stonewalling by the ARVN CID. I knew no more on August 25 than I did on June 3. My emotional attachment to the case, however, lasted right up to the day before I departed Vietnam, the last time I saw Phan Thi San, co-owner of the Caribe Diamond Works.

San was the most beautiful woman I met in Vietnam, and she wasn't even Vietnamese. Her mother was Chinese and her father French. In her heritage, she reflected the history of the domination of Vietnam by outsiders. She had grown up in Vietnam, but had received a Catholic education and been exposed to international culture her entire life. She spoke English perfectly. She also spoke French, Chinese, and Vietnamese, but I was in no position to know how well. She had the physical features of an Oriental beauty and the body of a French model. Her skin had an olive hue, like a Mediterranean woman's skin. Her soft, coal black hair cascaded down to and around her shoulders and neck. She was beautiful.

As co-owner of the Caribe Diamond Works, San also represented Vietnam's history. The Chinese had possessed a virtual stranglehold on Vietnam's economy. Through a long history of economic presence in Indochina and favorable governmental activities under French colonial rule, the Chinese thrived. By the early 1950s, they made up about a tenth of the population of Vietnam while controlling four-fifths of the retail commerce and over half of all its capital, an accomplishment for which they earned the title "Jews of the Orient." By the mid-1950s, growing anti-Chinese sentiment forced many Chinese to Vietnamize their names, but their economic strength remained. That's how a beautiful French-Chinese woman with a Vietnamese name ended up selling jewelry in Chu Lai's main post exchange. Because some Vietnamese thieves decided to steal nearly $60,000 in jewelry from her business, I had the good fortune to become her lover for the rest of my time in Vietnam.

My relationship with San was completely different than any relationship I had with any other Vietnamese woman. First, I had absolutely nothing—economically speaking—that San wanted. She was wealthy; far wealthier than a poor enlisted guy like me. She would never ask me for a Sears Roebuck catalog: she had access to anything I could have ordered for her. As well, she certainly wasn't going to ask me to marry her and take her back to the States. From the beginning of our relationship, we both understood that someday I was going back to the States. To be perfectly honest, if I had been inclined to bring back a war bride, she would have been the one. But we never discussed that issue. Besides, because of her considerable economic assets in Vietnam, I doubt if she would have even entertained leaving with me. I think she would have stayed in Vietnam.

Also, she knew from the beginning of our relationship that I was a Number 10 GI. For instance, she knew my seeing her wouldn't stop me from having sex with other women on or off post. So, from the very beginning of our relationship we both knew that I wouldn't be buying her things, taking her to the States, or be faithful to her. Knowing all that up front made our liaison the best I had during the war.

Once or twice a week, San and I would meet at my hooch. We'd spend a couple of hours together. Then she'd have to leave to take care of her financial interests. One afternoon after we'd made love, I was lying on my back on the bunk. San was sitting up, straddling me. Around her neck she wore an ivory, gold-trimmed Buddha pendant hanging from a gold chain. She called it a lavaliere. She took it off and bent toward me to place the chain over my head. "Wear this for good luck," she said as she kissed me. I've worn her lavaliere since that day in 1971. I've only had it off when I had the chain repaired a couple of times. It's the only souvenir I have from the war, and it's my good luck charm. It got me through Vietnam in one piece and it got me through twenty-seven years on the LAPD. I have no sentimental reason to continue to wear it; I just do.

Sex, whether with a Tina, Kathy, or San, was nothing more than a diversion. We worked long hours in Vietnam, under third-world conditions (although those of us in the CID certainly had it better than the grunts), overlaid with the possibility, at least, that the war itself would intrude into our lives. So sex, virtually free and readily available, diverted us from the realities of our lives in the war. It wasn't, however, the only diversion. The reason the Army trained me and sent us investigators to Vietnam was to combat drugs, another diversion for the troops. Those of us that refused to participate in the drug scene, however, found another diversion in alcohol, and we drank plenty of it. Spinning off from the alcohol use were the fights, rowdiness, and general buffoonery that alcohol causes in young men's lives.

Whenever I went to one of the clubs, I liked to go with Clyde Kingston. He was a Southern, black, athletically built sergeant. He used words as if each cost him money. If it had, he'd have spent very little each month. When he did speak, what he said was well worth the money spent. He also wore a gold chain necklace from which dangled three small golden gloves. He claimed that he'd won his state's golden glove championship three consecutive years. His physique said he wasn't lying. I saw him in action one night and know he was telling the truth.

Kingston and I were drinking one evening at the civil engineers' club when a fight broke out. The club manager herded the antagonists outside where the fight resumed. We moved out with the crowd just to watch. It quickly became obvious that the fighters were not evenly matched. The bigger and stronger of the two brawlers landed punches faster than the other guy could react. Finally, the underdog fell to the ground. He tried to get back up but had energy enough only to get on his hands and knees. Just then his subduer kicked him in the head. The kicker's approach and force made him look like a football place kicker. The guy on the ground had been knocked cold.

Kingston and I had seen enough. Kingston grabbed the kicker and tried to pull him away from the unconscious soldier, whom I grabbed and tried to drag away from further harm. The kicker turned on Kingston. With a flurry of jabs to the head, Kingston knocked the guy out cold. Two of his buddies then jumped Kingston. He neutralized both of them with an equally impressive flurry of punches. Within seconds of the first kick to the one soldier's head, three more GIs were lying unconscious on the ground. By the time the MPs arrived, everyone, except the knocked-out troops on the ground, had disappeared. Kingston and I went back into the bar and started drinking again. "You're pretty good," I said to him. I think I was gushing. He smiled, reached inside his shirt to pull out the three golden gloves, jiggled them out in front of him, and said, "Yeah." If I'd ever had a reason to doubt his boxing stories, which I hadn't, that night would have made a believer out of me.

Although Kingston never had to prove himself to anyone, Ralph Colbert was always betting everyone that he could perform this or that fantastic—or vulgar—feat. Colbert was a tall, probably 6'3", slender, white Mississippian. Someone started calling him Slim and it stuck. (Nicknaming him "Slim" made sense because he was, well, slim. We had another guy who told everyone his nickname was Doc. As it turned out, his nickname was Doc because he liked the name Doc; it had nothing to do with anything else. Whenever he met somebody, such as the first time I met him, he introduced himself as Doc. I asked him, "Why Doc?" I figured there had to be a reason similar to why we called Slim "Slim."

"I just think it's a cool name and I like it," he replied. So we called him Doc. He's one of the few guys I've ever known that nicknamed himself.) Anyway, Slim's willingness to subject himself to bizarre undertakings provided pure entertainment for the rest of the MPIs and CID agents.

One of his capers involved a three-inch Vietnamese cockroach. One day a bunch of us sat drinking at a club. Slim was there dressed in a uniform adorned with love beads and peace medals. I'm not sure how he got away with that, but he always wore the beads and peace medals while in uniform. He had a necklace or two, a couple of bracelets on each wrist, peace medals pinned to his breast pockets, and so forth. No one ever told him to get rid of his decoration when in uniform, so every time I saw him, he wore the beads and medals.

As we sat drinking, a three-inch cockroach crawled across the top of the bar. Usually cockroaches are in a big hurry to get anywhere and would normally scurry across a bar. But not this fellow. Slim picked up an empty beer glass and turned it upside down over the cockroach. The cockroach clawed helplessly at the sides of the glass while walking in circles.

Doc asked, "What are you going to do with this cockroach now that you've caught him?"

"I'll bet I can eat him," Slim said, smiling.

"I'll bet you won't," said someone else jumping into the conversation.

A lively bantering ensued pitting Slim against everyone else at the bar. Finally, he'd made six $100 bets that he'd eat the cockroach. Six hundred dollars in MPC lay on the bar top. Slim didn't have enough MPC to cover the bets, but everyone knew if he lost he'd pay up. After all the bantering and betting finished, Slim tilted the glass, raising up its edge so the cockroach could crawl out. Just as its head and antennae cleared the rim of the glass, Slim slammed the glass down and decapitated the bug. He then lifted up the glass and picked up the cockroach by its back legs. He tipped his head back and dropped the cockroach into his open mouth. Expressionless, he chewed the cockroach and chased it down with a beer.

One of the bettors called foul. "You said you were going to eat the cockroach, and there's still part of it on the table," he said while jabbing his finger toward the cockroach's head. "I'm not going to pay up because you didn't eat the whole fuckin' cockroach."

Slim reached down and picked up the head by one of the antennae. He tipped his head back and dropped the head into his open mouth.

Once again, he chewed and then chased the head with a swig of beer. "Any more whiners?" he asked the bettors. Silence. He picked up the pile of MPC, smiled at everyone and walked out the door. Outside he stuck his finger down his throat and threw up.

The next day Slim started getting concerned about his eating a cockroach. One of his buddies called a doctor to find out what the biological effects might be of eating one. The doctor said that although he didn't recommend the eating of cockroaches, the many diseases that they carried probably wouldn't affect someone stupid enough to eat one. Slim had made an easy $600 MPC by being stupid enough. He wouldn't fare so well with his next antic.

One night the movie *Coolhand Luke* starring Paul Newman was shown at a club. One of the memorable scenes in the movie is when Paul Newman, as a result of a challenge in a chain gang camp in the South, eats fifty hard-boiled eggs. Slim figured if Paul Newman could do it, so could he. He stated that he didn't think that eating those eggs was such a big deal, and then the bantering began. MPC came out of pockets, and very shortly Slim had bet ten guys $25 MPC each that he could eat fifty hard-boiled eggs. All agreed that he'd accomplish this amazing stunt the next evening.

In preparation for this Herculean feat, Slim decided to eat nothing the next day until the appointed time that evening. Another MPI acted as his second and went to the mess hall to convince a cook to hard-boil fifty eggs. That night at the EM Club, Slim sat down with a kettle full of peeled, hard-boiled eggs on the bar and started eating. The ten bettors hovered around him. Thirty rubbernecks stood nearby. At first it looked as if Slim would make another $250 MPC. He gobbled down the eggs non-stop. At about egg number thirty-five, however, Slim slowed down considerably and started looking sick. His eyes rolled back, his cheeks puff out the way they do when one is trying to hold down vomit. He was not looking good, but he was determined to eat all fifty eggs. When Slim got to egg forty, we could see that he was forcing himself to swallow as he fought to keep from vomiting. Egg forty-two did him in: when the eggs came back up, they did so with no warning, and he threw up with no control all over the bar. Slim paid out $250 MPC to the bettors and walked out of the bar. The club manager raged. Slim had left quite a mess.

In so many ways, we were all Number 10 GIs. The exploitative nature of our interaction with the Vietnamese—and not just the sex and our attitude toward them, but that they were our surrogates fighting what our government had decided was a global struggle against communism—left all of us looking like ugly Americans. Futhermore, the Vietnamization of the war occurring during 1971 meant that we were about to leave our surrogates to fend for themselves. If such interaction with the Vietnamese didn't make us look ugly enough, our interaction with each other did: drinking for some, drugs for others, the fighting, and even throwing up hard boiled eggs. There wasn't a lot going on in 1971 to make our mothers proud of us. Whatever was going on, however, largely became irrelevant when Nature decided to reclaim the environs of Chu Lai.

CHAPTER 10   TYPHOON HESTER

During the early evening hours of October 22, 1971, Chu Lai head-quarters received notification that Typhoon Hester was three hundred miles southeast of Chu Lai, heading our direction at sixteen knots. Next morning the typhoon was two hundred forty miles closer, bearing down on us at thirty-five knots. By noon, October 23, the full force of Typhoon Hester (ninety knot winds made it a category 2 typhoon) ripped, tore, and shredded Chu Lai. At 7 p.m., the eye of the storm engulfed us and an eerie calm settled over the post. A lone helicopter made a quick sojourn over the base so the brass on board could survey the damage to the area, then returned to the airfield to be battened down for the second visit by the typhoon. A couple of hours later, the winds picked up again and Hester completed the destruction of most buildings that had survived her first assault. By midnight, the storm passed over Chu Lai and darkness enveloped the powerless post.

A warning system comprised of runners, sirens, loudspeakers, and telephone calls on the morning of October 23 told all the soldiers on Chu Lai of the impending storm and ordered them to take cover in fortified bunkers. The idyllic location of our hooch on the precipice overlooking the South China Sea now became a disadvantage. Our hooch would be one of the first hit by the front edge of the storm. As the winds picked up, my three hooch mates and I grabbed what provisions we could from our makeshift living room and moved into the bunker directly north of our front door. The full force of the storm that hit at noon temporarily diminished in our minds the war and any other activities of humanity. Mother Nature, Typhoon Hester reminded us, is far more powerful than any act of humankind, including war. The sheets of rain driven by a fierce wind beat unmercifully against the sand bags, railroad ties, and culvert that protected us. The deafening roar inside the bunker reached into every corner of my body and reminded me that I was mortal, too.

When the calm that accompanied the eye of the storm gave us a reprieve, we left the bunker to survey the damage. Our hooch was destroyed. The corrugated metal roof was gone. Sheets of roofing lay strewn over the hill to the west and north. Most of the plywood siding was gone too, ripped from the skeletal two-by-fours. I walked up the three steps into what remained of the structure. Pieces of furniture lay on the floor or smashed against the upright two-by-fours. As I walked toward the back of the hooch to the bedroom, I saw the South Vietnamese regimental flag still hanging tacked to the joists above where my bed used to be. It hung swollen with rainwater like a giant water balloon. Just as I entered the room, the flag burst in the center along its whole length, splashing its captured rainwater on the floor in front of me. Only a limp, torn flag remained tacked to the joists.

If I had been philosophical—which I was not—I might have drawn some comparison between the renting of the flag and the torn temple curtains on the day of Christ's crucifixion. I might have thought that the torn flag augured the end of the South Vietnamese nation. It was, I could have said, a sign from nature and the gods that all of America's military power couldn't save South Vietnam. The gods had spoken: South Vietnam would be torn asunder and there wasn't anything we Americans could do about it. I could have, but I didn't. Instead I cursed the storm for destroying the one war souvenir I'd hoped to take back to the World. Besides, the flag was the least of my concerns. More importantly, when the wind tore off the roof of our hooch, it took with it more than $1,800 in MPC I'd hidden in the rafters.

One of the great advantages for me in Vietnam (among the many that made the war so enjoyable) was my lack of expenses. Unlike many of the noncommissioned officers my age, I didn't send money home to a wife and a houseful of kids, or to pay child support or alimony, or to nest it away to put kids through college. And, thanks to Uncle Sam, I lived free of charge, no housing costs and no grocery bills. I had no expenses other than cigarettes and booze. At fifteen cents for a pack of cigarettes and a dime for a beer, those expenses were minimal. So every payday, I received my full pay (plus combat pay), paid no taxes, and had no expenses.

Consequently, the soldiers who knew me soon learned that I had money to lend them. I hadn't intentionally set out to become a personal banker in Vietnam. It happened only because one of my hooch mates was always broke and needed a loan. I don't know what he did with his money, but he never had enough of it to make it from one payday to another. So I started lending money to him, and once word got around that I had the money to lend, other soldiers asked for loans, too. I don't know how many usury laws I broke, but I'm sure I violated a few Army regulations along the way. As my business increased, I needed money readily available for my customers. That's when I began hiding MPC in an envelope and tucking it in the rafters above the Vietnamese flag over my bed. That way I didn't have to make a trip to the American Express Bank every time someone needed a loan. I had a lucrative business going until Typhoon Hester blew the roof and my hidden MPC cache to smithereens.

The typhoon also destroyed my jeep. When the storm hit, the jeep was parked in front of the hooch. I sat in the bunker and watched as the canvas top was torn off and flew west toward Laos. The front windshield glass exploded under the force of the wind. Flying debris pelted the jeep unmercifully. It hadn't been much to look at before the typhoon, but it was a total wreck after the storm. I would shortly be leaving Chu Lai and thought about fixing it up to take along. After the storm, a mechanic convinced me that it was a hopeless cause, so when I did leave, I left the jeep sitting on the hill overlooking the South China Sea.

On the morning of October 24, Americal soldiers began surveying the damage caused by Hester. Chu Lai lay in ruins. Seventy-five percent of Chu Lai's 4,055 buildings were destroyed or had sustained severe damage. Many of the buildings were nothing but two-by-four skeletal frames. Many had been blown off their two-foot stilts. Engineers estimated that tens of thousands of plywood sheets and corrugated metal roofing sheets would be required to repair the buildings. Not an outhouse remained standing. Mess halls that hadn't been blown away had burned in fires caused by a mixture of gas leaks and falling metal sheets. The interlocking steel planks (called PSP for pierced steel planking) that served as aprons along Chu Lai's runways had blown away like pieces of paper. Revetments housing aircraft collapsed; many of the aircraft inside them sustained heavy damage. Electrical power and water supplies ceased. The buildings that housed emergency generators lay in ruins. As a consequence, thousands of pounds of meat and other perishable rations spoiled in mess hall and depot lockers. Tops had blown off guard towers; some towers wobbled precariously. Whole sections of fencing lay on the ground; fence posts had snapped off at ground level. For five days, QL1 remained impassable; bridges and sections of the road were washed away. Amazingly,

Hester only took one American life: A captain had braved the storm to check on his troops when a falling piece of metal roofing crushed him in a building he'd entered.

The Vietnamese people fared far worse: our two-by-four, metal-roofed, plywood buildings proved much stronger than wattle-and-thatch homes. Initial reports estimated that the typhoon had destroyed over fifteen thousand Vietnamese homes and damaged another seventeen thousand. The Army issued rice and provided piasters to the families whose homes were destroyed. For the Vietnamese, too, the loss of life had been minimal considering the ferocity of the storm: twenty-six Vietnamese died and another 265 people suffered injuries.

Over the next few days, more Americans and Vietnamese died, but those deaths were never counted in the official tally of Typhoon Hester's body count. For example, around 10:00 the morning of October 24, a young soldier walked in knee-deep water ahead of a truck traveling on QL1 when he stepped into a washout, was swiftly carried away by the current, and drowned. Other soldiers died in similar accidents those first few days after the storm. Other than sitting out the storm in the bunker, the most vivid memory I have of the storm is seeing a soldier's body dangling beneath a helicopter en route to the morgue. The dead soldier had been lashed to a rope suspended from the helicopter when he was plucked out of a flooded area where the chopper couldn't land. The image of the body doubled over with a rope tied around the waist, swaying ten feet or so beneath the helicopter, has always stuck with me. Even now when a helicopter flies overhead and I glance up, I sometimes imagine that soldier's swinging body beneath it.

In the grand scheme of things, despite virtually destroying Chu Lai, Typhoon Hester had little effect on the American war effort in the area. Six months earlier, on April 13, 1971, MACV earmarked Chu Lai for closure in support of Vietnamization, i.e., turning the war over to the South Vietnamese. Hester proved to be merely an inconvenience for Chu Lai's last month of American active service.

Euphemistically and officially, MACV called Chu Lai's deactivation a "redeployment" under the Ninth Increment Republic of Vietnam Redeployment Plan—Keystone Oriole CHARLIE. For the most part, Americal units and materiel were slated for movement to Fort Lewis, Washington, or Da Nang, roughly ninety miles north of Chu Lai. In only a few months, Americal had gone from a 14,000-strong combat force located at 23 landing zones and fire support bases, as well as

Chu Lai proper, employing over 5,000 Vietnamese nationals, to a small residual force protecting American contractors running the electrical power plant for the ARVN who assumed command of Chu Lai on November 27, 1971. By the time Typhoon Hester hit on October 23, nearly half the American soldiers had already been redeployed. The typhoon barely hampered redeployment operations. An official after-action report stated, "Although the physical damage suffered by the base was extensive, the effect on the movement of personnel and equipment out of Chu Lai was minimal. A total of nine units were delayed from one to three days because of rough seas." Even Mother Nature could not interfere with America's retreat.

Certainly, the greatest disruption caused by the redeployment was economic. For six years, the United States government pumped $50 million into the local economy just to build the post. And tens of thousands of American GIs had spent millions of dollars more on everything from blowjobs to haircuts to heroin. People in the small agrarian communities surrounding Chu Lai had learned trades to work on the post or had otherwise provided services to satisfy young GIs' appetites, whatever those might be. In the span of just a couple of months, the GIs and the post were gone.

From the outset, military planners knew that great economic hardship would be forced upon the local residents, but there was simply no good way to retreat from the area and not leave them in a lurch. In June the plan called for a cut to the civilian employment rolls by not replacing any local who left a job. Then in August, a hiring freeze went into effect. Yet in September, the civilian workforce still numbered more than five thousand, roughly the same number of locals employed in May. Obviously, influential locals and their American friends had tried to forestall the inevitable.

That inevitability included more than just the loss of income. It also meant the withdrawal of the protection the American military offered the Vietnamese nationals (VN). Through psychological operations, the Army hoped to convince locals that the redeployment of the American soldiers demonstrated the growing strength of the government of South Vietnam. No one believed it, least of all the VNs working on post or the South Vietnamese soldiers. To get the most out of what little time remained with the Americans, pilfering increased dramatically. Theft of MPC and black-market items by Vietnamese civilians became such an epidemic that eventually enlisted American troops replaced VNs who had worked as cashiers and clerks in the clubs, post exchanges, and other service organizations. However, the problem of pilfering by South Vietnamese soldiers was much more difficult to control and far more dangerous.

By August, redeployment plans were well laid and well known, even though the actual movement of troops had not yet begun. ARVN troops (not just as individuals, but entire squad-size units) began brazenly loading up their trucks with building materials and driving off post. When stopped by MPs, the ARVN soldiers became belligerent, if not indignant, over the fact that the retreating Americans dared stop them from removing materials from a base that was soon to be theirs.

One such incident in mid-August nearly erupted into violence. At around 2 p.m., August 16, a battalion engineer making a routine check of a storage area found in it two ARVN officers, twelve ARVN enlisted men, and two Vietnamese high school students with five two-and-a-half ton trucks. The Vietnamese had stripped most of the metal roofing off the buildings in the area, loaded the metal sheets onto their trucks, and were convoying out of the area when the engineer stopped them. He radioed for the MPs, who responded quickly. The ARVN major in charge of the foraging operation became belligerent, chambered a round into his M-16, and threatened to shoot the MPs if they didn't let the convoy continue. One of the quick talking MPs managed to defuse the situation and convinced the major to accompanying him to the MP Law Enforcement Desk to clear up the confusion.

Once at the office, the major was pointedly told that he was not to steal US government property. He again loaded a round in his M-16 and threatened to shoot the MPs. This time MPs overpowered and subdued him. They eventually turned him and the rest of the unwelcome looters over to the ARVN MPs, who no doubt enjoyed a good laugh at the major's expense. My assignment to Turkey years earlier had prepared me well for such international law enforcement relations.

Even the Kit Carson Scouts got involved in the pilfering. The Kit Carson Scouts (KCSs) were young Vietnamese men employed by the Army to lead American troops through the countryside in search of Viet Cong (VC). Many were themselves former VC fighters, but also a number were local young men who grew-up in the area and knew the terrain and how to move around it. In much the same fashion as General George Crook had used Apache scouts to track Apache bands in America's Southwest a century earlier, the KCSs were incredibly useful allies in ferreting out VC. Of all the Vietnamese, America's retreat from Vietnam left the abandoned scouts in the most precarious position.

The redeployment of the Americans from Chu Lai offered the KCSs few attractive alternatives. The former VC among them could be returned to prisoner of war status. Any of them could be drafted into the ARVN. And, of course, the seemingly unstoppable, potentially victorious VC and North Vietnamese Army (NVA) regulars would not look kindly upon one of their own countryman who'd so effectively collaborated with the enemy. Consequently, incidents of desertion in the KCS units skyrocketed. Possessing draft deferment papers, an acknowledgement of their service with the Americans and something that would be taken from them as the Americans readied to leave, many hoped to blend into the civilian population, thus preventing any of the unsavory alternatives awaiting them.

Some of the scouts used the opportunity as well to feather their nests with plunder from the ungrateful Americans. For example, on September 29, an MP stopped two KCSs departing the post in a pickup. During a search of the vehicle, the MPs found an assortment of tools, mess hall utensils, bedding, clothing, a camera, and M-16 ammunition. The two were probably leaving the post for the last time. The MPs apprehended them and turned them over to the KCS unit. The incident no doubt only delayed their inevitable desertion.

The pilfering by Vietnamese civilian employees, tensions between the ARVN and American troops, and desertions by KCSs increased as the imminent departure of the Americans loomed on the horizon. The only cooperation in the area seemed to be from the enemy. "During the period 1 September to 27 November," the official after-action report noted, "there were no attacks against U.S. bases [including Chu Lai and its twenty-three outposts]." The report went on to conclude that this fact demonstrated the "continued weakening of the enemy." That's a stretch. My guess is the VC and NVA were simply biding their time. Why would an army want to risk losses against an adversary in full-fledged retreat? Clearly, the VC and NVA were waiting patiently for the day that the KCSs were dreading so much: the final departure of the Americans from Chu Lai.

After Typhoon Hester nearly destroyed Chu Lai, the pace of the redeployment accelerated. On November 1, the USO shut down its operations; nine days later, so did the American Express Bank. By that time, all the clubs, enlisted and officer, had closed. As of November 14, over twelve thousand troops had been redeployed, leaving roughly two thousand in Chu Lai. Days later the curtain began closing around America's four-year operation. The after-action report continues:

> As intelligence indicated a strong possibility of a rocket and sapper attack on Chu Lai Combat Base during the last few days before final redeployment, precautionary measures were taken to improve the defensive posture of Chu Lai. Patrolling, ambushing and air cavalry operations were intensified west of Chu Lai; Vietnamese employees were arbitrarily discharged five days before the final redeployment [November 22] to reduce possible intelligence risks; a curfew forbidding any movement between 1900-0600 hours was instituted; and defensive forces were withdrawn from the perimeter at night, except for listening posts, and positioned around five small 'enclave' areas into which the remaining troops and vital installations were concentrated.

Such was the death rattle of the once great symbol of American power situated along the sandy beaches of the beautiful South China Sea in Quang Tin Province.

On November 25, troops evacuated the final three outlying firebases west of Chu Lai. By 10:30 the morning of November 27, the remaining soldiers departed Chu Lai, except for a small contingent to protect remaining contracting operations and an even smaller group of brass to conduct the ceremony turning over the post to the ARVN, an event that occurred at noon.

From the beginning of the redeployment on September 10 through November 27, virtually all troops and materiel had departed by sea or air. However, as the after-action report noted, "[A] single road convoy of Military Police vehicles completed [the Army's] disengagement from Chu Lai." My sole involvement in Operation Keystone Oriole CHARLIE was as part of that convoy.

Typhoon Hester and the continuing redeployment of Chu Lai's American forces virtually shut down CID operations. Hester's winds blew our office off its stilts. Troops were leaving faster than we could identify witnesses or suspects. Crime doesn't take a holiday, but our investigation of it certainly did. By mid-November, all we knew for sure is that our operations would be moved to Da Nang. The 23rd MP

Company (CI) would cease to exist, and we would be integrated into the 8th MP Company (CI) in Da Nang.

On November 25, a deuce-and-a-half and a five-ton truck arrived at what remained of our office. We spent the day loading desks, chairs, filing cabinets, and other miscellaneous furnishings onto the trucks. My biggest concern, however, was the loading of our evidence locker, a CONEX container.

CONEX containers were metal shipping crates designed to stack inside a ship's hold. They were used to ship war materiel to Vietnam, but once in-country, they became the most versatile "buildings" around. Creative GIs converted them into storage sheds, clinics, garages, PXs, mailrooms, and whatever else GIs needed that would be enclosed, lockable, and already assembled. They were rectangular and came in a variety of sizes. The standard size I saw in Vietnam, however, was about seven feet high, roughly six feet across, and a little over eight feet in length. Like a semi-trailer, they had two metal, hinged doors at one end that were latched with a pivoting bar. The doors could be locked with a padlock.

When CID opened an office at Chu Lai, one of these CONEXs was placed along the side of the CID building and transformed into an evidence storage locker. Someone had welded eight metal shelves, each about two feet deep, on the inside walls (four shelves on each side) running the full length of the container. The shelves were designated "A" through "H," and spaces on each shelf were numbered "1" through "8." An agent logged evidence into a green-covered ledger book that contained columns for location (e.g., "Shelf A, slot 5"), date, case number, suspect—if any, description of the item, and final disposition of the case and evidence. Because evidence must have a chain of custody (a record of everyone who ever had control of the evidence) from the time the police acquire it until the case is completed (including all legal action), only one agent could have access to the evidence locker. This agent, called the evidence custodian, kept the only key to the padlock used to lock the CONEX, logged-in all evidence, saw that evidence was properly disposed of when cases were closed, and, most importantly, ensured all the paperwork was completed and filed. ("Disposing of evidence" meant returning it to a rightful owner, returning it to the Army [weapons, for example], or destroying it, as we did with drugs.)

Being evidence custodian was not a sought-after job. It involved a lot of administrative work that none of us wanted. The job was, therefore, assigned by the time-honored military tradition of giving it to the Fucking New Guy (FNG). That poor son-of-a-bitch would then keep the job until just before it was his turn to rotate back to the States. Around that time, the next FNG who showed up got the padlock key and the job. Unfortunately when I arrived at Chu Lai in February, I was the FNG, and the old evidence custodian was within a couple of days of leaving. When Strawberry indoctrinated me into the unit, he made sure that I understood the FNG rule.

So my first few days at Chu Lai were spent with the evidence custodian in the stuffy hot CONEX inventorying and signing for every piece of evidence. There was plenty: drugs, knives, live hand grenades, handguns, rifles, ammunition, watches, cameras, wallets, broken bottles, clothes, beer cans, stereo components, speakers, jewelry, pieces of wire, sheets of paper, envelopes, and on and on and on. The old custodian and I accounted for every piece of evidence that, according to the logbook, was still in the CONEX. For four years, custodians had logged in evidence. For four years, cases had been adjudicated. For four years, custodians had failed to dispose of the evidence. I was signing for evidence belonging to cases in which the subjects had returned to the States two and three years earlier. Hell, they were going to school at Berkeley on the GI bill and I was signing for their three-year-old heroin! I swore then that I would not turn over all that shit to the next FNG. Damn it, I would do the job right. By November, however, all I'd accomplished was to push old evidence to the back of the shelves and to log in the new stuff. If it hadn't been for Hester, a few months later I would have turned over the key to the CONEX to some poor FNG who'd have inherited all that shit in the evidence locker. But with the deactivation of Chu Lai, my primary job was to escort the CONEX evidence locker—which, remarkably, was unfazed by Hester—to Da Nang.

On November 26, a soldier operating a forklift picked up my CONEX locker and set it on the bed of the five-ton truck. I tied the container to the truck bed with a couple of log chains. Before loading the CONEX onto the truck, I'd tried to tie down evidence on the shelves inside, but realized that was a futile undertaking. As the forklift tipped and jostled the CONEX in place, I could envision the evidence (don't forget the hand grenades) falling off the shelves. I yelled a couple of times at the forklift driver to be careful (actually, "Watch what the fuck you're doing," was more like it), but then I realized that the bumping and jerking along QL1 wouldn't be any better. I resigned myself to the inevitable mess that would be inside the CONEX once I got it to Da Nang. Just before noon on November 27, I threw my duffle bag onto the back of a deuce-and-a-half and climbed into a passenger bus loaded with CID agents and MPs. Thirty minutes later, we lurched along in the middle of an MP convoy of dozens of vehicles, the only overland convoy involved in the deactivation of Chu Lai, heading north on QL1. Like millions of GIs before me and since who've ridden anywhere in an Army bus, I leaned my head against a window and went to sleep.

Chu Lai had been a creation of the Vietnam War. Before US Marines splashed ashore on the beach of what became Chu Lai in 1965, it didn't exist. With our departure in 1971, its future was in question. Undoubtedly, the agrarian communities, the rice paddies, the sand dunes, the rivers and streams, the fishing weirs, the water buffaloes, the farmer, his wife and their children, and the beautiful beaches that were there a century before 1965 would remain, resilient as ever. Chu Lai's entire lifecycle had, to that point, revolved around the Americans' war. That was not the case with Da Nang, which held an historic place in Vietnam's history, although outsiders influenced its founding as much as they had Chu Lai's. (An update: Chu Lai survives. After the fall of Saigon in 1975, the post fell into disrepair and was virtually abandoned. By the early 2000s, Vietnam's economic recovery inspired the government to renovate the airfield and environs. Today it is called Chu Lai International Airport. Very near where my hooch sat overlooking the South China Sea is a resort.)

About twenty miles south of the city of Da Nang sits the ancient port city Hoi An. It had served as the economic center of that area of ancient Vietnam where trading ships from all over Asia converged. The Europeans first arrived in the area in the fifteenth century. As Asian junks had done for centuries, European caravels began unloading trade goods at this ancient trading port. Eventually, the river allowing access to the port began silting up, and the European traders, who had switched to larger trading ships, found it more and more difficult to get to Hoi An. The logical mooring and discharging location for the Europeans was the Bay of Da Nang to the north. Soon, because of European needs, the port city of Da Nang sprang up to accept the trade goods disgorging from the large ships. Quickly Da Nang became the new international trade center and Hoi An became a quaint ancient city. One Vietnamese scholar explains:

Hoi An still plays an important role, principally because of the unique historical and cultural values it has created. Parts of the town—streets, alleys, the harbour, houses, religious constructions—still stand relatively intact, and one will be surprised by their architectural richness and variety. Most of the other ancient cities have been affected by time and weather. Destroyed or rebuilt, they have almost nothing to tell about their past existence, with the exception of a few palaces, temples or tombs. But Hoi An is a unique case in Vietnam and a rare case in the world in terms of conservation.

By being off the beaten path of QL1 and having lost its purpose as a trading center, Hoi An escaped the destruction of the twentieth century wars that so mauled and mutilated the rest of the country.

Da Nang had not been so lucky. It sits squarely at a pivotal point of the country. Situated halfway between Hanoi and Saigon (now Ho Chi Minh City), QL1 runs through it, and the Bay of Da Nang was as enticing in the twentieth century as it had been to European traders trying to find a replacement harbor for Hoi An. Back in 1965 when Americans watched the black-and-white images of the first landing of US Marines to hit the beaches of Vietnam, they splashed ashore on Da Nang's beaches. From Da Nang, South Vietnamese patrol boats launched to attack North Vietnamese bases—attacks preparatory to the Maddox incident that led to the Gulf of Tonkin Resolution. And it was to Da Nang that displaced South Vietnamese flocked during the war, and cowered in at the very end of it. In 1965, 228,035 residents called Da Nang home. When I arrived there in November 1971, nearly twice that number (430,639) were crammed into the city. During the final death throes of South Vietnam in 1975, more than a million Vietnamese crushed into Da Nang seeking safety from the invading North Vietnamese Army. The next year, repatriation and rehabilitation efforts by the unified government of Vietnam brought that number down to 330,575. Indeed, Da Nang had not been spared any of the scourges of war.

The old city of Da Nang sat on the western side of the mouth of the Song Han (Han River) in the southeasterly corner of the bowl formed by the Bay of Da Nang to the north of the city. A narrow strip of land east of the river ended at the South China Sea at a place called China Beach. The strip of land contained a number of military installations, some American—Marble Mountain Airfield, for example—some Vietnamese, and, if television can be believed, a large number of sexy American nurses. I rarely ventured to that side of Da Nang and, therefore, cannot vouch for the accuracy of the old television series called *China Beach*.

Southwest of the old city of Da Nang laid a huge military complex containing Da Nang Air Base—from where "freedom birds" soared toward the World—and numerous smaller military installations, both American and Vietnamese. As one traveled north past these compounds, military temporary architecture—the same style as at Chu Lai—gave way quickly to an eclectic mix of French colonial and "war refugee" design. Most buildings were only one-story high. A few more prominent government administrative buildings, schools, temples, pagodas, churches, and even a cathedral, stood over one-story, but not many did. Many residents lived in temporary houses built on rivers, canals, marshes, and even over sewer canals. (Canals covered with concrete composed most of Da Nang's sewer system. Much of the covering concrete had broken open exposing sewage canals through which sluggish human waste, animal offal, and other refuse collected as a repugnant sludge.)

Streets were narrow, mainly unpaved. Electricity and water services to the city, not counting the military installations, were sporadic and unreliable. Traffic bottlenecked at Cau Nguyen Hoang, the one bridge spanning Song Han and thus connecting east and west Da Nang. Traffic cops—called "white mice"—dressed in white uniforms and, wearing white helmet liners and white gun belts and holsters, danced a fandango while standing on a pedestal in the center of major intersections. Somehow their movements, at first undecipherable to a newcomer, directed a collection composed of every third world conveyance imaginable, as well as a bevy of modern military vehicles, to move through the intersections.

"Slicky boys," young, pre-teen Vietnamese boys, accosted every American vehicle that had to stop in these intersections, and stole anything that wasn't tied down. They'd steal your spare tire. They'd steal the jerry can off the back of your jeep. They'd try to reach in to grab anything lying on the seats. And, of course, there was always the possibility that one of the slicky boys would toss a hand grenade into the backseat of a vehicle. One of the first survival tactics I learned in Da Nang was to carry mace. Anytime I was creeping along in traffic, or stopped dead, I kept an eye out for the slicky boys. When one ran up to my jeep to try to take something, I'd hose him down with the aerosol can of mace. I don't recall that anything got stolen out of my jeep.

Slicky boys, white mice, large permanent buildings, open sewer canals, traffic congestion, the smells, the sounds, all these were so much different from the rustic, agrarian Vietnam that surrounded Chu Lai. Likewise, I found my job in Da Nang equally different from the one I had at Chu Lai.

I never investigated one crime in Da Nang. To my knowledge, none of us from the 23rd Americal MP (CI) investigated any crimes once combined with the 8th MP Group (CI) at Da Nang. The latter agents saw us as interlopers. As with the CID agents in Saigon whom I'd met upon arriving in Vietnam, the Da Nang agents saw themselves as big city cops and us as country bumpkins. So for my last three months in the war, I worked little and partied often.

When the MP convoy arrived in Da Nang, we went directly to one of the many American military compounds in the area. My CONEX was unloaded and set beside a similar CONEX evidence locker belonging to the Da Nang CID office. I soon learned that the Da Nang evidence custodians had done a much better job of disposing of evidence over the past four years than we Chu Lai bumpkins had. Because Da Nang belonged to the 8th MP Group (CI) headquartered at Long Binh, inspectors periodically showed up to check over the evidence and procedures related to the proper disposal of it (as well as all other CID functions). Evidence custodians, therefore, kept meticulous records, disposed of evidence at the appropriate times, and, in short, kept a well-maintained evidence locker. Because we at Chu Lai weren't under the 8th MP Group, no inspector ever looked at our locker. The result, as I mentioned earlier, was successive evidence custodians pushing old evidence to the back of the shelves and logging in the new stuff, creating an absolute mess.

The jostling by the forklift, both getting the CONEX on and off the flatbed, and the jolting, bumpy ride up QL1 hadn't improved the situation. When I opened the doors, I found nearly everything thrown on to the floor of the middle aisle. It would take me weeks to sort through the mess.

Unfortunately, when I opened the door to the CONEX, standing next to me was a warrant officer of the Da Nang office—if he wasn't in charge of the office, he certainly made it seem so. He was a Jack LaLanne-look-alike if there ever was one. (For younger readers, Jack LaLanne was a fitness guru before fitness became fashionable. He had an Arnold Schwarzenegger-like body—or, Arnold has his—and hosted a fitness program on television in the 1950s and 1960s.) The LaLanne-look-alike was also a martial arts master of some flavor. He had nailed a board covered with a piece of leather to a telephone pole outside of the CID office. For an hour or so a day, he went out to the pole and punched the board. The punching apparently did nothing for his disposition; he was always in ill humor.

When I swung open the doors, he exploded.

"What the fuck is all that shit?" he yelled.

Without confessing that it was four years' worth of shit, I told him that we had a lot of crime at Chu Lai, and I would be putting all the evidence back in order and disposing of the evidence from the recently adjudicated cases.

"You're goddamned right you will," he growled. "You ain't dumping that shit on us. You get rid of it."

Da Nang's CID evidence custodian also had been standing with us. Turning to him, the warrant officer shook a finger in his face and snarled, "Don't let these motherfuckers from Chu Lai give you one piece of evidence that doesn't have a proper chain of custody or that belongs with a case that has already been adjudicated." He then turned and stormed away. The evidence custodian looked at the mess in my CONEX, shook his head, and said, "Good luck," as he, too, walked off.

I spent practically every day of the rest of my time in Da Nang trying to put all the evidence in the right spots on the shelves according to the logbook listing, trying to determine which cases were still active and which already adjudicated and closed, and getting rid of evidence. The former task was monotonous and time-consuming, but fairly straightforward: check the tag on the evidence, find its location listed in the logbook (for example, Shelf A, slot 5), and put it there. The second task, however, proved much more difficult.

I divided the cases associated with the evidence into three categories: cases I could prove had been adjudicated and closed; cases still pending; and, cases about which I didn't have a clue what their status was. Regarding the first cases, using what records we'd salvaged from Chu Lai or copies of those records filed elsewhere, I identified victims who'd lost property to thefts, such as watches, jewelry, stereos, or whatever. Then I'd send a message to Army Personnel to find the last known addresses of the victims. After four years, that meant most of these victims were out of the Army living back in the States. Once I had those addresses, I sent messages to the nearest Army posts asking

CID agents there to try to verify that the former soldiers still lived at the last know addresses. If all that went well, I'd box up a piece of evidence from a theft occurring years before and mail it back to its rightful owner. I'm sure the receipt of such boxes containing watches, jewelry, cameras, and so on surprised many former soldiers.

The second category of cases, those still open and not yet adjudicated, were easier to handle. I made sure that the evidence sat at right spots on the shelves and followed those cases for the few months I had remaining in Vietnam. If a case was adjudicated before I left Da Nang, I disposed of the evidence. Of these cases, I ultimately turned over less than a dozen to the Da Nang evidence custodian. I'm sure the Jack LaLanne-look-alike found even that disturbing.

But for the majority of the evidence, I could find no records to determine the status of the cases. The typhoon had destroyed most of our CID records, as well as any records held by Chu Lai's legal office. I made the decision that if I couldn't find records for a case, it was closed. So if it was a closed case, I could dispose of the evidence. But first, a military lawyer had to sign the destruction forms. Fortunately, I found an Army lawyer willing to work with me to dispose of the evidence; and dispose of it we did.

Whatever the status of the case, I had a number of options for disposing of the evidence: as mentioned, if I could identify a rightful owner, I sent him the property; if I couldn't identify an owner, I destroyed the property (I broke it into pieces, usually) and threw it away; if it was Army property, such as a weapon, I returned it to the Army supply system; if it was contraband, such as AK-47s or old hand grenades, I turned it over to the Army's Explosive Ordinance Disposal (EOD) unit for destruction; if narcotics, I destroyed it. To do the latter, I got a fifty-five--gallon drum and some cans of diesel fuel. I threw packages and vials of heroin, kilos of marijuana in plastic bags or pre-rolled cigarettes, and an assortment of other drugs into the barrel, soak it all with the diesel fuel, and lit it. I probably broke a few Army rules doing it that way, but it got rid of evidence.

God, I hated that job of disposing of evidence so damn much. But because we weren't being assigned any cases by the Da Nang office, that's the only official job I had. To break up the monotony of all the administrative bullshit associated with disposing of the evidence, I started generating my own cases. That didn't please the Da Nang CID agents, but even they couldn't argue with success.

The easiest police work for me to do without actually being assigned cases was the physical security survey. These surveys were security audits of a commander's area of responsibility. To conduct such a survey, an agent would target a military unit, find out who the commander was, and then notify him that a security survey was about to take place. There was nothing secret about it. Commanders usually weren't happy to have such an audit because their careers might be on the line if the evaluation showed lapses in their security. Regardless, my intent wasn't to jeopardize their careers, but rather to test their security and have a little fun in the process.

There was a format that one had to follow for such a survey. An agent had to document the company's mission, the types of equipment that it had, any reported losses, the level of security, and the physical layout of the place, such as perimeter fences, guard towers, and so forth. After accomplishing these preliminaries, the rest of the inspection was as thorough or shallow as an agent wanted to make it. In Da Nang, I liked making them thorough because that was the only adrenalin rush left for me.

My goal, then, was to test the security of the area. That is, to see if I could sneak in, steal something, and get back out. Back in the States, doing such an activity was no big deal. There guards frequently walked their posts with empty weapons. Vietnam was very different: guards were armed with weapons and had plenty of ammunition. Guards in towers had M-60s and guards on walking posts had M-16s. Moreover, many of the guards, especially the cherries, were scared shitless. They were seeing "gooks" jumping out from behind every bush, climbing through wires, and who knew what else.

Someplace along the line while I was still in Chu Lai, I got the idea that we should steal equipment from a unit we were surveying. That usually meant stealing a vehicle. I figured that the administrative details, such as reporting losses, physical layout and so on, were merely window-dressing. If we really wanted to know how good the security was, we needed to challenge it. For my first couple of these adventures, I had to go it alone. I couldn't get another agent to go with me—nobody. When I suggested it, the response was, "You're crazy. You're fucking insane. Those guys have guns." I knew that, but I relied on the fact that they would recognize me as a GI, despite a justifiable homicide I'd investigated on a GI who was shot crawling through a motor pool fence. Nevertheless, I rationalized that I wasn't short, I didn't look Asian, I didn't have black hair. Surely they'd recognize me as a GI, I told myself. So at night, I would steal a vehicle from a company's motor pool.

My intent wasn't to harass commanders and guards. Rather, it was to address the very real problem the Army had in Vietnam of vehicles disappearing. All over Vietnam, it was not uncommon to see a Vietnamese driving down the road in an American military vehicle painted orange or some other ridiculous color. But the Vietnamese weren't the ones stealing the vehicles. Most often I found that some GI strung out on heroin was looking for easy money, and to get it sold stolen Army vehicles on the black market.

That's why I decided to start stealing vehicles as a part of a security survey. Then I could prove to commanders that their physical security had big holes in it. Besides, frankly, it was a lot of fun. So once I arrived in Da Nang and couldn't have any more fun investigating narcotics cases, I decided to conduct physical security surveys, a procedure that included stealing vehicles.

Some nights that meant sneaking into a motor pool. On other occasions, I would walk into a motor pool during the day and then hide there until night. Other times, I'd put on a uniform and walk through the front gate. Regardless of how I got into the motor pool, my next step was to steal a vehicle. Sometimes I would take someone else with me (after I'd been successful a number of times, other agents wanted to get in on the fun and glory that went with my brand of "security survey"). Sometimes we'd push the vehicle to sneak it out the gate. Other times, I'd start the engine and drive out. Anytime a vehicle left a motor pool, the driver was supposed to have a "trip ticket," a white piece of paper that showed that the trip out of the motor pool was authorized. The ticket also documented one's destination, the vehicle mileage, the time of departure, the expected trip time, and so forth. A driver was supposed to show this ticket to the guard at the motor pool gate and at the main gate to the post. If I had to deal with a guard, usually I'd just wave a white piece of paper out the window and the guard would let me go through the gate. So much for the security enhancement of the trip ticket.

There were certainly a number of ways for me to steal vehicles; I was limited only by my imagination. Not once did I get caught and not once was I unsuccessful. During my year in Vietnam, I stole around two dozen vehicles. Most of them I stole during the three months I spent in Da Nang. I stole jeeps, ambulances, and trucks—three-quarter ton, deuce and a half, and five-ton trucks. The biggest thing I ever stole was a semi-tractor. After I'd steal a vehicle, I'd write up a report that I gave to the commander detailing what I'd stolen, how I did it, and who—if I knew whom—had been negligent and, therefore, contributed to my success. Correcting the problem was entirely the responsibility of the commander. I don't know if any of the problems got fixed; I wasn't around long enough to do follow-up surveys.

One of these adventures that I remember with great amusement involved my stealing a three-quarter ton ambulance, the kind used in the old television series *M.A.S.H.*—a big green box behind the cab, a red cross with a white background painted on the box's sides, top, and doors. To steal it, another agent and I put on uniforms over our civilian clothing, and after dark we sneaked into a motor pool. In it was parked a whole row of these ambulances, maybe a dozen or more of them. We picked one out and got into it. One didn't need a key to start the engines in these ambulances. In place of a key, there was a toggle switch. I flipped the toggle switch and started the engine. There were guards in the towers, and as I started the engine, I watched for their reaction. They never paid any attention to us. There were mechanics working on other vehicles, so there wouldn't be anything unusual about an engine starting. I then drove out of the motor pool without a trip ticket or any authorization. It had been too easy.

Our goal now was to get the ambulance off the post. To do that, we'd have to drive through the main gate where a guard was supposed to stop us and check our trip ticket. When we got to the front gate, a young private stopped us. That was good; that's what he was supposed to do.

"Where you goin'?" he asked.

"Just heading into town. We're hoping to get laid."

My partner laughed and yelled, "Fuckin' yea!"

The guard asked to see our trip ticket, and I told him we didn't have one.

"Well do you have any authorization to leave post?"

"No," I told him.

"Then, I can't let you go," he pronounced authoritatively.

"Oh, come on," I pleaded. "I've been cooped up on this fucking post for a week and I'm hornier than hell. I just want to go down and spend a little time with a whore."

"I can't let you go."

"Come on, man," my partner cajoled him, "all we want is a little pussy. We'll be right back."

We bantered back and forth for fifteen minutes. I even offered to bring him back a whore if he wanted one.

"We'll bring her back and you can get a blowjob right here in the back of our ambulance," I said. "We'll even pay for it," added my partner.

I'm not sure if the proffered sexual favor turned the tide or he just got tired of arguing with us. He stepped back from the ambulance and with a wave of his hand said, "Go ahead. Get the fuck out of here."

I drove out the gate and went around a corner to be out of sight of the guard. "What a dumb shit," my partner said laughingly. We stopped and stripped off the uniforms revealing our civilian clothes underneath. We turned the vehicle around and headed back to the gate. There we showed our CID credentials to the stunned young man and told him to call the sergeant of the guard. Once the sergeant arrived, we explained what had happened, and the private was relieved of his post. We returned the ambulance to the motor pool and the next day filed our report with the commander. What makes this incident so memorable is that the young private who tried to stop us from going off post was the only guard who ever challenged me. Yet, in the end, he did no better than any of the guards who simply let me go. If I could steal two dozen Army vehicles and drive them off post with virtually no problems, how easy was it for the drug- or money-motivated GI to do the same? Very easy. That's why one saw so many Vietnamese driving around in wild-colored Army vehicles. The financial impact of all these stolen vehicles to the American taxpayers must have been tremendous.

Another incident that demonstrates how easy it was to steal Army vehicles involved my stealing a semi-tractor; and I didn't even know how to drive one. Once I crawled into the cab and saw all the buttons and switches, I wondered how I'd ever drive it off post. First, I had to figure out how to start it. I then played with the gears to get it moving in the right direction. I was sure that I'd get caught this time as I was jerking my way across post heading toward the gate. Once again, the guard looked up at me in the cab and waved me through the gate. No trip ticket, no questions. I knew I had been lucky to get that far, so about twenty feet outside the gate I stopped because I knew I'd wreck the son-of-a-bitch. I crawled out of the cab and went about my normal routine identifying myself and so on. This time, however, I had to find a real driver to take the tractor back to the motor pool.

Admittedly, stealing vehicles was the most exciting thing I did in Da Nang, or, for that matter, was allowed to do by the Da Nang CID office. But that was OK. I so enjoyed stealing vehicles that I was getting all the adrenalin rushes I needed. It really was an incredible exciting thing to do given that armed guards could have—actually should have—shot me as I either crawled through their fences or drove off with their vehicles.

Besides cleaning up and disposing of evidence in my CONEX and stealing vehicles as a result of security surveys, the only other thing I did the whole time I spent in Da Nang was party. And we did hard. I'd spend an eight-hour day disposing of evidence and a few hours in an evening one night a week stealing vehicles. Other than that, I partied. There was nothing else to do.

When I arrived at Da Nang, I was assigned a bed in an open-bay hooch with over a half a dozen other CID agents. An attempt had been made to partition the hooch into separate rooms. There still wasn't enough privacy for my liking. I knew I wouldn't be staying there long. Nevertheless, my first job was to find a hooch maid. I'd done so well at Chu Lai that my hooch mates thought I could do well in Da Nang too. I didn't. I hired a young woman who'd obviously been scarred by war; she had a cute face, but from the neck down to her feet, one could see that burn scars disfigured every inch of her skin that wasn't clothed. Her feet were burned, her hands, her arms, and her neck. I assumed she was equally scarred under the clothing. Probably the most compassionate thing I did in Vietnam was to hire her out of sympathy for her. Then she stole us blind. She took everything that wasn't nailed down. When I bought brand new underwear at the Freedom Hill Exchange, she stole it. She stole cassette tapes. She stole toothpaste. She stole deodorant. She stole anything. So much for my compassion. I fired her and hired another. In the meantime, what I was most interested in was getting out of that crowded hooch and moving to an isolated place such as I'd had at Chu Lai.

Unlike Chu Lai, though, Da Nang actually had nightlife. Da Nang had bars, restaurants, a variety of clubs, and a hundred other diversions for any young man unfettered by a moral code. I quickly adapted to my new surroundings.

Within twenty-four hours of arriving in Da Nang, I learned that much of its nightlife revolved around B-girls. B-girls (short for bar girls) hustled drinks from GIs. A GI would pay exorbitant prices for bourbons for himself and glasses of tea for a B-girl just to have the privilege of drinking with a woman. As the night went on, the prices increased as the customers got drunk. Bar owners paid B-girls a percentage of the drinks they got GIs to buy. Many, but not all, of the B-girls were also prostitutes. Bars frequently had small rooms on the second floor or, lacking that, down a back hallway. As a night wore on, B-girl prostitutes and their customers migrated to these rooms. On any given night, I watched a B-girl make a half a dozen or more trips to a back room with different customers.

However, my most intriguing night with a B-girl had absolutely nothing to do with sex. It was about the healing quality of an Oriental cure for the common cold. I had been in Da Nang not long when I caught an awful cold. I was at a club, and I was coughing constantly. Every nerve ending on my body hurt like hell. One of the B-girls told me that she had a cure for me. But there was a catch.

"We'll go to upstairs room," she said in her broken English, "so you pay for me like we going upstairs to fuck."

Sex was the furthest thing from my mind that night. "It's OK," she assured me. "I've got good medicine for you." So I shelled out the money to her boss man and we went upstairs.

Once in the room, she introduced me to what I later learned was called coining. She had me take off my shirt and sit cross-legged on the floor. There was a knock at the door, and someone from the kitchen delivered a kettle of boiling hot water. She set the kettle in front of me. She took a blanket off the bed and draped it over my heading and the kettle so that I breathed in steam from the hot water. Then she took a coin and started rubbing it briskly across my back. I could feel the coin getting hotter than hell. I don't know how she held on to it, but she did. She continued rubbing my back for quite a while. Then she uncovered my head and told me to lie on my back on the bed. She took the same coin and started rubbing my chest with the same results. I could then see that she was leaving red marks all across my chest.

When she finished, I was very tired and still felt like hell. I left, not just a little puzzled about what I'd paid for, and went back to my hooch and straight to bed. The next morning I was feeling pretty good. I was on my way to the latrine to shave and shower when one of my hooch mates exclaimed, "What in the hell happened to you?"

"Nothing," I said, rather perplexed at his sudden outburst.

"Look in the fucking mirror!" he said gesturing at my chest and back.

I looked in the mirror. My chest and back looked as if I'd been flogged. The red marks I'd seen on my chest the previous evening, as well as the ones I hadn't seen on my back, were now all bruised black and blue. The coining had certainly left its mark on me, but my cold was gone. I don't know if there was any connection between my Florence Nightingale's remedy and my recovery from the cold. But I guess the coining may have acted like a mustard plaster—and I'm not sure a mustard plaster would cure a cold. Nevertheless, I felt much better the day after being coined. (As an aside, I know about cases in Los Angeles when school officials have reported child abuse against Oriental parents because it looks as if they've whipped their children. I suspect coining is responsible for some of those cases.)

Irrespective of coining, on my second night in Da Nang I met the B-girl that became pivotal to my Da Nang sojourn. She worked at a bar in the downtown area. I knew her only as Lin. The first night we met, she tried to hustle me. I wasn't as starved for female companionship as many GIs, so I wasn't interested in buying her tea. Neither was I interested in paying her for sex, although I'm not sure she was a prostitute. For whatever reason, I did, however, enjoy talking to her and apparently she enjoyed being around me. During that first night, she kept stopping at my table to talk, and the boss man kept scolding her and running her off. He wasn't making any money from me and wanted her to entice other soldiers to buy her tea.

The next couple of evenings, I stopped in the same bar and continued my flirtations with Lin. She'd figured out by now that she wasn't going to make any money off me, but, nevertheless, we were getting friendly. About the third or fourth evening, she invited me home with her after work. She lived in a hole-in-the-wall apartment down one of Da Nang's back streets. I spent that evening with her. The next morning as I left, I began thinking that, instead of finding a hooch on post similar to the one I had at Chu Lai, maybe I ought to find a place in Da Nang. Then I could live completely separate from the Army—except for work, I wouldn't be on post at all. I knew I'd be doing that bullshit administrative stuff to get rid of evidence. I couldn't stand the thought of being cooped up on post every evening after having had such a boring day at the office.

That night I returned to the club with one purpose in mind: to see if Lin knew a place I could rent in Da Nang. Between her dalliances with other GIs to hustle drinks, she stopped at my table and invited me to her place again. When she finished work, we went back to her little hole-in-the-wall apartment.

After having sex, we laid together on her little single bed when I asked her, "Do you know where I can rent a house?"

She thought for a moment, staring toward the ceiling. "Maybe," she said nodding her head.

"Let me know," I said.

The next night, Lin told me that she'd found a place. When she got off work around 1 a.m., instead of going to her little hole-in-the-wall place, she navigated as I drove the jeep along winding back streets, across major thoroughfares—such as they were—to a walled compound. (This meant driving in pitch-darkness. As a wartime measure, there were no streetlights or outside lights of any kind on. Windows for businesses and residences alike were shuttered, holding in all interior lighting.) The wall of the compound was made of some sort of blocks, such as cinder blocks, that were whitewashed. It stood several feet high. There were only two breaks in the wall. There was a big double wrought iron gate to drive through and a much smaller pedestrian gate next to it.

Lin reached in front of me and beeped the jeep's horn a couple of times. A mama-san appeared at the pedestrian gate. Lin walked over to the gate and spoke to the older woman. In a couple of minutes she returned to the jeep and said, "Twenty dollars a month OK?" I didn't know what I was getting for my twenty bucks, but if it got me a place to live off post, it would be worth it.

"Sure," I responded.

Lin yelled back toward the mama-san who then swung open the driveway gate. Lin walked ahead of me as I drove into the compound. I was duly impressed. Inside sat five homes of various sizes. The mama-san lived in one of them. Vietnamese families lived in the other three. The one that I'd just rented had two bedrooms with an adjoining kitchen and living area. All the rooms had bare cement floors. Neither bedroom had a door; curtains covered the doorways. The place had furnishings such as chairs, a table, two beds, lamp stands, and a two-burner camp stove in the kitchen. The house didn't have a bathroom, but located a short walk from it was a communal restroom with sinks and a shower that served all the residents. The compound had electrical power, too, supplied by a diesel generator. Just having electricity set the place apart from most residences in Da Nang.

The mama-san gave me a key that Lin told me unlocked the pedestrian gate. If I ever needed the locked driveway gate opened, she explained, I was to honk and the mama-san would open it for me, any-time day or night. (True to the mama-san's word, it didn't matter when I came home, I'd honk and she'd always open the gate for me.) When I had left Chu Lai, I couldn't imagine that I'd find anything better than my hooch overlooking the shimmering South China Sea. Now at 2:00 in the morning, I stood in the best-looking house I'd seen in Vietnam, and it belonged to me. And standing there with me was Lin, pretty and sexy, available and willing. I'd been in Da Nang exactly one week. Yes, this war just kept getting better.

At first I was concerned about the security of the house. None of the windows had glass in them. They were just open portals. When it rained or in the evening, I closed the jalousie shutters, but during the day I had wide-open windows. And the house had a wooden front door that couldn't be locked. So my house sat open for anyone who had access to the compound. Eventually, I would have almost all my clothes, stereo equipment, and nearly everything else I owned in that house. But my initial fears about losing anything were unfounded; I never lost a thing. I felt very secure in that house, not only from thiev-ery, but from the war as well.

Not surprisingly, Lin became a regular visitor to the house. She never actually set up housekeeping and she still had her job as a B-girl, but she was there regularly. She hadn't hustled me for drinks, nor prostituted herself to me for money. But in retrospect, she ended up spending much of her time in a very nice house as opposed to the hole-in-the-wall apartment she rented. So, maybe I did get hustled. But it didn't matter because she took good care of me. On my second day in the house, she showed up with pots, pans, plates, and flatware, and from then on did all the cooking, making the most fantastic meals. She introduced me to true Vietnamese culinary delights. She'd stop at an open-air market on the way to my house, buy all the ingredients for a great meal, and cook it for the two of us. And, of course, there was the sex, frequent, passionate sex. Lin was so concerned about my carnal desires that on days when she couldn't come to my house, she'd send one of her prostitute friends to spend the night with me—free of charge, of course. On other evenings when I'd find myself attracted to another young lady whom I wanted to bring to the house, Lin would make herself scarce.

News of my cornucopia of debauchery traveled at lightning speed through the CID and MPI offices. Shortly, my house became a frat house for CID and MPI cops, as well as a few medics who partied with us. I had to maintain some control over the whole concept of this frat house, so guys could only come there with my invitation. I was rather liberal in extending invitations, so many nights there would be six or seven of us partying at the house. Lin's responsibility was to provide the girls. She'd find out from me how many cops and medics would be at my house on an evening and would send enough prostitutes to accommodate them all. My guests would pay Lin or one of the whores for this service. The GIs also brought beer or hard booze as an entrance fee to party at the frat house. Truth is, I was running a pretty well organized and profitable house of ill repute, but I wasn't making anything from the venture, except for the free drinks and free sex. I suspect that Lin was getting a share of each of the whore's take for an evening, so she undoubtedly made out quite well. For all I know, maybe the mama-san received her share of the prostitutes' take too.

One of the guys who came with me from Chu Lai fell in love with one of these whores. He was engaged to a beautiful woman back in the States—a model, he claimed—and his parents were well-heeled. But none of that stopped him from falling in love with one of the whores Lin had sent over to the house to party with us. She was nothing but a 50 piaster (33 cent) whore, but he loved her. To make her monogamous, he'd pay her $5 or $10 a day—a gold mine to her—to keep her from going with other guys. I doubt that it worked, but he thought it did. She even gave him the clap once. He got medical treatment and then arranged for a medic buddy to get her treated too. The end result is that he fell so madly in love with her that he broke off his engagement with the model and did the paperwork to marry the whore and take her back to the States. "You marry me GI? Take me back to OOSA?" had worked for her.

The whole setup—the frat house, the whores, the drinking—would not have been possible if the Army hadn't designed different standards for the "watchmen" than for the common soldiers. Most soldiers had to live by rules. They had to abide by curfews. There were bed checks to ensure they were in their company areas. They couldn't leave post without authorization. But we cops had virtually no rules. We traveled on and off post at will. No one checked to see if we were snug in our beds. We had to have assigned sleeping quarters on the post, but no one checked to see if we ever used it. After renting the frat house, I used my bed on post only once or twice a week, if that.

We were allowed so much freedom because we were enforcing laws and, as enforcers, needed certain privileges to be effective in our roles. We (some of us, at least) abused those privileges and, as a result, lived life to the fullest.

We immersed ourselves in alcohol and sex. I've often said about my year in Vietnam that I doubt if I took a sober breath while I was there. That's certainly an overstatement, but it's true that I drank my way through the three months in Da Nang. The cops I associated with did, too. And we were the ones the Army had sent to the war to try to restore military order to a decaying—or decayed—Army. Two thousand years ago, Roman satirist Juvenal asked, "But who is to guard the guards themselves?"—better known now as "Who watches the watchmen?" For those of us serving in law enforcement in Vietnam, the answer was "no one." We weren't corrupt in the sense of breaking laws by using or selling drugs, by torturing suspects, extorting money, or any of a long list of possibilities. But we certainly bent Army rules to our advantage.

We could, and therefore we did, live by a completely different set of rules than those imposed on the other soldiers. In that regard, we were a privileged class. I wasn't an officer, but my guess is that many of them lived by rules different from the soldiers they commanded. In Neil Sheehan's *A Bright and Shining Lie* we learn that John Paul Vann lived by a different set of rules, too. My guess is that there were all sorts of privileged classes of Americans serving in Vietnam. Only the poor grunt was denied belonging to such a group. Only he was required to abide by the rules. But, as I've demonstrated, even many of them broke the law. Ultimately, then, there existed in Vietnam— in the year I was there at any rate—two broad groups of Americans: those who could break and bend the rules to live life as they chose, and those who broke the law through a variety of illegal activity. Many of my CID and MPI colleagues and I, belonged to the former group. Our opponents in our war against drugs in Vietnam belonged to the latter.

John Paul Vann had, according to Sheehan, "lost his compass." For me, it wasn't that I'd lost my compass, but when one is young, without many sexual morals, and invincible, it's a different compass that directs one's life. As strange as it sounds, my compass directed me to uphold the laws the Army had sent me to Vietnam to enforce, while allowing me to break any rules that stood in the way of my own hedonistic pursuits. I have never lived a life less restrained and scrutinized, yet more exciting and pleasurable, than my year in Vietnam.

MY FINAL DAYS

Four or five days before leaving Vietnam I hosted my last party at the frat house. It was a rouser of a party with agents, MPs, medics, whores for everyone, and booze, a lot of booze. Much to my delight, I had hosted a full-blown saturnalia.

The oldest reveler there was a CID warrant officer. About forty-five years old, ancient by our standards, he had spent nearly a quarter of a century in the Army, and looked every bit the Italian-American he was so proud of being. Well past midnight, he became agitated over one of the prostitutes. He thought she'd taken a liking to him and got quite upset when he found her engaging in a sexual act with one of the medics. Nothing anyone could do or say would calm him down. Finally, he pulled his .38 pistol out of his holster and threatened to shoot the next guy that he decided was fucking with him. (One of the dangerous downsides to partying with CID agents is that we carried our revolvers with us all the time—sober or drunk. This night that fact nearly cost us dearly.)

The more we tried to calm him down, the more agitated he became. Despite my own inebriated state, the waving gun had a sobering effect on me. I knew that if I didn't do something quickly, the old man would shoot someone. When I saw my moment of opportunity, I rushed him while I focused on getting one thing accomplished—getting my hands on the gun. A revolver can only shoot if the cylinder can turn. I knew if I could grab the cylinder of the weapon, I would buy enough time for others to help subdue him. As he and I struggled with the weapon, two guys jumped in, and we took the gun away from him. Fortunately, the incident ended without anything but his ego bruised. A buddy took him home and the party ended. The near tragedy had been too much; it sapped our enthusiasm. Luckily, though, I would leave the frat house with a better "final" memory of the place that had provided so much joy during my stay in Da Nang.

Shortly after my arrival to the city, I learned that Phan Thi San had moved her Caribe Diamond Works from the destroyed PX on Chu Lai to one of the local post exchanges in the Da Nang area. During my three months in Da Nang, San and I would meet at my house or one of the clubs and enjoy each other's company. That I was having such a great time in Vietnam, coupled with my relationship with San, motivated me to ask the Army to extend my time beyond the normal one-year tour. I wanted to remain in the war, but the Army thwarted my every attempt to stay there. I eventually resigned myself to returning to the World.

On January 22, 1972, two days before I left Vietnam, San and I met at my house. It would be my last time in the frat house and my last time with her. San and I never talked about my leaving. We had a couple of drinks and made love. I took off the ivory and gold-trimmed Buddha lavaliere she'd given to me at Chu Lai and handed it to her. She told me to keep it. I walked her to the pedestrian gate where she gave me a quick kiss and hurried down the street. I threw everything I owned into the back of my jeep, honked for the mama-san to open the driveway gate, and drove back to post. I packed all my stuff to be sent back to the States, stood in line to fill a specimen bottle while standing at the pee trough, and, later, boarded a Freedom Bird heading home.

It was hot that day in Vietnam. Steamy, sweaty heat. Mercury bubbled to the top of thermometers and humidity drenched everything. Within twenty-four hours, I was deplaning in Bismarck, North Dakota, where the wind chill drove the temperature below zero. I've never been so cold in my life.

No one spit on me when I got back to the States. No one called me a baby-killer. I've never felt deprived of any sort of gratitude from my country. I don't collect a disability from the VA for having seen ugly scenes of humanity or being shot at. (I've seen inhumanity as bad in Los Angeles as I saw in Vietnam, and have been in as grave danger, too.) I don't feel compelled to wear fatigues and cry about my experiences at some rap session at a VA clinic. I'm not a bum—I've worked, paid taxes, and continued to serve my community. I don't think anyone owes me anything for my year in the war. And the Vietnam vets whom I've worked with over the years would say the same.

There are a million stories that could be told about wartime service. Some noble, some not so noble. Regardless, I think all veterans of our nation's wars—those past and those present—have earned the right to be proud Americans, proud of serving their country in whatever capacity. I also believe that most Americans appreciate that service. It really is time to get past the victim-veteran mentality that has haunted the Vietnam veterans. In telling my story, I have but one purpose: to tell the truth about one soldier's wartime experiences. The myths, and in some cases the lies, told by veterans or wannabe veterans have captured the headlines, the attention of the public, and the money for veteran's programs. The truth is that for many of us serving in Vietnam, it really was the best of times. Another truth is that not everyone who served there is a hero.

THE END

The author spent his formative years on a farm in North Dakota. Here he is as a toddler with his father, a veteran of the Korean War, standing in front of a granary on the family farm eight miles north of Hettinger.

AFTERWARD

BY

LARRY C. SKOGEN

When my brother Gary departed for Vietnam, my parents and I bade him farewell at the Bismarck, North Dakota, airport. A year later our cousin met him at the Bismarck airport on his return flight from Vietnam. The next day I met up with Gary at our cousin's house in Bismarck and drove him back to Hettinger. I'm not sure what I was expecting, but I know that my impression was that a year at war hadn't changed him much. He was still my big brother, and still my hero.

Gary and I had never really been close as brothers. The seven years that separated us meant that we grew up in virtually different worlds. Our parents sold the family farm when Gary was nearly finished with high school. His entire growing-up experience involved doing farm work: driving tractor, haying, plowing, working with sheep, milking cows, sundry daily chores, and the host of farm work that many agrarian North Dakotans grew up doing.

When our parents sold the farm, they bought a hardware store in Hettinger. I was ten years old when we moved into town. I remember it as one of the worst days of my young life, as I wanted to remain on the farm. But then, I wasn't old enough to be doing much farm work, and what I did was modified for someone under ten years of age. I did more farm work as a teenager doing summer work on relatives' farms than I ever did on our family farm. So I grew up in a hardware store where we worked hard, but it was very different from grueling, weather-exposed, lifecycle work on a farm. From those growing-up differences, the lenses I look through at life are very different from Gary's lenses.

Then, shortly after we moved to town, Gary eloped with his first wife. I was eleven years old. Thus ended my growing up with an older brother. There's not much in common between two brothers whose ages are separated by seven years (seven crucial years from childhood to adulthood), one growing up on a farm and the other growing up in town (albeit a small North Dakota town), and one working on the family farm and the other in the family hardware store. But the lack of commonality in our lives didn't prevent me from always admiring him as my big brother.

The family lore about Gary's bravado, fearlessness, and immunity to pain created for me the perfect super-hero. After slicing his hand with a hunting knife, he had the doctor sew him up without use of anesthetic. When he accidentally shot himself in the leg, he dug the bullet out with his knife, a fact only discovered by our parents when blood poisoning set in. As a teenager, he was the first to jump out of his car with crowbar in hand to take on any comers when trouble brewed on Main Street. And teenage girls adored him. I used to get caught in the middle when he was two-timing them. One girlfriend would ask me, the little brother, what I knew about another girl she'd heard he was seeing. I knew nothing, of course. He was everything I was not. A friend who knows us both maintains that we have perfect yin and yang symmetry.

The distance between us created by lack of commonality rapidly disappeared when I enlisted in the military in May 1972, a mere three months after his return from Vietnam. Not surprisingly, I volunteered to go into law enforcement, just like my big brother. By fall 1972, I was wearing a sidearm and working in law enforcement at Lowry Air Force Base, Colorado. I quickly gained an acquaintance with the military Gary had described to me, but about which I had comprehended little.

On that drive from Bismarck to Hettinger when Gary returned from Vietnam, he talked a lot about his wartime adventures. He was excited and enthusiastic about what he'd experienced over the past year. But his conversation was so peppered with military jargon and acronyms, as well as cop lingo, that I had trouble following his stories. My experience in Colorado changed all that.

A uniform and a badge quickly immersed me into a military gone awry. Drug overdoses, suicides, assaults, and near riots filled our evening police blotters. Gary had talked about racial problems, but until I witnessed police dogs being used to break up racial brawls at the enlisted clubs, I hadn't comprehended the width of the divide. Gary had talked about suicides, but until I witnessed it happening at Lowry, it had been an abstraction. Gary had talked about the plague of drugs in Vietnam, but until I witnessed the superabundance of drug busts and overdoses as a cop myself, I had no understanding of the depth of the scourge in our military. Thus as I began to understand his year in Vietnam and the jargon and lingo, for the first time we could really talk.

Almost overnight our brotherly conversations took on a whole new tone. He wasn't talking at me, while I tried to comprehend what he'd experienced; he was now talking with me—and I understood his wartime experience with a fresh appreciation. And so for years we talked.

After six years in enlisted law enforcement, I earned my bachelor's degree and received a commission as an Air Force officer. I left the law enforcement field and spent four years as a weapons system operator. During those four years, I completed a master's degree in history and parlayed that into a position on the faculty at the United States Air Force Academy. From there I received an assignment to complete my Ph.D. in history at Arizona State University. In that program I spent untold hours doing original research at libraries, government repositories, and the National Archives. Relative to Gary, what I learned in my program is that his stories could be documented.

As an aspiring historian listening to Gary's stories, I often thought that he could write a great book full of crime, sex, and drugs, but that there were many unknowns, gaps really, in his recollections. After having gone through my Ph.D. program—and learning how to do original research—I told him that he should write a book and I would help him. I would do the original research necessary to fill in the blanks, shore up the arguments, and, in general, help him set the cadence to the narrative.

Brothers Larry (left) and Gary Skogen have what one friend calls "perfect yin and yang symmetry," as evident in this picture as the two review research documents from Gary's time served in the Vietnam War. Larry Skogen, who holds a Ph.D. in history from Arizona State University, verified the crime narratives in this book by checking records in the National Archives and Records Administration.

We began this journey as we had always done: Gary talking and my listening and asking questions. This time, however, I had a tape recorder. Twenty hours of taping provided the gist of this book. I transcribed the tapes and marked those things for which I believed I could find substantiating or additional evidence. As luck has it, I was then temporarily assigned to Norfolk, Virginia. Every chance I had to break from my military duties, I headed to Washington, DC, and the National Archives and Records Administration.

On my very first visit to the National Archives facility at Suitland, Maryland, I requested police blotters from Chu Lai. The very first folder I received contained onionskin copies of those blotters dating from Gary's first month at Chu Lai. As I flipped through the copies, I found a tri-folded, single page tucked inside. It had been filed in the wrong place, it appeared to me. I took that page out of the folder, unfolded it, and found that I was holding a CID report completed and signed by Gary over twenty years earlier. I'm not superstitious, but at that moment I figured the gods were sending me a message: complete this project. That report wasn't of particular interest and doesn't have a part in this book, but the sign was clear to me.

As you have read this book, then, the stories of Gary's exploits have been substantiated by archival research. The court-martial quotations are from the court-martial record. The sources for information about Firebase Mary Ann, Typhoon Hester, drug abuse reports, CID investigation reports, and so forth, are all listed in this book's bibliography. Memoirs tend to be hazy recollections of lives lived in the misty past. That is not the case here.

My research in the official record of the Vietnam War demonstrated to me that Gary's recollections, while certainly containing gaps and lacking an exactitude required in historical works, were all very accurate. The additional archival materials allowed him simply to fill in gaps and to create a much more accurate picture of his year in the war. Because of his accurate recall about events captured in the official record, my assumption has always been that his recollections about his personal exploits—the partying, the women, and the testosterone-driven adventures—were equally accurate. I leave it to the readers to decide if they agree with my conclusion.

In the end, and most importantly, this is Gary's story. I'm pleased to have been able to contribute to this project as an historian, researcher, and writing consultant. I enjoyed every step of this journey. After all, I got to do it with my hero.

SELECTED BIBLIOGRAPHY

PRIMARY SOURCES

Clerk of Courts, U. S. Army Judiciary, Arlington, VA. *Vietnam War Era Courts Martial Records.*

Comptroller General of the United States. *Drug Abuse Control Program Activities in Vietnam.* Washington, DC: Department of Defense, August 11, 1972.

Geography and Map Division, The Library of Congress, Washington, DC.

Marine Advisors, Inc. *An Oceanographic Survey of Da Nang Bay and Chu Lai, Republic of Vietnam.* La Jolla, CA: Marine Advisers, Inc., 1965.

National Archives and Records Administration, *Records of the Office of the Chief Signal Officer, Record Group 111.*

National Archives and Records Administration, *Records of the Office of the Secretary of Defense, Record Group 330.*

National Archives and Records Administration, *Records of the Department of Defense—Interservice Agencies, Record Group 334.*

National Archives and Records Administration, *Records of the United States Forces in Southeast Asia, 1950-1975, Record Group 472.*

National Committee for the International Symposium on the Ancient Town of Hoi An. "Ancient Town of Hoi An: International Symposium held in Danang on 22-23 March 1990." Hanoi: Foreign Languages Publishing House, 1991.

National Institute for Urban and Rural Planning. *Data Book Danang City.* Hanoi: Ministry of Construction, 1994.

National Personnel Records Center, St. Louis, Missouri. *Vietnam War Era Military Personnel Records.*

United States Army Criminal Investigation Division, U.S. Army Crime Records Center, U.S. Army Criminal Investigation Command, Fort Belvoir, VA. *Criminal Investigation Reports, Chu Lai, February 1971–October 1971.*

United States House of Representatives. "Hearings before the Select Committee on Crime." 92nd Congress. Serial No. 92-1. June 1971.

Washington Headquarters Services, Directorate for Information, Operations and Reports. "Department of Defense, U. S. Casualties in Southeast Asia." Washington DC: Government Printing Office, 1985.

SECONDARY SOURCES

BOOKS

Bowers, Ray L. *The United States Air Force in Southeast Asia: Tactical Airlift.* Washington, DC: Office of Air Force History, 1983.

Burkett, B. G. and Glenna Whitley. *Stolen Valor: How the Vietnam Generation Was Robbed of its Heroes and its History.* Dallas, TX: Verity Press, Inc., 1998.

Cima, Ronald J., ed. *Vietnam: A Country Study.* Washington, DC: Headquarters, Department of the Army, 1989.

Cortesi, Lawrence. *The Magnificent Bastards of Chu Lai.* New York, NY: Kensington Publishing Corp., 1986.

Ebert, James R. *A Life in a Year: The American Infantryman in Vietnam, 1965-1972.* Novato, CA: Presidio Press, 1993.

Hagen, Margaret A. *Whores of the Court: The Fraud of Psychiatric Testimony and the Rape of American Justice.* New York, NY: HarperCollins Publishers, 1997.

Halberstam, David. *The Best and the Brightest.* 1969. Reprint, with a new introduction by author, NY: Ballantine Books, 1993.

Holland, Tom. *Rubicon: The Last Years of the Roman Republic.* New York, NY: Anchor Books, A Division of Random House, Inc., 2005.

Kolko, Gabriel. *Anatomy of a War: Vietnam, the United States, and the Modern Historical Experience.* NY: Pantheon Books, 1985.

Nolan, Keith William. *Sappers in the Wire: The Life and Death of Firebase Mary Ann.* College Station: Texas A&M University Press, 1995.

Prugh, George S., Major General. *Law At War: Vietnam, 1964-1973.* Washington, DC: Department of the Army, 1975.

Reporting Vietnam. 2 vols. NY: Literary Classics of the United States, Inc., 1998.

Sheehan, Neil. *A Bright Shining Lie: John Paul Vann and America in Vietnam.* NY: Random House, 1988.

Smith, Clark and Don Watkins. *The Vietnam Map Book.* Berkeley, CA: Winter Soldier Archive, 1981.

Sorley, Lewis. *A Better War: The Unexamined Victories and Final Tragedy of America's Last Years in Vietnam.* NY: Harcourt Brace & Company, 1999.

Stanton, Shelby L. *Vietnam Order of Battle.* Washington, DC: U. S. News Books, 1981.

Summers, Harry G., Jr. *Historical Atlas of the Vietnam War.* New York, NY: Houghton Mifflin Company, 1995.

Tuchman, Barbara W. *The March of Folly: From Troy to Vietnam.* NY: Alfred A. Knopf, 1984.

ARTICLES

Douglass, Joseph D., Jr. "Red Cocaine: Drugging of the American Military." *Soldier of Fortune,* June 1991, 64-67.

Downey, F. Gerald. "NVA Surprise at Fire Support Base Mary Ann." *Vietnam,* December 1995, 46-53.

Grover, David H. "Twilight of the Troopship." *Vietnam,* December 1995, 30-36.

NEWSPAPERS

Bismarck Tribune (North Dakota)
Christian Science Monitor
Denver Rocky Mountain News
Navy Times
Pravda
The New York Times

UNPUBLISHED

Karis, Daniel G. "Criminal Investigation Activities [in] World War II and Vietnam[:] Battlefield Implications." Master's thesis, U. S. Army Command and General Staff College, 1988.

Weimer, Daniel. "Drug Abuse and the Heroin Epidemic Among American Soldiers in the Vietnam War, 1970-72." Master's thesis, Kent State University, 1996.

WEBSITES

www.archives.gov
www.no-quarter.org
www.weather.unisys.com/hurricane/w_pacific/1971

INDEX